Newfoundland and Labrador English

Dialects of English

Series Editors
Joan Beal (University of Sheffield)
Patrick Honeybone (University of Edinburgh)
April McMahon (University of Edinburgh)

Advisory Board
Laurie Bauer (Victoria University of Wellington)
Jenny Cheshire (Queen Mary, University of London)
Karen P. Corrigan (Newcastle University)
Heinz Giegerich (University of Edinburgh)
Peter L. Patrick (University of Essex)
Peter Trudgill (University of Fribourg, UEA, Agder UC, La Trobe University)
Walt Wolfram (North Carolina State University)

Volumes available in the series:
Robert McColl Millar, *Northern and Insular Scots*
978 0 7486 2317 4

David Deterding, *Singapore English*
978 0 7486 2545 1

Jennifer Hay, Margaret Maclagan and Elizabeth Gordon, *New Zealand English*
978 0 7486 2530 7

Pingali Sailaja, *Indian English*
978 0 7486 2595 6

Karen P. Corrigan, *Irish English, volume 1 – Northern Ireland*
978 0 7486 3429 3

Sandra Clarke, *Newfoundland and Labrador English*
978 0 7486 2617 5

Forthcoming titles include:

Bridget L. Anderson, *Smoky Mountain English*
978 0 7486 3039 4

Newfoundland and Labrador English

Sandra Clarke

Edinburgh University Press

© Sandra Clarke, 2010

Transferred to digital print 2015

Edinburgh University Press Ltd
22 George Square, Edinburgh

Typeset in 10.5/12 Janson
by Servis Filmsetting Ltd, Stockport, Cheshire, and
printed and bound by CPI Group (UK) Ltd
Croydon, CR0 4YY

A CIP record for this book is available from the British Library

ISBN 978 0 7486 2616 8 (hardback)
ISBN 978 0 7486 2617 5 (paperback)

The right of Sandra Clarke
to be identified as author of this work
has been asserted in accordance with
the Copyright, Designs and Patents Act 1988.

Published with the support of the Edinburgh University Scholarly Publishing
Initiatives Fund.

Contents

Acknowledgements

This volume, the first to present a comprehensive overview of Newfoundland and Labrador English, would not have been possible without the input of many. Its foundations were laid almost half a century ago by such researchers as George Story, E. R. ('Ron') Seary, John Widdowson and, in particular, William J. Kirwin, whose continued dedication to local language as Director of Memorial University's English Language Research Centre serves as a genuine inspiration. Their efforts, spearheaded by the folklorist Herbert Halpert, were instrumental in the establishment of the Memorial University Folklore and Language Archive (MUNFLA). Recorded materials housed in MUNFLA, which represent all areas of Newfoundland and Labrador, have proved an invaluable resource in establishing the structural features of the region's traditional speech varieties, as Chapters 2 and 3 of this volume attest.

Over the years, my research on Newfoundland and Labrador English has benefited considerably from the help of my Memorial University colleagues. Throughout his career, Harold Paddock served as an excellent source of knowledge on local varieties. Upon retirement, he also made available his largely unpublished regional linguistic atlas materials; these are now being developed as the online Dialect Atlas of Newfoundland and Labrador English (DANL), with the funding support of Memorial University's Institute of Social and Economic Research, along with its J. R. Smallwood Centre. I am also very grateful to Philip Hiscock and Robert Hollett, with whom I have collaborated on DANL and other local language projects spanning the past decade. For them as well as me, this work has yielded many insights into the regional and temporal patterns of spoken English in Newfoundland and Labrador.

I am also deeply indebted to a number of Memorial University Master's-level linguistics students whose excellent theses, though little-known outside the region, provide considerable information on patterns of language variation and change in rural Newfoundland. A listing of these – by no means exhaustive – includes Wade Colbourne, Eloise (Lemire) Hampson, Linda Harris, Catherine Lanari, Amanda Newhook and Ronald Noseworthy. I also owe thanks to the many Memorial undergraduate students who, over the years, have provided valuable local data, particularly with respect to traditional and contemporary lexical items.

The audio files at http://www.lel.ed.ac.uk/dialects/, which correspond to the speech samples of Chapter 7, have generously been made available by Winnifred Flynn, Philip Hiscock, Eloise Lemire and Harold Paddock. I am extremely grateful to them, as I am to their interviewees. I also thank the Canadian Broadcasting Corporation (CBC) for allowing me to reproduce three of the Chapter 7 speech samples, originally broadcast on CBC Radio in Newfoundland and Labrador.

I extend my thanks to the editors at Edinburgh University Press – notably Esmé Watson – along with the editors of the *Dialects of English* series – and in particular Joan Beal, for her comments on an earlier draft of this book. I am grateful to my colleague Gerard Van Herk for reviewing several chapters.

Last but far from least, I owe an enormous debt of gratitude to my husband, Don Tarrant, who produced the figures and cover photos for this volume. This contribution, however, pales beside the encouragement and support that he has provided during the writing of this book.

1 Introduction: history, geography and demography

Newfoundland and Labrador, located at the northeastern extremity of the North American continent (see Figure 1.1), became a province of Canada in 1949. As Britain's oldest transatlantic colony as well as Canada's newest province, the region has had a long history of European settlement. This chapter presents an overview of European settlement history in Newfoundland and Labrador and outlines the principal reasons why the English spoken there constitutes a unique variety in the English-speaking world.

1.1 Newfoundland and Labrador English as a distinct speech variety

> My advice if you ever go to Newfoundland take either a translator or be prepared to ask everyone to speak very slowly. (http://www.languagehat. com/mt/mt-comments.cgi?entry_id=1614, posted by Nena, 5 November 2004)

The English spoken in Newfoundland and Labrador – officially known up to 2001 simply as Newfoundland – has long been acknowledged as distinct. Though recognisably North American, Newfoundland and Labrador English (NLE) is often perceived by residents of mainland Canada as sounding more Irish than Canadian. Yet such a conclusion masks the considerable linguistic variation to be found within the province: in fact, NLE has been recognised by linguists as displaying one of the greatest ranges of internal variation in pronunciation and grammar of any global variety of English (Kortmann and Szmrecsanyi 2004; Schneider 2004). Present-day varieties of NLE extend from the standard, Canadian-like speech of many younger, urban middle-class residents of the province to the conservative, and decidedly non-standard, varieties still to be found in many small rural communities, particularly, but by no means exclusively, among older generations. Extensive

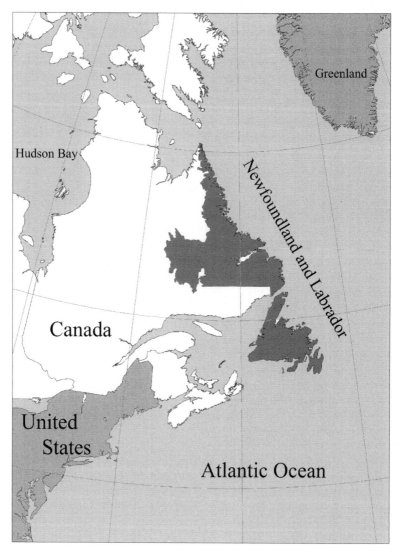

Figure 1.1 Newfoundland and Labrador in northeastern North America

internal variation has characterised the language of the region for centuries. Thus in 1836 the English clergyman Edward Wix (1836: 168)
commented that the inhabitants of neighbouring bays, separated by
only a few miles, differed 'as much as if they were of a different nation'.
Newfoundlanders and Labradorians themselves have long been aware
of the existence of regional dialect differences: Dewling and Shorrocks

(1999: 2) observe: 'Each harbour developed its own dialect; and each would make fun of its neighbour's "misuse" of what it considered proper English.'

For many North Americans, the differences separating NLE from their own varieties of English are sufficiently great to cause comprehension difficulties. Almost a century ago, a visiting American writer, George Allan England, remarked (1925: 323) that the language of Newfoundland fishermen was virtually unintelligible, a fact that he attributed their 'thick and mumbling tone'. A contemporary American writer, Robert Finch, observes:

> In St. John's and in most of the towns on the Avalon Peninsula, local speech exhibits a strong Irish rhythm and lilt. In the more remote and largely English settlement of the outer bays, the accent is less flamboyant; but that, if anything, makes it more foreign to an outside ear. Something is swallowed – some say it is the vowels, some say the consonants. To my ear it seemed to be both, so that often what I heard was a seamless, continuous growl, or else a staccato burst of fricatives, plosives, and glottal stops, devoid of any vocalized sound. In fact, I am still not sure whether I eventually came to understand the accent itself or merely began to decipher it from context. (Finch 2007: 57)

Almost four decades ago, the Survey of Canadian English, which investigated nationwide reported usage by school students and their parents of a wide range of lexical, pronunciation and grammatical features, found Newfoundland to be 'more distinct in its speech habits from the rest of Canada than are the other areas from each other' (Warkentyne 1971: 196). Even today, it is not unusual to see subtitling of the speech of rural Newfoundlanders and Labradorians in television programming designed for the broader North American and world markets.

The often-remarked upon distinctiveness of NLE derives from a combination of factors: historical, economic and geographic. From an historical perspective, the region experienced earlier European settlement than did much of the North American continent; in addition, its European founder populations displayed extremely localised origins in Britain and Ireland. Geography has also played an important role, since Newfoundland and Labrador occupies a peripheral and geographically marginalised location within North America. From the early seventeenth to the late twentieth centuries, the area's economy was largely intertwined with the cod fishery, which for a considerable number of the rural population involved small boat and inshore fishing methods. As a result, the population of Newfoundland and Labrador has always been sparse and scattered; even today, it remains small by world standards. The province's total population currently stands at just over half a million (505,469, according to Statistics Canada census figures for 2006), despite the fact that its land mass (almost 406,000 sq. km) is larger than those of Japan or Germany. The continental portion of the province, Labrador, is even more sparsely settled: though three times the size of the island of Newfoundland, it contains only about 5 per cent of the province's total population.

Since regionally-based variation is a fundamental characteristic of NLE, and since much of this variation derives from the settlement history of Newfoundland and Labrador, section 1.2 provides a brief overview of European settlement. Section 1.3 distinguishes four major regions of the province on the basis of differences in their European settler origins. Section 1.4 outlines the NLE varieties covered in this volume.

1.2 From European discovery to the present: an historical overview

The area now referred to as Newfoundland and Labrador has been known to Europeans for over 1,000 years. First discovered by the Norse around AD 1000, and rediscovered by the English-sponsored Venetian explorer Zuan Cabotto (John Cabot) in 1497, the area hosted a migratory fishery from the beginning of the sixteenth century. This early fishery was pursued by western Europeans of various nationalities, among them Basques, French (Bretons and Normans in particular), Portuguese and Spanish. Apart from the French, however, none of these groups ever attempted permanent settlement; their legacy remains primarily in a host of toponyms (see Table 1.1 for some examples). Place names of Portuguese or Spanish origin cluster principally in the eastern and southeastern regions of the island of Newfoundland, while the small number of Basque toponyms are located primarily in the island's northern and western regions, as well as in southern Labrador. The many French place names are to be found in all parts of coastal Newfoundland and southern Labrador and attest to the long presence of the French in the region. The French have also left a legacy of family names, including a number from the Channel Islands – among them Gr[o]uchy, Gushue, LeDrew, LeGrow, LeMessurier, Noel, Puddester (from Poingdestre) and Renouf. In addition, early European fishermen and whalers have left their mark in a handful of words that relate to the fishery. From Portuguese or Spanish, for example, come *quintal* (pronounced 'kental', meaning '112 pounds of fish') and *baccalao* 'cod-fish',

Table 1.1 Some Newfoundland and Labrador place names of non-English origin (Sources: Seary 1971; Hamilton 1996)

Origin	Examples
Portuguese (and Spanish)	Bonavista; Conception Bay; Cape Race (*cabo raso*, 'flat or barren cape'); Fermeuse (*fermoso* 'beautiful'); Renews (*ronhoso* 'scabby' or *arenhosa* 'sandy'); Ferryland (*farelhao* 'steep rock', but possibly French *forillon* 'cape, point'); Fogo (*fogo* 'fire'); Labrador; Placentia
Basque	Cap Dégrat; Ingornachoix Bay; Port au Port; (West and East) St. Modeste (*samedet*)
French	Baie Verte; Barachois/Barasway; Bay l'Argent; Cape Anguille; Conche; Croque; Forteau; Griquet; Harbour le Cou; Harbour Mille; Hermitage; Isle aux Morts; Jacques Fontaine; La Scie; Lamanche; Port-de-Grave; and numerous settlements with initial word *anse* ('bay, cove') (as in l'Anse-au-Clair, l'Anse-au-Loup)

borrowed with the meaning of 'dried and salted cod', and also existing in the form *Baccalieu* in local place names.

In 1583, the island of Newfoundland was officially claimed for the English Crown by Sir Humphrey Gilbert, thereby becoming England's first overseas transatlantic colony. The English too, however, were initially more interested in the region from the economic perspective provided by a migratory or seasonal cod fishery rather than as a location for the planting of new settlements. Nonetheless, under royal charter, several attempts at colonisation were to follow, sponsored by the Society of Merchant Venturers and the London and Bristol Company. These include Cuper's Cove, now known as Cupids (1610), and Bristol's Hope (1618), both in Conception Bay. Along the Atlantic coast of the Avalon Peninsula, Renews was established in 1615, followed by the 'colony of Avalon' (present-day Ferryland), which in 1621 was founded by George Calvert, later Lord Baltimore (see Figure 1.2). Though these charter and proprietary colonies proved largely unsuccessful, permanent English settlement on the island has been continuous since this period (Pope 2004).

The earliest English-speaking settlers in what is now central and eastern Canada came primarily from the American colonies to the south, when Loyalists wishing to remain within British North

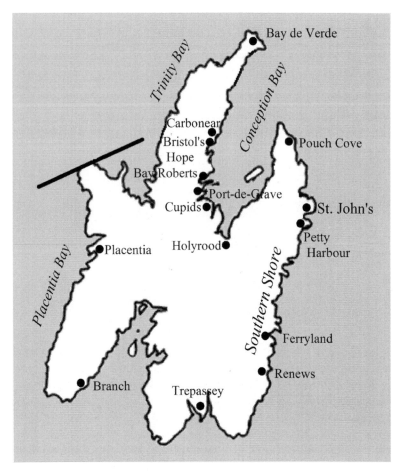

Figure 1.2 The Avalon Peninsula of Newfoundland

America migrated northwards in the period 1776–93, following the American Revolution. No such influx, however, affected the island of Newfoundland. Rather, Newfoundland's earliest non-aboriginal population came to the area directly from two highly localised sources: the southwest counties of England – in particular Dorset, Devon, Somerset and Hampshire – and the southeast counties of Ireland – specifically, the southern portions of Waterford, Wexford, Carlow, Kilkenny, Tipperary and Cork. The reason for this lies in the migratory fishery, which in the seventeenth and eighteenth centuries was centred in the 'West Country' (that is, southwest England), especially in such Devon and Dorset port cities as Dartmouth, Teignmouth and Poole, along with the Channel Islands. From approximately 1675, a number of West Country ships began to stop regularly at towns along the southeast coast of Ireland, in particular the port of Waterford, to take on provisions as well as migratory workers. Fishery workers typically served for two successive summer seasons, overwintering in Newfoundland. In time, a number of these seasonal workers, both English and Irish, took up permanent residence. Through the eighteenth century, however, permanent settlement remained small: Handcock (2000a) estimates that by 1750 the summer population of the island was less than 10,000, and the overwintering population only half that number.

Up to the mid-eighteenth century, English settlement was largely limited to the eastern, and particularly the southeastern, portion of the island. This area, the so-called English Shore, extended from Trepassey in the south to Bonavista and Salvage in the north (see Figure 1.3 for community locations). Competition and wars with the French were in some measure responsible for this situation. In 1662, the French had established a colony at Plaisance (now Placentia), which they abandoned in 1713 under the terms of the Treaty of Utrecht. However, they were to retain fishing rights over much of the Newfoundland coastline; the area known as the 'French Shore' encompassed the entire northeast coast of the island up to 1783, when it was redefined to include the western and northern coasts. French rights to the onshore fishery in these areas, which were not to end until 1904, impeded English settlement expansion.

During the first four decades of the nineteenth century, the permanent population of Newfoundland underwent a substantial increase, from about 19,000 in 1803 to over 96,000 by 1845 (Mannion 1977a). Its two principal sources, however, remained southwest England and southeast Ireland. Handcock (2000b; see also Handcock 1989) states that 80–85 per cent of the English immigrants known to have settled in Newfoundland originated in the south and southwest of England; approximately half of these came from 'Wessex' (Dorset, Hampshire and Somerset, with Dorset migrants being by far the most numerous), and another 35 per cent, from Devon. Irish migrants to Newfoundland, likewise, originated principally within a fifty km radius of the city of Waterford (Mannion 1977a). As a result, Newfoundland displays a greater degree of homogeneity in its European founder population than perhaps anywhere else in English-speaking North America.

The nineteenth century also saw changes in the area's political status. In 1832 Newfoundland obtained a colonial assembly, and in 1854 became a self-governing colony with the granting of responsible government by the British. It was to remain a colony until it acquired the status of a Dominion in 1907.

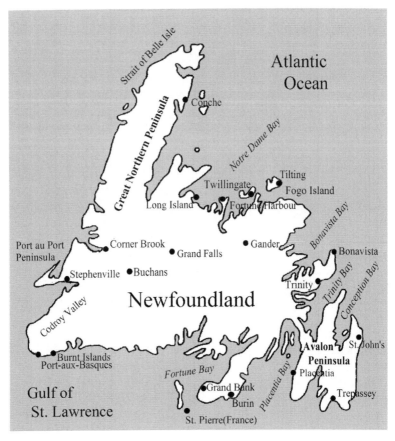

Figure 1.3 The island of Newfoundland

After the mid-nineteenth century, English and Irish migration to Newfoundland declined considerably; the prime economic resource, the cod fishery, was to peak in the 1880s. The precarious nature of this resource-based economy meant that the substantial late nineteenth- and early twentieth-century migrations of Europeans to North America were to pass Newfoundland by. By 1884, 97 per cent of Newfoundland's population was native-born (MacLeod 1990), and, since that date, this proportion has not changed dramatically. The 2006 census of Canada (Statistics Canada 2007) indicates that less than 6 per cent of the province's population had not been resident in Newfoundland and Labrador during the previous five years, the vast majority of these coming from elsewhere in Canada. And while the 2006 census shows that, for Canada as a whole, almost 20 per cent of residents were born outside the country, this figure decreases to less than 2 per cent for the province of Newfoundland and Labrador.

In 1949, when Newfoundland's status changed from 'Britain's oldest colony' to 'Canada's 'youngest province', much of its population remained scattered along 18,000 miles (29,000 km) of coastline, in some 1,300 small rural 'outport' communities which depended chiefly on the fishery. The island's interior had remained largely unknown to all but the indigenous Beothuk and Mi'kmaq groups until the early nineteenth century; the first successful European crossing of the island, by William Epps Cormack, was not made until 1822. However, the interior was slow to open up. The establishment of the Geological Survey of Newfoundland in 1864, under the direction of Alexander Murray and James P. Howley, led to further exploration with a view to assessing the rich mineral and forestry resources. In 1898, a trans-island railway was completed, which provided the first means of transportation of both residents and resources between the east and west coasts. The opening of the interior led to the construction of the mill towns of Grand Falls in 1909 and Corner Brook in 1925, along with the mining town of Buchans in 1927. However, inland communities remained relatively few in number, with much of the population continuing to draw its livelihood from the sea.

The 1950s brought considerable social change, including a government-sponsored – and often bitterly resented – programme of resettlement which by 1975 had led to the loss of some 300 of the province's outport communities, most of which had fewer than 300 inhabitants (Handcock 1994). Declining cod stocks dealt a major economic blow in 1992 in the form of a total moratorium on the northern cod fishery. Currently, many small outports are in serious decline as younger generations, deprived of a future in the fishery, are out-migrating in large numbers not only to urban Newfoundland but, even more so, to Canada's western provinces, which until the 2008–9 economic downturn had been enjoying an unprecedented economic boom.

Despite increasing urbanisation and population decline, the settlement history of Newfoundland and Labrador, along with its marginalised geographical location, have provided ideal conditions for dialect preservation. Throughout the region's long history, the economics of the inshore fishery contributed to the existence of a small and scattered population; coastal outport communities – a few of which to this day remain accessible only by water – were highly endocentric in nature and displayed dense local networks. While economic necessity led to seasonal out-migration on the part of many working males, and hence some measure of dialect contact (via the spring seal hunt on the northeast coast, the Labrador summer fishery, winter employment in logging camps in the interior, or pursuit of the fishery on the Grand Banks and out of Nova Scotia and New England ports), ties with the world outside the local region were relatively weak. As a result, despite linguistic change subsequent to initial settlement, Newfoundland and Labrador varieties of English remain on the whole remarkably faithful to their linguistic roots.

1.3 Settlement history and regional differences

In light of the generally conservative nature of NLE, the range of regional dialect variation that exists within the province today can best be understood within the context of its settlement history. On the basis of settler origins, the province may be divided into four broad regions: the Avalon Peninsula, with its mixed Irish–English linguistic heritage; the southern west coast, where the French, Scots and Irish constituted important founder groups; the largely southwest English-settled coastline, which comprises all the remainder of the island; and the continental portion of the province, Labrador, which displays a unique settlement history.

1.3.1 The Avalon Peninsula

The bulk of the province's present-day population resides on the Avalon Peninsula, which lies in the southeast corner of the island of Newfoundland (see Figures 1.2 and 1.3). This region includes the province's capital and largest city, St. John's, the metropolitan area of which contains more than a third (just over 181,000) of the total population of the province. The Avalon was the earliest part of the island to be settled by the English, and the roots of some of its communities date back to the early 1600s.

Many of the first settlers in the southern Avalon Peninsula, as well as Conception Bay and the St. John's area, came from Devon. The Avalon Peninsula – particularly the St. John's region – also served as the major destination for Irish seasonal fishery workers who embarked yearly out of southeastern Irish ports, generally on West Country ships. It likewise served as the destination of the subsequent waves of permanent settlers from southeast Ireland, whose numbers peaked in the first three decades of the nineteenth century. By 1836, the Irish comprised half of the total population of the island; three-quarters of them were concentrated in St. John's and the surrounding area, from the communities of the 'Southern Shore' (the stretch of Atlantic coastline south of the capital city) to those of Conception Bay (Mannion 2000).

Though some of the Irish who came to Newfoundland are known to have spoken Irish Gaelic as their first and even sole language, documentation is sparse (cf. Kirwin 1993). However, in parts of the Avalon Peninsula, the Irish language lingered on at least until the First World War (Foster 1979). Today, the entire coastline of the southern Avalon Peninsula, from Placentia in the west to just south of St. John's in the east, is populated almost exclusively by descendants of the original Irish settlers and constitutes the 'Irish Avalon' linguistic area. Despite considerable in-migration to St. John's from non-Irish-settled areas of the province since the 1940s, the traditional accent of the capital city clearly displays its Irish heritage. The northern Avalon, along with the west coast of Placentia Bay, represents a mixture of southwest English and southeast Irish settlement, the dual linguistic heritage being obvious in many of the major towns – among them the Conception Bay North community of Carbonear, as documented by Paddock (1981). Nonetheless, one unique English-settled enclave remains: the area of Conception Bay centred around Port-de-Grave/Bay Roberts, which represents the heartland of several linguistic features that have been infrequently documented in Newfoundland and Labrador. Notable among these is the (variable) deletion of post-vocalic /r/ (see Seary et al. 1968).

1.3.2 The southern west coast

Outside of Labrador, the portion of the island's west coast which lies between Corner Brook to the north and Port-aux-Basques to the south (see Figure 1.3) constitutes the most ethnically-mixed region of the province. In addition to the southwest English and the Irish, its European founder populations included two groups whose first language was not English.

In the northerly part of this area, encompassing the Port au Port Peninsula and Stephenville, many present-day residents trace their ultimate ancestry to France. These residents descend from French-speaking Acadians who, after about 1820, migrated to the region from Cape Breton in Nova Scotia. Augmented by French from the island of St. Pierre, off Newfoundland's south coast, along with some deserters from French fishing vessels, these settlers became the majority population in the area by the late nineteenth century. Some intermarried with the aboriginal Mi'kmaq population, who had migrated from Nova Scotia several centuries earlier (Mannion 1977a). Somewhat further south, the Codroy Valley became home after 1840 to Scots Gaelic speakers searching for agricultural land. This group likewise came to Newfoundland

directly from Cape Breton, to which their ancestors had emigrated from
the Scottish Highlands some generations earlier (Ommer 1977).

Oral narratives of descendants of the latter group born by the turn of
the twentieth century include mention of their learning Gaelic as a first
language. Today, however, Scots Gaelic has all but disappeared from
Newfoundland (Bennett Knight 1972; Foster 1982) and no fluent speakers remain. Newfoundland French, however, has proved more resistant.
French in this area experienced considerable decline after the establishment in 1941 of an American air force base in Stephenville. In the town
itself, which to that date had been 95 per cent French-speaking, the
huge influx of English speakers that followed resulted in rapid anglicisa-
tion and the loss of French as a first language within a generation. Even
the more remote villages of the Port au Port Peninsula were not spared:
by the mid-1980s only 10 per cent of the population of the peninsula
– a mere 700 or so – claimed French as a mother tongue (Waddell and
Doran 1993; see also Charbonneau and Barrette 1994; King and Butler
2005). Since the 1970s, however, the bilingual policies of the Canadian
government have gone some way towards combating this attrition. A
French language school system was introduced on the peninsula, along
with French language media and other services. It remains to be seen
whether the renewed sense of cultural and linguistic identity that has
emerged among French Newfoundlanders in recent years will be sufficient to stem the tide of French language loss.

At present, descendants of the original Acadian and Scots settlers
in western Newfoundland speak varieties of English that appear to be
very similar to those of other groups in the region, though these have
not been investigated in any detail (cf. Chapter 2). The attrition of these
languages, along with the aboriginal languages of the province (see 1.3.4
below) – coupled with the low rates of in-migration from outside the
country – means that Newfoundland and Labrador is the province of
Canada with the highest percentage of speakers who claim English as
their sole mother tongue (97.6 per cent, according to the 2006 census of
Canada (Statistics Canada 2007)).

1.3.3 The English-settled coastline

As noted in section 1.2, early English settlement on the island of
Newfoundland was largely confined to the area known as the 'English
Shore', consisting of the east coast of the Avalon Peninsula, along with
a handful of communities in Trinity and Bonavista Bays. North of
Bonavista, English settlement expansion was hindered, since the French
retained fishing rights to all of the remainder of the northeast coast.

Nonetheless, the early eighteenth century saw English encroachment into Bonavista Bay, as well as further north into eastern Notre Dame Bay (in particular, the islands of Twillingate and Fogo; see Figure 1.3). In 1783, by the Treaty of Versailles, the eastern boundary of the 'French Shore' was pushed to the western extremity of Notre Dame Bay, allowing for English expansion into this area.

Since the fishery and trade along the northeast coast, from Trinity to Notre Dame Bays, were largely controlled by the merchant firms of Poole, more than three-quarters of the settlers in this region originated in the counties of Dorset, southern Somerset and southwestern Hampshire (Handcock 2000c; cf. Handcock 1977). The Poole–Waterford connection also brought about the transport of small numbers of southeast Irish to this coast. Some eventually settled in the larger towns – Trinity and Bonavista and their environs in particular – resulting in an ethnically mixed settler pattern analogous to that of some of the larger settlements of Conception Bay. Others settled in what became Irish rural enclaves, among them Tilting on Fogo Island (the Irish roots of which were established in the 1750s) and Fortune Harbour in Notre Dame Bay. Further north, an Irish presence in such coastal communities as Conche on the Great Northern Peninsula dates to approximately 1800.

English – more specifically Wessex – migrants were also dominant elsewhere in coastal Newfoundland (other than on the Avalon Peninsula and the southern west coast). However, settlement came generally later to these areas, in part because the French continued to hold titular fishing rights to much of the remainder of the island. The settler base of these later Wessex migrants tended to be slightly different from that of the earlier settled northeast coast, since it was concentrated in northern Dorset and southern Somerset (Handcock 1977, 1994). In addition, migrants from the Channel Islands figured more prominently among the founder populations of the south and northwest coasts, where Jersey firms often played an important role in the local trade and fishery. The later settlement of these areas also resulted in some degree of secondary migration from Newfoundland's east coast: thus Conception Bay fishermen and their families formed a substantial segment of the nineteenth-century population of northern Newfoundland, including the area south of the Strait of Belle Isle (Thornton 1977). In short, despite Wessex dominance, the settler mix along the south, northwest and northern coasts of the island was somewhat more complex than along the northeast coast. Moreover, nineteenth-century in-migration remained very sparse in these areas. Even today, the south coast remains one of the most isolated regions of the island, with some fishing communities still possessing no road connections to the outside.

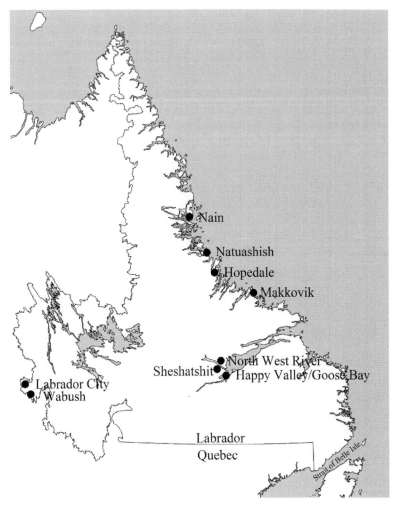

Figure 1.4 Labrador

1.3.4 Labrador

The southern coasts of the continental portion of the province, Labrador (see Figure 1.4), were known to Basque and Breton whalers and fishermen from the first half of the sixteenth century. By the early 1700s, the French had also established a presence in the area in the form of fishing and fur trading posts. Only towards the end of the Seven Years' War in 1763, when Labrador became a British territory, did migratory fishermen and traders from southwest England and the Channel Islands begin to build summer stations in the southern parts of the region. Though in 1809 coastal Labrador was transferred to Newfoundland by Britain, it was not until 1927 that the current inland boundary between Labrador and Quebec was formally resolved.

Through the nineteenth century, the Labrador fishery continued to be pursued on a largely seasonal basis by fishermen not only from England, but also from the island of Newfoundland, particularly Conception and Trinity Bays and the northeast coast. After about 1830, however, small numbers of summer fishermen and their families began to take up year-round residence in coastal southeastern Labrador, including the area to the north of the Strait of Belle Isle, the westernmost part of which today lies within the province of Quebec.

In the southern interior of the Labrador Peninsula (the Hamilton Inlet/Lake Melville region), a very small permanent English settler base had been laid in the late eighteenth century, supplemented by a handful of French trappers and fur traders. In 1836, the Hudson's Bay Company established two fur-trading posts in the area and brought in workers from Scotland, especially the Orkneys, as well as other parts of Britain. Some of these employees remained permanently, marrying into the two local indigenous groups, the Innu and the Inuit; this has resulted in a mixed or Métis population, traditionally referred to as 'settlers' (though within the Labrador context, the term 'settler' has increasingly taken on the meaning of 'non-aboriginal'). Farther north, from the late eighteenth century, Moravian missionaries, who had previously worked among the Inuit in Greenland, established mission stations and settlements at several coastal sites. Small numbers of European trappers and traders followed, and a mixed population also established itself in the more northerly coastal areas. At the turn of the twentieth century, however, the total population of Labrador remained very small (under 4,000).

Ethnically and linguistically, then, Labrador represents a more complex picture than the island of Newfoundland. Outside its southerly coastline area – which drew primarily either on secondary settlement from Newfoundland or else directly on the same southwest English and southeast Irish sources as did the island – its European population stemmed from more disparate source areas in the British Isles, as well as from France. Linguistic residues of language contact are apparent in the English spoken in Inuit coastal communities in the form of a small number of phonetic features, as well as some lexical borrowings. Today, the Inuktitut language, a member of the Eskimo-Aleut linguistic family, is in serious decline in Labrador. Despite ongoing attempts at revitalisation, it constitutes a first language only among older Inuit, principally in the communities of Nain and Hopedale. The Innu language, a sub-variety of Algonquian, is somewhat less threatened as it still represents the home language of most of the approximately 1,500 residents of the two Labrador Innu communities of Sheshatshit (or Sheshatshiu) and Natuashish.

The present-day population of Labrador remains at under 30,000, more than half of it concentrated in two urban areas: Labrador City–Wabush near the western border with Quebec and Happy Valley–Goose Bay to the east, in the Lake Melville area. Goose Bay was established during the Second World War as a Canadian air force base, while Labrador City was founded in the 1950s by the Iron Ore Company of Canada. The employment opportunities offered by both towns drew workers from many areas of Newfoundland and Labrador, Francophones from the province of Quebec and migrants from even further afield. This has resulted in some degree of dialect levelling; though the Newfoundland base of Labrador English is unmistakable, the speech of at least some younger urban Labradorians is more 'mainland'-like than that of their peers on the island of Newfoundland.

1.4 A note on the terminology used in this volume

A single volume dedicated to 'British English' or even 'regional British English' would be difficult indeed: Where to begin? Which varieties to cover and to what extent? A work that attempts a description of the spoken English of Newfoundland and Labrador faces a similar problem. Not only is there considerable regional variation which by and large correlates with settlement history and ethnicity (in particular, southwest English vs. southeast Irish origins), but such social factors as age or rural vs. urban residence – not to mention gender and socioeconomic background – also figure prominently in clarifying the considerable range of linguistic variation evident within the province.

As a result, the two chapters that follow – which deal with NLE pronunciation and grammar, respectively – aim to cover not only features of 'standard' NLE (henceforth SNLE), but also those typical of the two major regional varieties of Newfoundland and Labrador. The abbreviation NIE ('Newfoundland and Labrador Irish English') is used to refer to everyday varieties spoken in areas of the province settled by the southeast Irish – principally but not exclusively, the southern Avalon Peninsula. NBE ('Newfoundland and Labrador British English') refers to comparable varieties of southwest English origin, which, as we have seen, occupy much of the remainder of coastal Newfoundland and Labrador. This distinction is particularly useful when it comes to the more traditional rural varieties found within the province, varieties often labelled 'non-standard'. The Irish vs. southwest English distinction also proves useful with respect to standard NLE varieties. Despite the lack of investigation into regional standards in NLE, these differ phonetically, to at least some degree, between the Irish-dominant southern Avalon Peninsula region and the remainder of the province, in which the Irish presence is minimal. Thus the speech of the capital, St. John's, as well as of major towns on much of the Avalon Peninsula, shows several characteristics of Irish origin which are not the norm in standard urban varieties elsewhere in the province, in such centres as Corner Brook, Grand Falls–Windsor or Happy Valley–Goose Bay.

In the following chapters, the terms 'traditional' and 'conservative' are used interchangeably to refer to features which, only a generation or two ago, were much more in evidence, particularly but by no means exclusively in rural Newfoundland and Labrador. These often echo the features of their founder varieties in southwest England and southeast Ireland. Though still used by conservative (or traditional) speakers, many such features are today in decline among younger generations. Some are almost totally recessive. The term 'vernacular' is used in this volume to refer to spontaneous or casual, everyday speech styles; while these are frequently associated only with 'non-standard' speaker usage, this term should also be understood here as encompassing the informal styles of 'standard' speakers as well.

This volume will give minimal coverage to contact varieties of English in the province, for the simple reason that these varieties have not yet been subject to systematic investigation. This is particularly the case for the English spoken in parts of Labrador, which at the levels of pronunciation and prosody (see Chapter 2) bears traces of its aboriginal language substrates. That said, an example of such a variety is provided in Chapter 7 (7.4.2), in the form of a speech sample from an elderly resident of the largely Inuit Labrador community of Makkovik.

Additional references

Newfoundland Historical Society (2008), *A Short History of Newfoundland and Labrador*, Portugal Cove-St Philip's NL: Boulder Publications. (An exellent and highly readable introduction to the history of the region, from prehistoric times to the present day.)

Web resources

http://www.heritage.nf.ca/home.html
   Information on the history, geography, economy and culture of Newfoundland
   and Labrador
http://www.colonyofavalon.ca
   Information on one of the earliest Newfoundland settlements, the 1621
   'Colony of Avalon' (present-day Ferryland)
http://www.irishdiaspora.net/ or http://ics.leeds.ac.uk/papers/vp01.cfm?outfit
   =ids&folder=158&paper=159
   Brian McGinn's online paper 'Newfoundland: the most Irish place outside of
   Ireland', which provides a brief overview of the Irish presence in
   Newfoundland, along with a discussion of the language (Irish vs. English)
   spoken by early Irish migrants
http://www.labradorvirtualmuseum.ca
   Information on the history and culture of Labrador

2 Phonetics and phonology

This chapter sketches the range of variation exhibited by the vowel and consonant systems of contemporary NLE. In terms of its pronunciation – and despite the fact that Newfoundland and Labrador (NL) did not join Canada until 1949 – NLE is clearly a North American variety. As we shall see, both Irish- and English-origin speech in the province (NIE and NBE, respectively) share many phonological features, particularly with respect to their vowel systems. This situation is not as surprising as it might appear given the historical relationship between southeast Irish English and the traditional English spoken in the western regions of southern England (Hickey 2002). As we shall also see, however, NIE and NBE differ in terms of a number of consonant and vowel features, some of which are highly salient.

NLE is currently undergoing considerable change, the general direction of which is a shift, on the part of younger generations, away from traditional local community norms towards more geographically widespread or supralocal forms. While this chapter includes some mention of the features of innovative NLE, language change is treated in greater depth in Chapter 5.

Since accurate description of sounds and sound change requires a specialised vocabulary, along with a set of specialised International Phonetic Alphabet (IPA) sound symbols, this chapter is by far the most technical of the volume. For those without a phonetics background, section 2.1 below provides an introduction to basic phonetic terminology. That said, much of the chapter should be accessible to non-specialists, given the inclusion of Wells' (1982) 'keyword' approach to vowel representation, as outlined in the following section.

2.1 Phonetics and phonology: some basic terminology

Phonetics is the study of actual speech sounds, each of which is represented as a unique phonetic symbol, within square brackets [ ].

Phonology, on the other hand, investigates how these sounds are organised and structured in any human language. Sound segments that contrast to produce differences of meaning in a language are called **phonemes**, and are represented within slashes, / /. In English, for example, the initial sound of *pit* contrasts with the initial sound of *bit*; thus for English, /p/ and /b/ are separate phonemes.

A fundamental distinction in English, as in most languages, opposes consonants and vowels, which are distinguished by degree of closure (constriction) of the mouth and jaw area (the vocal tract). Vowels are articulated with less mouth/jaw closure than consonants. Vowels in isolation can form a complete syllable, as in the *a* of *a book*; consonants cannot. However, a handful of consonants – those produced without turbulence in the airflow, including the **sonorants** /m/, /n/, /l/ and /r/ – may also function as **syllabics** (that is, as complete syllables) when not followed by pronounced vowels, as in *rotten* or *bottle*. In addition, vowel production typically involves vibration of the vocal cords located within the larynx (voice box) – that is, vowels are **voiced** sounds. While many consonants in English are also voiced, most voiced consonants typically have a **voiceless** counterpart (e.g. voiced /b/ as in *bit* and voiceless /p/ as in *pit*; voiceless /k/ as in *cut* and voiced /g/ as in *gut*).

Phonetically, consonants are also described in terms of the degree of mouth/jaw opening involved in their production (**manner of articulation**), as well as their articulatory position, normally the position where the tongue comes into greatest proximity to the roof of the mouth (**place of articulation**). Most varieties of English, including NLE, have the same consonant system. A listing of NLE consonants is provided in Table 2.1, along with the IPA phonetic symbol for each, its phonetic features and examples of words in which it occurs.

Differences in manner of articulation produce several different consonant types, as seen in the table. **Stops** (also known as **plosives**) are sounds which involve complete closure or blockage of the airstream, whether via tongue contact with the roof of the mouth (/t, k/, etc.) or lip-closure (as in /p/ and /b/). If mouth closure is also accompanied by the escape of air through the nose, the result is a **nasal** stop, such as /ŋ/, spelled 'ng', as in *sing*. If closure is not complete, air compression may create turbulence or friction, yielding **fricatives** such as /f/ or /v/; those that involve high friction, or a hiss-like sound, are referred to as **sibilants** (/s/, /ʃ/, /z/, as illustrated by *sit, shoe* and *dozen*). Table 2.1 also includes sounds that are termed **approximants**, that is, intermediate between consonants and vowels. These include two **glides**, /j/ and /w/, along with two (sonorant) **liquids**, /l/ and /r/. /l/ is a **lateral**, in that, despite tongue contact with the roof of the mouth, its production

Table 2.1 The consonant phonemes of NLE

Symbol	Place	Manner	Voicing	Sample words
/p/	bilabial	stop	voiceless	*pit, spat, supper, stop*
/b/	bilabial	stop	voiced	*big, bring, rubber, rib*
/t/	alveolar	stop	voiceless	*tip, stay, better, pot*
/d/	alvcolar	stop	voiced	*dig, rid, redder, mud*
/k/	velar	stop	voiceless	*kettle, cap, school, pocket, sick*
/g/	velar	stop	voiced	*get, great, logger, frog*
/m/	bilabial	nasal stop	voiced	*much, smell, swimmer, some*
/n/	alveolar	nasal stop	voiced	*not, snore, dinner, ton*
/ŋ/	velar	nasal stop	voiced	*singer, winger, long*
/f/	labiodental	fricative	voiceless	*fit, phone, coffee, stuff, tough*
/v/	labiodental	fricative	voiced	*vet, clever, drove*
/θ/	interdental	fricative	voiceless	*thistle, ether, bath*
/ð/	interdental	fricative	voiced	*this, brother, bathe*
/s/	alveolar	fricative	voiceless	*sin, spot, messy, divorce*
/z/	alveolar	fricative	voiced	*zip, dessert, buzz, rose*
/ʃ/	palatal	fricative	voiceless	*ship, shrine, threshold, mesh*
/ʒ/	palatal	fricative	voiced	*pleasure, vision, beige*
/h/	glottal	fricative	voiceless	*help, hot, Ohio*
/tʃ/	palatal	affricate	voiceless	*chicken, pitcher, touch*
/dʒ/	palatal	affricate	voiced	*job, widget, fudge*
/l/	alveolar	approximant	voiced	*like, sled, dollar, ball*
/r/	(post) alveolar	approximant	voiced	*right, shrimp, barren, door*
/j/	palatal	approximant	voiced	*yard, yet, unit*
/w/	labiovelar	approximant	voiced	*wedge, swell, award*

involves the escape of air at both sides of the tongue. In English, particularly NLE, /r/ is frequently pronounced as a **retroflex**, via the curling back of the tongue tip towards the palate.

With respect to place of articulation, consonants in which only the lips are involved as articulators are referred to as **bilabial** (e.g. /m/, /p/). The primary articulator, however, is the tongue, and the point of greatest closure near the roof of the mouth may range from the tooth area (**dental**) to the gum ridge directly behind it (**alveolar**), through to the soft palate (**palatal**) and the back of the mouth (**velar**). Involvement of the lower lip and upper teeth produces **labiodentals** (/f/ and /v/), while protrusion of the tongue between the teeth produces the **interdental** *th* sound, noted /θ/ when voiceless and /ð/ when voiced. Consonants like /h/, which do not involve the teeth or lips as articulators, but simply the glottis at the top of the windpipe, are referred to as **glottal**.

Phonetically, vowels are typically described in terms of three dimensions: their height (the degree of mouth/jaw opening accompanying their production); their place of articulation, from the front to the back of the mouth; and whether or not the lips are also involved in their articulation. Table 2.2 lists the principal vowel phonemes of standard NLE. On the height dimension, progressing from a relatively closed to relatively open mouth position, English vowels may be described as **high** (or close), as in *see* or *sit*; **mid**, as in *say, set*; and **low** (open), as in *pot* or *paw*; a further distinction within the mid range contrasts **high mid**, as in *say, go*, and **low mid**, as in *set, but*. The place dimension in English is three-way, contrasting **front** vowels, as in *sit* or *sat*, with **back** vowels, as in *put, go, loose*, and intermediate or **central** vowels, as in the NLE articulation of a word like *got*. Most back vowels in English also display some degree of lip **rounding** (contrast lip position between the high back vowel in a word like *soup* and the high front vowel in *seep*).

English vowels are also described as **tense** or **lax**. The tense vowels, as in *see, make* or *go*, are often referred to as 'long', while the lax vowels, as in *sit, set, got* and *put*, are known as 'short'. In addition, English contains three obvious **diphthongs**, or non-simple (non-pure) vowels. These involve a change of sound quality during production, generally through the addition of an **upglide** in the form of tongue raising towards the end of the vowel. They are 'long i' as in *wide* or *try*; the sound written 'ou' or 'ow' in words like *loud* and *crowd*; and the 'oi/oy' of words like *poison* or *joy*. However, the so-called tense vowels of English are also typically pronounced as diphthongs rather than 'pure vowels' (**monophthongs**), as they would be in languages like French or German.

Table 2.2 The principal vowel phonemes of standard NLE

Symbol	Key-word(s)	Height	Place	Rounding	Tense-ness	Sample words
/iː/	FLEECE	high	front	unrounded	tense	*peek, peak, believe, police*
/ɪ/	KIT	high mid	front	unrounded	lax	*sick, symbol, build*
/eɪ/	FACE	high mid	front	unrounded	tense	*rate, day, they, beige*
/ɛ/	DRESS	low mid	front	unrounded	lax	*rest, measure, friend, says*
/æ/	TRAP/ BATH	low mid	front	unrounded	lax	*sack, path, dance*
/a/	LOT/ CLOTH/ THOUGHT	low	central	unrounded	lax	*dock, dog, soft, lawn, bought, caught, tall*
/ʌ/	STRUT	low mid	back	(un)rounded	lax	*luck, rough, tongue*
/oʊ/	GOAT	high mid	back	rounded	tense	*go, goal, show, though*
/ʊ/	FOOT	high mid	back	rounded	lax	*put, took, could*
/uː/	GOOSE	high	back	rounded	tense	*tooth, move, group, rude*
/ə/	commA	mid	central	unrounded	lax	*the, ahead, seven*

Since the pronunciation of vowels may differ markedly from one English variety to another, vowels are most easily described with reference to a small set of **keywords** initially developed by Wells (1982) for both British and American English. This representational format – used extensively in Britain and elsewhere in the English-speaking world, though less frequently in North America – is the one that is adopted in this volume. Keywords for the principal vowel phonemes of NLE are provided in Table 2.2, as well as in the sections below. Following general practice, keywords are noted in small capital letters (e.g. FLEECE, GOOSE). Each keyword provides a shorthand for referencing a complete lexical set, that is, a set of words which are pronounced in the same way in any particular dialect. In contemporary English, for example, the FLEECE set includes not only many words spelled with -ee-, but also with -ea- (*meat, leak*, etc.), as well as a few other spellings (*p<u>ie</u>ce, s<u>ei</u>ze* or *pol<u>i</u>ce*). Though these words have different historical origins, they have all fallen together as tense /iː/ in most contemporary standard varieties.

The data on which this chapter is based derive from several decades of observation and analysis of NLE varieties from all areas of the province. The nine speech samples of Chapter 7 constitute a supplementary source, which are drawn on to illustrate particular features of pronunciation.

2.2 Vowel patterns

The phonological inventory of vowels in standard NLE (SNLE) – whether of Irish or southwest English origin – is identical to that of standard Canadian English (CE), which will serve as a further reference point. It is also identical with those varieties of standard or General American English which have undergone the *cot/caught* merger, that is, those in which there is no phonetic distinction between words like *cot* (or *Don*) and words like *caught* (or *Dawn*). Like the vast majority of North American varieties – which in this regard differ from standard British English, a variety usually referred to today as RP (Received Pronunciation) – SNLE does not distinguish between the vowels of the TRAP and BATH sets (other than, for some speakers, via vowel lengthening in BATH words).

In terms of Wells' (1982) lexical sets, the NLE vowel system consists of:

- six lax vowel phonemes (KIT; DRESS; TRAP/BATH; LOT/CLOTH/THOUGHT; FOOT; STRUT)
- four tense vowels (FLEECE; FACE; GOAT; GOOSE)
- three diphthongs (PRICE; MOUTH; CHOICE).

Standard NLE, whatever its ancestry, also exhibits the typical North American set of vowel contrasts before /r/:

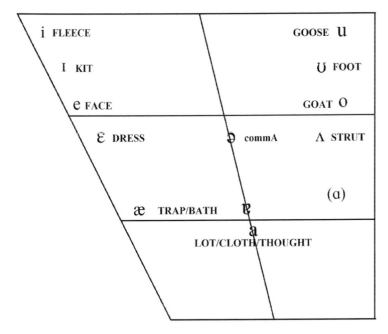

Figure 2.1 A chart of NLE vowels, showing their approximate location in vowel space

- six pre-/r/ vowels (NEAR; SQUARE; START; NORTH/FORCE; POOR/CURE; NURSE/lettER).

Note that the keyword POOR has been added to Wells' (1982) keyword CURE to represent the /uːr/ lexical set. This is because after a palatal (as in *cure, pure* or *sure*), the vowel of the sequence /uːr/ is frequently centralised and unrounded in CE, as in American English, to sound more like the vowel of *fir*. Note also that all of the above represent stressed vowels, that is, vowels that are given their full quality. A final sound, consisting of the mid central vowel, termed 'schwa' /ə/, occurs in unstressed syllables and is represented by the final syllable of Wells' keyword commA.

Figure 2.1 positions the tense and lax vowel phonemes of NLE in vowel space or, to simplify, a side view of the mouth/jaw area. In this vowel chart, high vowels are represented towards the top of the figure and low vowels towards the bottom; front vowels appear on the left, and back vowels on the right. In light of the extensive variation in vowel pronunciation in NLE, Figure 2.1 provides only an approximation of 'normal' vowel production.

Although the phonological inventories of vowels in NLE and CE are identical, actual phonetic realisations may differ considerably. While these differences are most obvious among conservative or traditional speakers of NIE and NBE, many are also found in SNLE. They are particularly evident when it comes to the low lax vowels (that is, the vowels of the TRAP/BATH as well as the LOT/CLOTH/THOUGHT sets), along with the STRUT vowel. The following sections outline the major vowel features of NLE.

2.2.1 NLE lax vowels

Table 2.3 provides an overview of the chief phonetic realisations of the NLE lax (or 'short') vowels. By way of comparison, the typical phonetic articulations (variants) associated with standard CE are listed in the second column; the third column groups typical pronunciations in SNLE, whether of Irish or southwest English origin. Additional (or particularly frequent) variants that occur in broader, more traditional accents of Irish and English ancestry are listed in the final two columns of the table. As outlined below, a number of the realisations which appear in these last two columns are linguistically conditioned. Some are fairly recessive today, in that they are restricted to small numbers of generally highly conservative speakers; these are enclosed in angle brackets (< >).

To reflect the more central pronunciation of the LOT/CLOTH/THOUGHT class in SNLE, it is represented in Table 2.3 (as in Table 2.2 and Figure 2.1) with the phonetic symbol /a/, rather than the retracted vowel /ɑ/, more usual across English varieties.

2.2.1.1 The KIT and DRESS lexical sets

One day when I was small in Beaumont North my buddy and I were going to the well for a turn of water. Suddenly my friend halted to ask me if I had ever heard of the old saying 'Wher dere's a well dere's a way' ... He then declared that this saying was 'some true'. 'Did you', he concluded, 'ever see a well dat didn't 'ave ne'er pat' ('didn't have no path') goin' up to 'en?' (Paddock 1982a: 71)

Despite the overlap between *will* and *well* in the above anecdote, speakers of SNLE – like standard speakers elsewhere in the English-speaking world – distinguish high lax stressed /ɪ/, as in KIT, from mid lax /ɛ/, as in DRESS. Yet as the third column of Table 2.3 indicates, both of these front vowels may exhibit some degree of raising in SNLE, at least in Irish-settled areas of the province. For many speakers of NLE, in fact,

Table 2.3 Phonetic realisations of the NLE lax vowels

Lexical set (<Wells 1982)		CE (Canadian English)	SNLE (Standard NLE)	NIE (conservative Irish-origin NLE): additional pronunciations	NBE (conservative English-origin NLE): additional pronunciations
KIT	/ɪ/	ɪ	ɪ, ɪ̞	iː	iː ɛ̝
DRESS	/ɛ/	ɛ	ɛ, ɛ̝	ɪ	ɪ, ɛ̝ɪ, æ̝
TRAP/BATH	/æ/	æ(ː)	æ(ː), æ̝(ː)	ɛ̝	ɛ̝, ɛ̝ɪ, <aː, ɑː>
LOT/CLOTH/THOUGHT	/a/	ɑ(ː), ɒ(ː)	ɒ(ː), a(ː), ɑ(ː)	ɒ̝(ː), a̝(ː)	ɒ̝(ː), a̝(ː)
PALM	/ɑ/	ɑː, ɒ(ː)	ɑː, ɒ̝, aː	æ(ː)	æ(ː)
FOOT	/ʊ/	ʊ	ʊ	ʊ̞, ʌ, u(ː)	ʌ, u(ː)
STRUT	/ʌ/	ʌ	ʌ, ʌ̝	a, ʌ̝, ʌ̞	a ʌ̝

/ɪ/ often undergoes tensing (manifested by raising along with lengthening) in two grammatical morphemes: verbal *-ing* (e.g. [*they're*] *going*), regularly pronounced with [ɪn] or [iːn]; and possessive *his* [hiːz], which may sound like *he's* (as produced by Speaker 7, in 7.4.2), possibly by analogy with this latter form.

In more traditional varieties of Irish ancestry, KIT and DRESS tensing are widespread. The DRESS set may also exhibit simple raising towards the KIT vowel, particularly before nasal and oral stops, so that *pen* may be pronounced like *pin*, and *bet*, like *bit*. KIT tensing and DRESS raising are well exemplified by Speakers 3 and 4 from Chapter 7 (see 7.2), both speakers of conservative NIE, in such words as *in, wind, system* (Speaker 4) and *dead, west, confectionery* (Speaker 3). In NBE, however, there is evidence of a more complex system of distribution which is conditioned both phonetically and perhaps, to a lesser degree, lexically. Thus depending on their context, the KIT and DRESS vowels may display not only raised and/or tensed articulations, but also lowered and/or retracted ones. KIT tensing to an [i(ː)]-like pronunciation as in the FLEECE set is most obvious in NBE in several following consonant environments: voiced velars (as in *dig*); alveopalatals (*fish*); labiodentals (especially the word *if*, though also elsewhere, as in *skiff*); and alveolar nasals (particularly the word *in*). In at least some varieties of NBE, KIT tensing occasionally occurs before /l/, particularly in the word *hill*. That this tendency may have been more widespread in previous days is suggested by the existence of such highly recessive NBE past tense forms as *loadied* ('loaded') or *fittied* ('fitted'). While the phenomenon of DRESS raising is more frequently attested than KIT tensing, its environments differ: it is most evident in NBE before a following stop or affricate, as in *set, when* or *ledge* pronounced with the [ɪ] of KIT words. Thus conservative NBE Speaker 1 (7.1.1) raises the DRESS vowel in words like *met* and *collectin'*, while Speaker 2 (7.1.2) raises it in such words as *red, head* and *vege(ta)bles*.

As to the opposite tendency, KIT and DRESS lowering/retraction, this occurs most frequently in NBE before the lateral approximant /l/, as in *will* pronounced like *well* (illustrated in the anecdote from Paddock cited above), or *tell* pronounced with an [æ]-like quality. For some speakers of NBE, KIT lowering also occurs before at least some fricatives, as when *with* is pronounced somewhat like 'weth' [wɛθ] on the part of Speaker 7 from northern Labrador (7.4.2). This tendency is also exemplified by the slight retraction and lowering of *different* (and, occasionally, *fishermen*) on the part of traditional NBE Speaker 1 (7.1.1). DRESS lowering likewise may occur before a fricative, as in *question*, or in the pronunciation of *seven* as something approaching 'savn' on the part of Speaker 1, as well as younger Speaker 9 (see 7.1.1, 7.5.2). DRESS lowering may also be found before a voiceless velar, as when the first syllable of *breakfast* is pronounced with [æ], to sound like 'brack'.

In short, the parallel phonetic conditioning, yet wide range of variation, of /ɪ/ and /ɛ/ in conservative NBE indicate a tendency towards extensive overlap, if not partial merger, of these two vowels. Thus Speaker 5 (7.3), representing an /r/-deleting NBE variety from Conception Bay, has a tendency to slightly retract and lower the KIT vowel in a word like *knit*, thereby producing a very similar vowel to his occasionally raised DRESS-word pronunciations (as in *stretchin'*). For Speaker 2 from the northeast coast, the (DRESS) vowel of *red* is articulated as higher than the (KIT) vowel of *trimmed*. Speaker 6, from coastal Labrador (7.4.1), has a tendency to lower the stressed vowel of *winter* (though not the vowel of *thing* or *sting*), yet raise her /ɛ/ tokens before many other stops (as in *pet, nettle*), and occasionally before fricatives (*yes*). Likewise, Speaker 7, from somewhat further north in Labrador (7.4.2), has a more raised vowel in *get* than in the pre-nasal environment of *swim*. Merger has been hindered, however, by the effects of standard English, along with its spelling system. Thus while the phonetic tendencies described above are still in evidence among rural speakers in areas of the province settled by the southwest English, contemporary speakers are on the whole aware of standard pronunciations, and tend to produce standard-sounding realisations in their more formal styles.

2.2.1.2 *TRAP/BATH*

As noted above, like the vast majority of North American varieties, NLE is characterised by the non-differentiation of TRAP and BATH words, that is, by the use of /æ/ in both lexical sets. And as in many North American varieties, the vowel may be lengthened in the BATH set – that is, in words such as *laugh, last, dance* and *grant*, where /æ/ is followed by either a fricative or a nasal plus consonant. In this regard, NLE differs from southern British English, which in the late seventeenth and eighteenth centuries underwent lengthening and retraction of the vowel in many BATH words, resulting over time in its present-day RP realisation as [ɑː] (a development termed by Wells 1982 the TRAP/BATH split).

Even in its standard varieties, NLE typically displays a somewhat tensed, fronted and raised articulation for the TRAP/BATH vowel. This is an obvious feature of many of the speakers found in Chapter 7, whether they represent conservative NBE (e.g. *happy, happened, half, cash*, as articulated by Speaker 1, or *cans* from Speaker 2), conservative NIE (as in *salmon* or *that's* from Speaker 4), or more innovative speech (as in stressed *class* from younger Speaker 9). This feature marks NLE within the Canadian context, particularly as the retraction of /æ/ is a feature of innovative CE via the ongoing set of lax vowel changes known as the Canadian Shift (Clarke et al. 1995). While in NLE the fronting and raising of /æ/ occurs in all environments, it is perhaps most apparent before a nasal consonant (as in *lamb* or *land*); among the two younger speakers in section 7.5, it is particularly obvious in this environment (as in their articulations of *camera's, and, Ramea*). It also occurs in a handful of lexical items – notably, *catch*, which is generally pronounced with an [ɛ]-like vowel. In conservative NBE, /æ/ typically undergoes both raising and diphthongisation before a voiced velar, as in *bag* ([bɛ̈ig] or *plank* [plɛ̈iŋk].

In no doubt conscious imitation of the prestige British model, a handful of older educated St. John's residents exhibit a more retracted, [ɑː]-like pronunciation in the BATH set. Yet this more retracted realisation also occurs historically in one conservative enclave variety of NBE, a variety centred in the north shore Conception Bay region of Bay Roberts/Port-de-Grave (Seary et al. 1968), in such BATH-set words as *path, glass* and *dance*. This early settled Avalon Peninsula dialect area also constitutes the heartland of post-vocalic /r/-deletion in NL (see 2.3.4, as well as 7.3). Its use of two phonological features emblematic of contemporary standard southern British English (RP) may have been reinforced in the past by the association of this area with the New England states, where these two features are also common.

2.2.1.3 LOT/CLOTH/THOUGHT; PALM

As is also the case in standard CE, virtually all speakers of NLE display merger of the vowels of the LOT, CLOTH and THOUGHT sets. Thus words like *cot* and *caught* are pronounced identically, as are *collar* and *caller*. A few speakers of SNLE do maintain a contrast between LOT words on the one hand, and CLOTH/THOUGHT words on the other, whether via vowel lengthening in the CLOTH/THOUGHT sets or, more rarely, greater vowel retraction. The latter also appears to be the case for some of the NBE speakers who appear in Chapter 7: Speaker 5 (7.3) has a more retracted vowel in words like *call* and *small* than he does in such LOT words as *cotton* and *prosperous*; Speaker 2 (7.1.2) has a more fronted vowel in *stopper* than he does in *small* or *saw*. Even speakers for whom LOT, CLOTH and THOUGHT words are fully merged may display a more retracted variant in the PALM class (e.g. *psalm, calm*); however, this typically constitutes a learned pronunciation, since in traditional NLE varieties PALM words belong to the TRAP/BATH set and are pronounced with /æ(ː)/.

Even more so than for the TRAP/BATH set, the articulation of the vowel of LOT/CLOTH/THOUGHT distinguishes all varieties of NLE from standard CE. In CE, the merged vowel is pronounced with [ɑ(ː)] or its rounded counterpart, [ɒ(ː)]. In NLE, however, the merged vowel is considerably more fronted and unrounded, a legacy of its southern Irish and southwestern English heritage (cf. Wells 1982; Wakelin 1988); it is typically articulated in central mid-low to low vowel space, i.e. as [ɐ(ː)] or [a(ː)]. These more fronted articulations are apparent in almost all the speech samples presented in Chapter 7: from *bottle, stopper* and *long* as pronounced by conservative NBE Speaker 2 (7.1.2), through *water, awful, rocks* and *job* (traditional NIE Speaker 4; 7.2.2), to the realisations of *population* or *lot* on the part of younger Speaker 9 (7.5.2). In short, speakers of SNLE possess a LOT/CLOTH/THOUGHT vowel that resembles the fronted realisation characterising the inland northern American cities that have undergone the vowel changes known as the Northern Cities Shift (Labov et al. 2006). Perceptually, SNLE *cot* occupies a similar vowel space to that of *cat* in innovative CE which, as noted above, is undergoing retraction of the TRAP/BATH vowel. As a result, misunderstandings are possible, as in the case of a St. John's resident whose first name, *John*, was repeatedly interpreted as *Jan* when he travelled to Toronto.

2.2.1.4 FOOT and STRUT

For many SNLE speakers, the FOOT and STRUT vowels are articulated as in many North American varieties, i.e., as high back rounded lax [ʊ] and low mid back unrounded lax [ʌ], respectively. For some speakers of SNLE, however – along with more conservative, and particularly NIE, speakers – the STRUT vowel is articulated differently from its often somewhat centralised CE counterpart: it is produced as a back, noticeably rounded [ʌ]-like vowel. As to the FOOT vowel, it may undergo raising and tensing towards the GOOSE vowel, in parallel fashion to the tendency noted for the lax front vowel /ɪ/. Again, this trend is associated more with Irish-settled areas of the province than with southwest English-settled regions. In NBE, in fact, FOOT tensing not only occurs less frequently, it also appears to be both phonetically and lexically conditioned. It is found among some conservative speakers for certain words in which the vowel is followed by voiceless velar /k/ (e.g. *book, cook, hook, look, took*), or else by voiced alveolar /d/ (e.g. *good, wood*). This pronunciation may well be an historical retention (cf. Wells 1982), since at least some of these words contained a long vowel in Middle English (and, in the case of a following /k/, for several subsequent centuries), which later underwent shortening in standard varieties.

In conservative NLE, the lexical incidence of /ʊ/ and /ʌ/ does not correspond to the distribution of these two vowels in standard North American varieties. A number of lexical items that today belong to the standard FOOT set form part of the STRUT set for conservative NBE speakers; these include *put, soot, took* and *look*. In NBE in addition, as well as for some SNLE and NIE speakers, an initial *un-* sequence tends to be pronounced not with the STRUT vowel, but rather with the [ɐ]-like vowel of LOT/CLOTH/THOUGHT. This affects the pronunciation of such lexical items as *until* and *understand*, along with the negative prefix; thus *untie* or *unlike* often sound like 'ontie' or 'onlike'. This feature may be heard, for example, in the realisations of *untangle* by NIE Speaker 4 (7.2.2), along with *unplug* on the part of younger Speaker 8 (7.5.1). A less retracted and often somewhat lowered realisation may also be heard in other environments on the part of NBE speakers, including words like *up* (Speaker 5) and *tumbler* (Speaker 2), along with *ultimate*, from Speaker 8.

2.2.2 NLE tense vowels

Table 2.4 provides an overview of the chief NLE pronunciations of the four tense (or 'long') vowels, as found in the FLEECE, FACE, GOAT and GOOSE sets. As Table 2.4 indicates, the typical phonetic realisations of these vowels are very similar in SNLE and CE (though on GOOSE in CE, see section 2.2.2.3). In both varieties, the FLEECE and GOOSE vowels – /iː/ and /uː/, respectively – display monophthongal to slightly diphthongised [ɪi/ʊu]-type pronunciations. (Although Table 2.4 does not indicate this, the lexical incidence of the FLEECE vowel extends to the final vowel in words like *happy*; that is, other than in very conservative speech, both

Table 2.4 Phonetic realisations of the NLE tense vowels

Lexical set (<Wells 1982)	CE (Canadian English)	SNLE (Standard NLE)	NIE (conservative Irish-origin NLE): additional pronunciations	NBE (conservative English-origin NLE): additional pronunciations
FLEECE /iː/	iː	iː, ɪi	<eɪ, eːə>	ɪ <eɪ, eːə, əɪ>
GOOSE /uː/	uː, ʉː	uː, ʊu, ʊ	ʉː, ʉʊ, ɵʉ, ɛʉ	ʉː, ʉʊ
FACE /eɪ/	eɪ, eː	eɪ, ɛɪ	ɛ̝ː(ə), e̞ː(ə)	ɛ̝ː(ə), e̞ː(ə), ɛ, æɪ
GOAT /oʊ/	oʊ, oː	oʊ, ɔ̝ʊ	ɔ̝ː(ə), o̞ː(ə)	ɔ̝ː(ə), o̞ː(ə)

CE and NLE display what Wells (1982) refers to as happY tensing.) As to the tense high mid vowels of FACE (/eɪ/) and GOAT (/oʊ/), both are typically upglided in SNLE, as they are in much standard CE, though Labov et al. (2006) and Boberg (2008) show that monophthongal pronunciations also occur in CE, particularly in central to western regions of the country.

As will be seen below, however, more conservative varieties of NLE differ in a number of ways from CE in terms of tense vowel production.

2.2.2.1 FACE/GOAT monophthongisation

A feature occurring in both present-day NIE and NBE, and particularly the former, is the realisation of the /eɪ/ and /oʊ/ phonemes without the upglided pronunciation that has characterised most standard varieties of English for the past 200 years. In open syllables, in which the vowel is not followed or checked by a consonant (e.g. *day, go*), the typical realisations are lengthened monophthongal [ɛ:] and [ɔ:]. Checked syllables (e.g. *date, goat, ghost*) often exhibit a schwa ([ə])-like inglide, which in some cases yields the perceptual impression of two syllables ('day-it', 'go-it'). Many obvious examples of non-upglided FACE and GOAT vowels are to be heard in the online sound files representing the two conservative NIE speakers in Chapter 7; these include *lane, Casey's, jokin', (on the) go* from Speaker 3 (St. John's; 7.2.1), along with *today, (sand)paper, hoses* and *boats* from Speaker 4 (Irish Avalon; 7.2.2). Less frequently, an inglided pronunciation also occurs among the traditional NBE speakers who appear in Chapter 7 – notably, in the articulation of *plate* by Speaker 2 (7.1.2).

Non-upglided variants can be found in all lexical items in the FACE and GOAT sets, whether their Middle English origin was monophthongal (that is, a simple vowel), as in *made*, or diphthongal, as in *maid*. Among speakers of NBE born a century ago, however, the distinction between these historically different types was often maintained phonetically via upgliding in *maid*-type but not in *made*-type words (see e.g. Colbourne 1982a). (Younger Speaker 9 in Chapter 7 provides evidence, however, that some varieties of NBE may still maintain the *made/maid* distinction via slightly different phonetic means, namely the height of the vowel nucleus; see 7.5.2 for details.)

Despite the fact that steady or monophthongal pronunciations of GOAT words are the norm among conservative speakers on the rural Irish Avalon Peninsula (see above, as well as Seary et al. 1968; Richards 2002), an alternative Irish-inherited realisation is found in at least one isolated NIE enclave variety. This is spoken in the community of Tilting on Fogo Island, Notre Dame Bay, an area otherwise settled almost exclusively by the southwest English. Here, an Irish-inherited relic pronunciation is preserved before /-ld/ in words such as *old*, which are produced with diphthongised [ɐʊ] or [ʌʊ] rather than monophthongal or inglided [o]/[ɔ] (cf. Wells 1982; Hickey 2007 for Irish English; this pronunciation of *old* is usually represented as 'oul(d)' or 'aul(d)'). Anecdotal evidence suggests that the diphthongised pronunciation in /-ld/ words was formerly a feature of the Irish-settled southern Avalon Peninsula; however, it is no longer attested in this area. The occasional articulation of *(you) know* with a lowered and somewhat unrounded vowel, followed by an upglide – as in *it may- it may you kno͟w* on the part of conservative NIE Speaker 4 (7.2.2) – may possibly constitute a remnant of this pronunciation feature, though the linguistic environment obviously differs. However, it is also the case that a similar lowered and unrounded pronunciation is occasionally used by the NBE speakers of Chapter 7, as in the realisation of word *snow* by Speaker 5 (7.3).

2.2.2.2 *The* FLEECE *set: recessive pronunciations*

You have all heard the one about the American hunter in Newfoundland who was amazed at the size of the things that his local guide called *ponds*. When the American asked what would be called a 'lake' his guide said that a 'lake' would be a hole in the bottom of a *tay-kittle*. (Paddock 1982a: 71)

The FLEECE set groups Modern English vowels that display two principal historical origins: the *-ea-* (*leak*) type, from Middle English low mid /ɛː/; and the *-ee-* (*leek*) type, from Middle English high mid /eː/. The Great Vowel Shift – which by 1600 had affected the entire system of long vowels in English – resulted in the raising of these two subsets, to /eː/ and /iː/, respectively. Subsequently, around 1700, the *-ea-* type raised to /iː/, and fell together with the *-ee-* type, in what Wells (1982) terms the FLEECE merger. Thus, both *-ea-* and *-ee-* words for the most part now sound identical in standard varieties of English.

A century ago in NLE, however, the FLEECE merger had not gone through to completion, since a mid, non-raised realization, which still occurs today in standard English in the words *break, great,* and *steak*, could often be found in the *leak* subset among traditional speakers of the period. Thus words such as *leave, beach, clean, leak* and *tea* were frequently articulated with an [e] or [ɛ] FACE-like vowel (as in the 'lake' and 'tay' representations in Paddock's anecdote above). While this conservative pronunciation has not entirely disappeared, it is now highly recessive, outside of 'performance' style (that is, exaggerated portrayal of local speech, for purposes ranging from local identity and solidarity to parody). It is best known in a handful of lexical items, among them *beat* and *beak*, which may be pronounced with [ɛː/eː(ə)] in both NIE and NBE – that is, similar to the pronunciations of *bait* and *bake* in contemporary standard English.

Even less common today is the appearance of the FACE vowel in the *meet* subset, whereby words like *indeed* or *needle* are also pronounced with [ɛː/eː(ə)], to sound like 'in-dade' or 'nay-dle'. This tendency appears to be more a feature of NIE than of NBE. Since words spelled with -*ee*- would have displayed a high [iː] or FLEECE-like vowel in many varieties of English for the past 400 years, it is possible that this represents a post-Great Vowel Shift lowering of high tense /iː/ in source varieties of NLE, as Wells (1982), indeed, suggests for Irish English.

Another unusual pronunciation within the FLEECE set occurs in a few regions settled by the southwest English, among them the Bonavista Bay island enclave variety documented by Harris (2006). This involves a centralised [əɪ]-like realisation for both *leak* (e.g. *tea, read*) and *leek* (e.g. *see, feed*) words. Whether this schwa-like pronunciation resulted from the lowering and retraction of a post-Great Vowel Shift /iː/ vowel (analogous to the development suggested in the previous paragraph), or directly from the retraction of a pre-Great Vowel Shift front mid tense /ɛː/ or /eː/, remains open to question.

2.2.2.3 GOOSE *centralisation*
Innovative CE displays a centralised articulation of the GOOSE vowel in environments other than before /l/ (Labov et al. 2006; Boberg 2008). Though /uː/ centralisation may also characterise the speech of more upwardly mobile segments of the Newfoundland population, speakers of SNLE generally retain a high back point of articulation for this vowel.

That said, GOOSE centralisation to an [ʉː]/[ʉʊ] pronunciation characterises a number of traditional speakers of NBE, in areas outside the Avalon Peninsula. Since GOOSE centralisation in southwest England is said to characterise only the traditional speech of Devon and (north) western Somerset (see e.g. Wakelin 1986) – areas which would not have had significant settlement input in other than the southeastern portion of the island, as outlined in Chapter 1 – it is unclear whether this feature is inherited or innovative. The conservative NBE speakers of Chapter 7 display both retracted and centralised realisations of /uː/, some of which may be phonetically conditioned. Thus Speaker 1 from the northwest coast (7.1.1) tends to centralise the post-alveolar vowel of *two*, yet not the vowel of *through*, which occurs after a retroflex /r/. Speaker 2 (7.1.2), from the northeast coast, has both a slightly centralised and a fairly retracted vowel in his various articulations of the word *spoon*. In terms of GOOSE centralisation, however, neither of these speakers compares with the degree of centralisation exhibited in words like *two* and *do* by Speaker 9 (7.5.2), a young female from a fairly isolated NBE-settled community in the southwest corner of the island, who nonetheless tends to retain a more backed vowel before /l/, as in *pool* and *school* (cf. Boberg 2008). Since other young female speakers outside the Avalon Peninsula have also been noted as exhibiting similar patterns of GOOSE centralisation, this may possibly represent a change in progress.

As to conservative NIE, although the two representative speech samples in Chapter 7 (Speakers 3 and 4) give no indication of GOOSE centralisation, a centralised and, at times, somewhat lowered realisation is well attested in areas settled by the southeast Irish, presumably reflecting source varieties in southeast Ireland (cf. Clarke 2004a). In NIE, while by no means limited to this environment, centralisation, often accompanied by diphthongisation, is particularly salient before /l/; thus for some speakers of NIE, *school* may sound like [skəwəl] ('skew-wel').

2.2.2.4 Tense vowel laxing

For many speakers of NLE, the lexical incidence of the GOOSE, FACE and FLEECE sets does not fully coincide with the distribution found in standard varieties elsewhere in North America: laxed vowel realisations are more prevalent in NLE, particularly for the GOOSE set. Among traditional speakers of NBE, laxing may also occur in some FLEECE and FACE words. For the FLEECE set, certain lexical items in which the vowel is followed by /p/ or /k/ (*keep, week, cheek* and *creek*) may be articulated with the [ɪ] of KIT; hence *creek* may sound like standard English *crick*, and *week*, like *wick*. For the FACE set, past forms such as *made* and *paid* may be pronounced with the [ɛ] of DRESS, as is the word *makin'* for Speaker 7, from coastal Labrador (7.4.2). As to the GOOSE set, lax pronunciations (as in FOOT) are found chiefly among older speakers of NLE (including SNLE), and both lexical and phonetic conditioning play a role. Lax /ʊ/ rather than tense /uː/ occurs, variably, in a number of lexical items in which the vowel is followed either by /m/ or /n/ (*broom, room, groom, spoon*) or by /f/ (*hoof, roof*). In conservative NBE, the lexical incidence of the lax vowel also extends to such words as *schooner* and *soon*; in addition, the lax variant is occasionally found before either /l/ (as in *foolish*) or a following stop (*hoop, food*, or – as again in the case of Speaker 7, from Labrador – *boot*). While lax /ʊ/ is by no means unknown in words like *room* or *roof* in mainland CE (as, indeed, in many standard varieties), it appears to be used much less frequently than in NLE. This is suggested, for example, by the 1972 Survey of Canadian English, where Newfoundlanders reported considerably more usage of the lax or short pronunciation in the word *roof* than did Canadian speakers as a whole (Warkentyne 1971).

2.2.3 NLE diphthongs

Table 2.5 presents an overview of the chief phonetic realisations of the PRICE/PRIZE, MOUTH/LOUD, and CHOICE lexical sets. Though Table 2.5 suggests highly similar pronunciations in both CE and SNLE, there are obvious differences between these two standard varieties.

2.2.3.1 PRICE/PRIZE, MOUTH/LOUD

CE is well known for the phenomenon referred to as Canadian Raising – that is, the use of mid rather than low vowels for the diphthongs /aɪ/ and /aʊ/ when these are followed by a voiceless consonant within the same syllable. Thus in CE, a word like *prize* – where the 'long i' diphthong is followed by voiced [z] – is typically pronounced [praɪz], with a low [a] diphthong nucleus. However, a word like *price* – with a following voiceless [s] – is pronounced [prəɪs] in CE, with a raised, mid [ə] nucleus. Similarly, *loud* contains the diphthong [aʊ], while its voiceless counterpart, *lout*, like *mouth*, is pronounced with [əʊ] or [ʌʊ] (or, in the exaggerated imitations by American speakers, very few of whom have this feature, as something approaching 'loot').

Table 2.5 NLE diphthongs

Lexical set (<Wells 1982)		CE (Canadian English)	SNLE (Standard NLE)	NIE (conservative Irish-origin NLE): additional pronunciations	NBE (conservative English-origin NLE): additional pronunciations
PRICE/ PRIZE	/aɪ/	aɪ, əɪ, ʌɪ	ɐɪ, aɪ, əɪ, ʌɪ	ʌ̣ɪ, ɔɪ	ʌ̣ɪ, ɔɪ
MOUTH/ LOUD	/aʊ/	aʊ, əʊ, ʌʊ, ɛʊ	ɐʊ, aʊ, əʊ, ʌʊ	æʊ, e/ɛʊ, æɪ	æʊ, e/ɛʊ
CHOICE	/ɔɪ/	ɔɪ	ɔɪ, oɪ	ɐɪ, ʌɪ, ʌ̣ɪ, əɪ, ɑɪ, aɪ	ɐɪ, ʌɪ, ʌ̣ɪ, əɪ, ɑɪ, aɪ

Like a number of North American varieties, NLE varieties typically display some degree of Canadian Raising for the PRICE diphthong; however, the situation is more complex in the case of MOUTH. Many speakers in areas of the province settled by the southwest English do exhibit a Canadian Raising pattern via the use of slightly higher nuclei in MOUTH words than in LOUD words, though the height differentiation between the two sets is often not as great as it is in CE (on this, cf. Boberg 2008). Thus Speaker 6, from coastal Labrador (7.4.1), has a somewhat higher, schwa-like nucleus in *out(side)* than she does in *cow*; likewise, for younger Speaker 8 (7.5.1) from central Newfoundland, the schwa-like vowel of *about* and *out* is more raised than the the [ɐ]-like vowel he uses in words like *around, found* and *thousand*. For some conservative NBE speakers, the difference between the MOUTH and LOUD sets is more marked. This is the case for Speaker 1 from the northwest coast of the island, who has not only raising in pre-voiceless environment, but also occasional backing and rounding. His *about* and *out* in *About this last – six or seven year I guess the bands have been gone out* (7.1.1) approaches the 'aboat/aboot' and 'oat/oot' pronunciations which are often associated with the neighbouring province of Nova Scotia (cf. Boberg 2008).

In the Irish-influenced NLE spoken in the area of the capital, St. John's, however, Canadian Raising is not the inherited norm for /aʊ/: thus the nucleus, though perhaps very slightly higher in pre-voiceless environments, is often not perceptually distinct in MOUTH and LOUD items. This is illustrated by the two traditional NIE speakers in section 7.1; for example, Speaker 3's pronunciation of /aʊ/ in (*and that's gone*) *out* is fairly similar to his pronunciation in *down*. The situation is complicated, however, by the fact that at least some upwardly mobile younger Newfoundlanders and Labradorians have been affected by the supralocal mainland Canadian Raising pattern, which appears to be gaining ground in the capital city and surrounding areas (Clarke 1991; D'Arcy 2005).

One additional striking NLE pronunciation of the /aʊ/ diphthong is illustrated by (younger) Speaker 9 (7.5.2) from the western portion of the island's south coast. Her realisations (as in *thousand, down, around*) are quite fronted, in that they tend to lie in the vowel space between front [ɛ] and central [ɜ]/[ɐ] (on the fronting of /aʊ/ in Newfoundland cf. also Boberg 2008). For this speaker, degree of fronting may possibly be more advanced in environments other than pre-voiceless, since her pronunciation of *about* is somewhat more centralised and schwa-like than fronted. In some communities, in addition, fronting of the diphthong nucleus may be accompanied by centralisation of the glide to [ʉ] or even [ɪ], as in the mixed south coast Irish-/English-settled Burin area described by Lanari (1994), where a word like *house* may sound like 'hice'. While Lanari shows that fronted [ɛ]-like articulations are associated with younger speakers, and while similar realisations have been noted for younger females particularly from English-settled areas off the Avalon Peninsula, there is evidence that /aʊ/ fronting in NLE is of long standing. Thus in a small southwest coast community not far from the home community of Speaker 9, Newhook (2002) found an [ɛ]-like pronunciation to be linked to women of all ages (as opposed to men). Fronted realisations also surface among traditional speakers in at least the southwestern portions of the Irish-settled Avalon, and are used as well by Speaker 5 (7.3), a traditional NBE /r/-deleting speaker from Conception Bay North.

Whether or not they make a height (and/or possibly a fronting) differentiation between pre-voiceless and other environments, for many speakers of NLE the nuclei of the PRICE/PRIZE and MOUTH/LOUD classes are never realised as fully low or open vowels; rather, they are never lower than mid low [ɐ, ʌ], etc. This is particularly evident among more traditional, and rural, speakers of both NIE (cf. Kirwin 1993) and NBE. Use of a non-low nucleus seems to be an inherited pattern, since it is also documented for Irish English (e.g. Henry 1957; Barry 1982), and is found in at least one other area of Canada settled by the Irish, the Ottawa Valley (Chambers 1975a). It is also not unknown in southwest England (Widén 1949; Upton and Widdowson 2006; cf. Wells 1982).

As to the /aɪ/ diphthong, several of the speakers in Chapter 7 reveal another striking feature of NLE. In both NIE and NBE, the nucleus of PRICE/PRIZE frequently undergoes some degree of backing, which may also be accompanied by rounding, the result typically being a wedge ([ʌ]) or rounded [ʌ]-like vowel. This feature was presumably inherited from both Irish English (cf. Henry 1957) and West Country English (Widén 1949). In the online audio samples that accompany this volume, the feature is by far most evident in (conservative NBE) Speaker 2 (7.1.2), whose articulations of words like *high*, *pie* and *wine* would probably be heard as 'hoi', 'poi' and 'woine' by speakers from elsewhere. More rounded articulations appear to be particularly favoured after a labial, as in *White's* from Speaker 3, and *while* from Speaker 4, both of whom represent conservative NIE (7.2). Retraction and possible rounding of the nucleus of /aɪ/ is a feature shared with conservative varieties in the neighbouring Maritime provinces of Nova Scotia and Prince Edward Island (on the latter, see Pratt 1982), along with parts of the eastern seaboard of the US. It is probably best known, however, as a characteristic of the speech of the so-called 'hoi toiders' (see e.g. Wolfram and Schilling-Estes 1997) of North Carolina's Outer Banks.

While /aʊ/ fronting and /aɪ/ retraction are perhaps the most salient characteristics of these two diphthongs in NLE, two other features are worth noting. Both NIE and NBE occasionally display glide weakening ('diphthong smoothing') before a following sonorant, so that words like *time, file* or *power* may be pronounced with just a lengthened vowel, resembling the monophthongal productions ('tahm', etc.) typically associated with the speech of the southern US. The final feature, which relates to the pronunciation of /aɪ/, is a traditional one which has undergone lexicalisation. In the lexical items *my* and *by*, the realisations [miː] and [biː] are common in NLE vernacular speech, as in many other vernacular varieties, when they occur in unstressed position, as in *me book, two-by* [biː]-*four*. These reflect pre-Great Vowel Shift pronunciations, since via this shift the high tense /iː/ vowel would have diphthongised, eventually resulting in the [aɪ]-like realisations today associated with the 'long i' vowel of the PRICE/PRIZE set. The same lack of participation in the Great Vowel Shift is responsible for the NLE pronunciation of *Pouch Cove*, a small community near St. John's, as 'Pooch [pʰ uːtʃ] Cove', that is, with the vowel of GOOSE rather than the expected MOUTH vowel.

2.2.3.2 *The* CHOICE *set*

Like standard speakers elsewhere, speakers of SNLE distinguish the CHOICE set (e.g. *toy, voyage, point*) from the PRICE/PRIZE sets by the use of a rounded mid back [ɔ] or [o] in CHOICE words (see Table 2.5). In vernacular styles, however, as well as among traditional speakers of both NIE and NBE, non-rounded nuclei are common in the CHOICE set. These range from the less salient [ʌ], through [ə], to the more lowered and stigmatised [ɐ] or even [a]; thus a word like *toy* may sound like *tie*. Illustrations from the speech samples in Chapter 7 occur in (NIE) Speaker 3's unrounded pronunciation of the word *Voisey's* (7.2.1), as well as (NBE) Speaker 5's articulation of *enjoy* (7.3). Unrounded pronunciations are particularly common in a handful of iconic lexical items, notably the address form and discourse marker *boy*, typically pronounced [bʌɪ] or [bɐɪ], and often written as 'b'y' (and, among some younger speakers, written and pronounced 'bah').

Since, as we have seen, the /aɪ/ diphthong may be realised with a similar range of nuclei, the result is considerable overlapping of the PRICE and CHOICE sets. For some non-standard speakers, near-merger may occur, at least in casual style. Typically, however, particularly in certain southwest English-settled areas (among them parts of the northeast coast), the two sets remain slightly distinct phonetically, in that PRICE/PRIZE words contain nuclei that are higher, more retracted and frequently more rounded, than those of CHOICE words. Thus Speaker 3 (7.2.1) has a more backed vowel in the word *pint* than in the word *Voisey's*, while for Speaker 5 (7.3) the wedge-like vowel of *nylon* is more retracted than the more centralised and lowered nucleus of *enjoy*. While this represents a pattern opposite to the one found in standard Englishes, the same distribution has been noted for conservative south-west English varieties (cf. Wakelin 1986).

2.2.4 Vowels before /r/ in NLE

Like standard speakers of CE, SNLE speakers display a six-vowel contrast in non-intervocalic pre-/r/ position, as represented by the lexical sets NEAR, SQUARE, START, NORTH/FORCE, POOR/CURE, NURSE/letteR. Table 2.6 provides a listing of the range of pronunciations which occur in SNLE, as well as in more conservative NLE varieties.

In vernacular styles, as well as in conservative NLE, this six-way pre-/r/ contrast is reduced to a four-way system. This results from two near-mergers. The first is of the NEAR/SQUARE sets, resulting in a single, non-low front vowel; thus *beer, bear* and *bare* may be pronounced identically. This merged vowel differs somewhat between NIE and NBE. In Irish-settled areas, it is more likely to be realised in the range of [i, ɪ] – that is, more similar, although not identical, to the pronunciation of *beer* than *bare/bear* in CE and other standard varieties, as in the pronunciation of *beer* on the part of Speaker 3 (7.2.1). In southwest English-settled regions of the province, a more open [ɛ]-like articulation is more common, resembling the pronunciation of *bare/bear* in most standard varieties of English. This latter pronunciation may be heard, for example, in the pronunciation of the word *clear* on the part of (NBE) Speaker 2 (7.1.2).

The second near-merger involves the back vowels. As in some varieties of North American English (with the possible exception of CURE words, as outlined in section 2.2 above), the articulations of the NORTH/FORCE and POOR/CURE sets are produced within the same vowel range. For conservative speakers – along with many SNLE speakers, at least in casual style – the resulting single back vowel is articulated as [o] or [ɔ]; thus the vowel of *poor* is pronounced with the more open vowel of *pore* (as well as of *force*), and *tour* sounds like *tore*. This mid rather than high pronunciation characterises, for example, the pronunciation of *sure* on the part of (NBE) speaker 1 (7.1.1). *Sure* being a CURE word, this realisation contrasts markedly with the centralised, schwa-like pronunciation of *sure* by Speaker 8 (7.5.1), one of the two younger speakers featured in Chapter 7.

Table 2.6 Phonetic realisations of non-intervocalic vowels before /r/

Lexical set (<Wells 1982)	CE (Canadian English)	SNLE (Standard NLE)	NIE (conservative Irish-origin NLE): additional pronunciations	NBE (conservative English-origin NLE): additional pronunciations
NEAR /iːr/	iː, ɪ, i̠, ɪ̠	iː, ɪ, i̠, ɪ̠	ɪ̠, e̥	ɪ̠; e̥
SQUARE /ɛr/	ɛ	ɛ, e	e̥ ə/ʌ (pre-vocalically)	e̥ ə/ʌ (pre-vocalically)
START /ar/	ɐ, ʌ	ɐ, ɐ̝	ɐ̝, æ	ɐ̝, æ
NORTH/FORCE /ɔr/	o	o, ɔ	(NORTH words) ɐ̝, æ	(NORTH words) ɐ̝, æ
POOR/CURE /uːr/	uː, ʉ	uː, o, ɔ; ʉ/ɚ (CURE)	–	–
NURSE (also lettER) /ɚ/	ə, ɜ	ə, ɜ	ə̝, ɵ, ʌ̝, ɔ̝	ə̝, ɵ, ʌ̝

Table 2.6 suggests considerable similarity between the pre-/r/ vowels of standard CE and SNLE. One obvious area of phonetic difference, however, is the greater fronting of the START vowel in NLE, parallel to the greater fronting of the TRAP/BATH vowel mentioned in section 2.2.1.2. As pointed out by Labov et al. (2006), relative to general CE, a fronted articulation of final or pre-consonantal /ar/ in words like *star* and *cart* occurs not only in NLE, but also in the speech of all four Atlantic provinces of Canada. This fronted pronunciation occurs in many of the speech samples provided in Chapter 7, from the word *large(r)* on the part of both (NBE) Speaker 2 and (NIE) Speaker 4, to the word *started*, as articulated by Speaker 6 from Labrador.

One further difference characterises conservative rather than standard NLE. This is the preservation of a non-rounded, START-like pronunciation in words in which in standard varieties of English /ar/ was retracted and rounded by assimilation to a previous /w/ (see Wakelin 1986 for the same feature in southwest England). Thus in traditional

NLE, the *ar* of words like *quarter* or *war* sounds like the *ar* of standard English *part* rather than the *or* of *port*. Several of the NBE speakers of Chapter 7 display this feature: Speaker 5 (7.3) has a non-rounded vowel in his articulation of *warm*, as does Speaker 2 (7.1.2) in *quarters*.

2.2.4.1 The NORTH/FORCE sets
While, like CE, SNLE displays a rounded vowel in the merged NORTH/ FORCE sets, this is not the case in traditional varieties of NIE and NBE. There, as in parts of West Country England (Wells 1982; Kirwin and Hollett 1986) and southeastern Ireland (Henry 1957; Hickey 1986), the NORTH vowel – but not the FORCE vowel – may be centralised and unrounded, yielding an [ɐ/æ]-like pronunciation. The result, among conservative speakers born prior to the mid-twentieth century, was a tendency to merge the NORTH and START sets, at least in casual style. Such speakers pronounced words like *north* as 'narth', and *port* as 'part'.

NORTH unrounding occurs frequently among the traditional speakers in Chapter 7, whether from areas of the province settled by the Irish (as in Speaker 3's articulation of *corner, north, George's*) or the English (as in *horse* from Speakers 5 and 6, along with partial unrounding of *sort* by Speaker 7 from Labrador).

NORTH unrounding is, however, a highly salient and socially marked feature, and it occurs much less frequently in present-day speech. In two small rural NBE coastal communities in which it has been investigated (Colbourne 1982a; Newhook 2002), unrounding of NORTH words was almost completely, if not totally avoided, in more formal styles.

2.2.4.2 Vowels before intervocalic /r/
Several vowel + /r/ sequences in CE, as well as in North American English in general, display different realisations when they occur before a vowel, as opposed to the pre-consonantal and word-final environments discussed above. The best-known of these involves the START and SQUARE sets, in the form of the *marry/merry/Mary* opposition. In NLE, as in CE, the historical opposition between low mid /ɛ/ and high mid /e/ has been lost before /r/, so that *merry* and *Mary* are identical. More recently, in much of CE, an additional change has occurred in that intervocalic /ar/ has fronted and raised to [ɛ], resulting in homophony between *marry* on the one hand, and *merry/Mary* on the other. In SNLE, however – outside of innovative urban speech among younger generations – the *marry* class continues to be articulated with a lower, more centralised [ɐ]-like vowel, so that pairs like *Harry–hairy* and *Barry–berry* remain distinct.

In standard CE, words in the NORTH/FORCE set are articulated in much the same way when the /or/ sequence is followed by a vowel (as in *borrow*) and when it occurs finally or pre-consonantally (as in *door* or *short*). In both cases, the /or/ vowel is in the range of high mid [o] to low mid [ɔ]. In SNLE, pre-vocalic /or/ tends to be lower and less rounded than /or/ in other positions: thus words like *orange*, *sorry*, *tomorrow* and *quarrel* are often produced with a vowel that approaches [ɑ] or even [ɐ]. (American English displays a similar pattern.) As to the NEAR set, in both CE and SNLE the vowel of intervocalic /ir/, as in *mirror*, may be more laxed ([ɪ]-like) than when either final (as in *fear*) or pre-consonantal (*feared*).

Traditional varieties of NLE display a feature that is today in considerable decline: vowel centralisation of the merged pre-vocalic /ɛr-er/ vowel, as in *merry–Mary*. Historically, what Wells (1982) terms the 'NURSE merger' resulted in the centralisation of many short vowels before final and pre-consonantal /r/ (as in *sir, learn, fern, nurse* and *word*), all of which today contain the same schwa-like vowel in most standard varieties, despite their different origins in earlier English. In some varieties, including conservative NLE, NURSE merger also affected /ɛr-er/ when it occurred before a vowel, at least in a number of lexical items. The outcome is that words like *very, berry* (and the anomalous *bury*) are produced with the /ɚ, ɝ/ vowel of *furry*, as demonstrated by the pronunciation of *very* by Speaker 6 (7.4.1). This same feature is found in many rural varieties of English; in Canada, according to the 1972 Survey of Canadian English (Scargill 1974), it is reported mostly in Newfoundland, along with the Prairie provinces in the west of the country.

2.3 Consonant features

NLE is distinct from CE not just in terms of its vowel features, but also its consonants. Once again, though the number of consonant phonemes of NLE is identical to that of standard CE (see Table 2.1), phonetic realisations may differ. Conservative NIE and NBE display a considerable number of non-standard consonant articulations, some of them shared (notably, TH-stopping), some of them not (e.g. the realisations of initial /h/ and post-vocalic /l/). Despite the generally held view that it is vowels rather than consonants that tend to differentiate accents from one another within the English-speaking world (cf. Wells 1982: 178), within NLE it is the consonant system that carries much of the phonetic distinction between varieties of southwest English origin and those with origins in southeast Ireland.

2.3.1 TH: /θ/ and /ð/

Their dialect was peculiar ... One of its traits was an inability to pronounce the th, which became t or d. Most of them were Wesleyans, and it was amusing to hear them fervently singing in their odd language: 'De ting my God dut hate, Dat I no more may do'. (Philip Henry Gosse, writing in the 1820s, as cited by Story 1982: 66)

As the above observation on the speech of the Conception Bay North area suggests, a well-known and long-standing feature of NLE is its tendency towards TH-stopping, or the articulation of the standard interdental fricatives as stops. Thus voiceless /θ/ as in _thin_ and _with_ may sound like _t_, as in _tin_ and _wit_, and voiced /ð/ as in _then_ and _other_, like the _d_ of _den_ and _udder_. This feature characterises the vernacular speech of all areas of the province, whether NIE or NBE, as attested by its frequent use on the part of all the traditional speakers who appear in Chapter 7. Before /r/, /θ/ is often palatalised and affricated, so that a word like _thrash_ is pronounced with initial [ʧ], creating homophony with _trash_ (but see also section 2.3.5.1 below); again, this is illustrated by the Chapter 7 speech samples, as in the pronunciation of _through_ by Speaker 1 and _three_ by Speaker 2 (both in 7.1).

TH-stopping occurs more frequently for /ð/ than /θ/: its incidence is particularly high in unstressed grammatical or function words (_the, that, this, those, their_ as well as _there, then_, etc.), where the stop realisation is phonetically less prominent. In such words it may be encountered, at least outside of very formal styles, among speakers from all socioeconomic levels. As Speakers 8 and 9 (7.5) demonstrate, this remains the case even for younger residents of the province. Such is the salience of this feature, however, that it is safe to say that today all speakers of NLE make some use of standard interdental variants in their formal registers. Yet as an iconic feature of NLE, TH-stopping is eminently 'performable' in contexts which, for whatever social reason, require overt indexing of Newfoundland identity.

Though not apparent in the conservative NIE speech samples provided in 7.1, other recorded data suggest that some traditional speakers – particularly those in Irish-settled areas of the province – may maintain a phonemic contrast between pairs like _thin_ and _tin_, or _then_ and _den_, via a phonetic realisation that differs from standard English, other than as spoken in Ireland. For such speakers, _th_-words are often realised as dental/postdental stops or fricatives (that is, with the tongue touching or approaching the teeth), rather than as the more retracted alveolar stops that occur in _tin/den_ words. However, perceptual discrimination is difficult in these cases, and, to date, no acoustic or experimental phonetic studies have been conducted to verify this observation.

Stopping is not the only process which affects interdental fricatives. NLE also displays TH-fronting, or the tendency to substitute the labiodental fricatives [v/f] for [θ/ð], resulting in the pronunciation of a word like *bath* as 'baf'. While TH-fronting is an important feature of innovative British English, its occurrence is infrequent in present-day NLE; along the largely Wessex-settled northeast and southwest coasts, it appears to have been a minority variant even among speakers born in the nineteenth and early twentieth centuries. From all available evidence, labiodental pronunciations are restricted in NBE to non-initial position, whether intervocalic (e.g. *Matthew*) or syllable-final (*bath, with, breathe*). In addition, in one relatively isolated area on the southwest coast where TH-fronting has also been documented, a highly unusual pronunciation has been observed (Newhook 2002). Here, [s] occurs as a variant of voiceless [θ] in non-initial position, so that the word *path* may be pronounced *pass*. Its voiced counterpart (e.g. *breathe* pronounced 'breeze') has not been attested, however. The [s] realisation is stigmatised in the local area.

Particularly when non-initial, /ð/ may also be subject to deletion in vernacular (notably NBE) speech. This is evident in the intervocalic position in such common lexical items as *whether, mother* and *father*, as well as word-finally in unstressed lexical items such as *with*. Perhaps the best-known lexical items to display this feature are the indefinite quantifiers *either* ('any') and *neither* ('none, no'). In conservative NLE, these are often realised as [ɛɹ/ɐɹ] (usually written *e'er* or *a'r*) and [nɛr/nɐɹ] (*ne'er/na'r*) (see section 3.3.3).

Because of both the salience and stigmatisation of TH-stopping in NLE, sporadic cases of hypercorrection also appear, as when the word *tong* is pronounced *thong*. One instance of hypercorrection, however, has become lexicalised. This is illustrated by the phrase *the once* (written as such, though often pronounced 'da once') which in NLE means 'immediately' or 'right away'. Historically, 'the' in this phrase does not come from the definite article *the*, but rather the preposition *to* (as also found in West Country English; see the *to* entry in the *Dictionary of Newfoundland English* (Story et al. 1990 [1982]), henceforth referred to as the *DNE*).

2.3.2 Initial H

My friend's mom is from Bonavista and is always really embarrassed when she accidentally says 'harm' instead of arm because people will know she's from Newfoundland. (http://www.greatbigsea.com/forums/133998/ ShowThread.aspx, posted by Caroldohn, 17 September 2008)

Newfoundlanders transpose H's unconsciously . . . Many of us have dropped an H in house and picked it up in hegg. (Strowbridge 2008: 2)

Within the province, among the most salient features of local pronunciation is the variable loss (and addition) of word- and syllable-initial /h/. This non-standard *h*-patterning, which characterises only NLE varieties of southwest-English ancestry, is among the most stereotyped of local features. It receives overt commentary from residents of the Irish Avalon, who stigmatise it as a rural feature (though they themselves often pronounce the name of the letter *h* as 'haitch', just as in Irish English). It is the butt of jokes, made ready use of by dialect imitators and in dialect performance and – as elsewhere in the English-speaking world – has even generated local sayings like 'Drop your aitches in 'Olyrood ("Holyrood") and pick 'em up in Havondale ("Avondale")', a variation on the Strowbridge (2008) example cited above.

In conservative NBE, in short, historical initial /h/ is frequently deleted in lexical words (e.g. *health, hungry, haul*); less frequently, non-etymological or 'intrusive' [h] is inserted prior to a word- or syllable-initial vowel (e.g. *oven* pronounced 'hoven', *easy* pronounced 'heasy'). In other words, [h] does not represent a segmental phoneme in NBE. Rather, it is a sandhi or liaison phenomenon, the presence of which as a syllable onset is favoured in two environments. The first of these involves stress: [h] is more likely to occur when the syllable in question is emphasised and given auditory prominence (as in *the hat, not the gloves*). The second involves syllable structure. The probability of [h] presence is greater after a vowel (as in *the end, I hope*), where its insertion would create an optimal syllable sequence involving vowel and consonant alternation, that is, a CV or consonant-vowel structure – than after a consonant (*that end, John hopes*). Despite lack of detailed studies on /h/ distribution in traditional southwest English varieties (cf. Kirwin and Hollett 1986 on the evidence offered by the Survey of English Dialects, or SED), there is some indication that they pattern in similar fashion. Harris (1967: 46), for example, reports [h] as a feature of 'pre-vocalic emphatic juncture' in a Devon dialect. In NBE, as well, both historical and intrusive [h] are somewhat more likely to occur before a non-rounded front or low vowel than in the environment of a following back rounded vowel, [ə] or [ʌ] (Whalen 1978).

In the speech samples provided in Chapter 7, initial *h*-deletion – noted in parentheses, as (h) – is an obvious feature of all the traditional speakers of NBE. This is the case not simply for unstressed function words like *him* or *her*, where /h/ is often deleted by standard speakers, but also in lexical words. It likewise turns up, though much more rarely (in *what (h)appened was . . .*) in the speech of younger (NBE) Speaker 9. Among the traditional NBE speakers, an intrusive [h] also occasionally occurs, almost always in a stressed syllable. The care with which Speaker 2 (7.1.2) articulates his repetition of the sequence *amber (h)andle*, which he initially pronounced as '*hamber (h)andle*', provides an indication of his awareness of the social meaning conveyed by the insertion of non-historical [h].

2.3.3 Post-vocalic L

Most speakers of SNLE, like those of other standard English varieties, use a 'dark' or velarised pronunciation of post-vocalic /l/ in words like *peel, towel* or *full*. In dark /l/ production, while the front of the tongue touches the alveolar ridge, the shape of the body of the tongue is similar to that of the high back FOOT vowel. This is phonetically quite distinct from the 'clear' or 'light' /l/ that occurs word-initially before a vowel (as in *lean, left*) in standard English; here, the body of the tongue assumes much the same shape that it does in the articulation of the high front FLEECE vowel.

In traditional varieties of NLE, however, the articulation of post-vocalic /l/ is one of the phonetic features that differ markedly between English- and Irish-settled areas of the province. In post-vocalic position, NIE has inherited from Irish English a clear rather than the usual dark articulation of /l/; thus this fronted pronunciation is the one favoured by Speaker 4 (7.2.2), in words ranging from *well* to *falls* to *whistle*. The clear variant is the traditional one in the province's capital, St. John's, particularly among older generations (as in such words as *Michael's* and *Hotel* by Speaker 3; see 7.2.1). Among younger speakers, however, its use is diminishing. Clear /l/ also occurs on the west coast of the island, in areas with French- and Scots Gaelic-speaking founder populations.

In NBE, however, a strongly velar quality is associated with post-vocalic /l/, with [ɫ] – that is, dark consonantal /l/ – being the typical realisation in all environments, as generally exemplified by the traditional NBE speakers of Chapter 7. Speaker 1's velar realisation of the /l/ of *myself* (7.1.1) contrasts strikingly with the clear /l/ of *itself* as produced by (NIE) Speaker 4 (7.2.2). Yet in parts of the English-settled coastline velar /l/ has become a vowel through loss of the front-of-tongue contact with the roof of the mouth (that is, vocalisation). The resulting vowel-like (vocoid) pronunciation is quite similar to the FOOT vowel; after low vowels, as in *tall* or *haul*, /l/ may simply disappear (just as it did in standard English *walk* and *talk*), though it may leave a trace in the form of vowel lengthening. In some regions of the province, the vocoid pronunciation of post-vocalic /l/ is virtually the only one encountered today, as in the isolated northeast coast island community described by Colbourne (1982a). That this realisation is of long historical standing is indicated by its appearance in recordings of NBE speakers born as early as the 1870s. Since post-vocalic /l/ vocalisation appears to be a fairly recent phenomenon in southern British English (Wells 1982: 259), it is possible that this development arose independently in English-settled areas of Newfoundland, though this remains to be investigated. The fact that vowel-like pronunciations are also making some inroads among younger, upwardly mobile speakers in St. John's attests to the ease with which dark consonantal /l/ may undergo vocalisation.

Despite the obvious settler origin-related regional distribution of dark vs. light post-vocalic /l/, there is considerable phonetically conditioned variation within NLE, as documented by Paddock (1982a). For example, in the Irish-settled southern Avalon Peninsula region, dark variants occur in some communities after a mid back vowel (as in *gold*) with clear variants most frequent in the environment of a preceding high front vowel (as in *feel*).

2.3.4 Deletion and insertion of R

A Newfoundlander may drop her R in one word and pick it up in another. Some people, besides Newfoundlanders, use R in fast and lost, but I've never heard anyone tell them to drop their R. (Strowbridge 2008: 2)

While pockets of post-vocalic /r/-deleting varieties exist in the neighbouring Canadian Maritime provinces, few outsiders are aware that NLE also possesses this feature. SNLE – like most North American varieties, along with most NIE and NBE – is generally described as 'r-ful', or rhotic. Indeed, NLE in general displays strong retroflexion of post-vocalic /r/ in words like *beer* or *port*, as well as intensified *r*-colouring on /ɚ/, in words like *letter* and *butter* (along with such words as *works*, as articulated by (NIE) Speaker 4 in 7.2.2).

That said, there are several regional enclaves on the island of Newfoundland which, until recently at least, have been characterised by a fairly high degree of post-vocalic /r/-deletion. The best known of these (see Seary et al. 1968) lies on the north shore of Conception Bay on the Avalon Peninsula. It is centred on the southwest English-settled community of Bay Roberts and the nearby Port-de-Grave Peninsula, though many communities throughout Conception Bay – including some very close to St. John's (and even a small pocket within the city) – exhibit some degree of /r/-deletion. In the Bay Roberts/Port-de-Grave area, traditional varieties regularly display variable post-vocalic /r/-deletion in all final (e.g. *par, pair, butter*) and pre-consonantal (*lord, feared*) environments. Speaker 5 (7.3), a traditional speaker from Port-de-Grave, provides a good illustration of /r/-deletion in this area.

As we have seen, this same regional enclave is also characterised by a feature that is extremely rare in NLE: the TRAP-BATH split (Wells 1982), that is, the retraction of /æ/ in words such as *grass* and *laugh*. Why this region in particular should exhibit such a constellation of features is not clear. The Bay Roberts/Port-de-Grave area was settled well prior to the loss of post-vocalic /r/ in much eighteenth-century southern British English (including the precursor of contemporary RP) and, in any case, settlers to this area would have originated in southwest England, where traditional dialects have remained rhotic. The explanation may lie, at least in part, in nineteenth- and early twentieth-century ties with the New England states, where these two phonetic features were common at the time. The vowel of Speaker 5's /r/-deleted word *yarn* is in fact very similar to the [aː]-like Bostonian pronunciation parodied in phrases like 'Pahk ya cah in Hahvad Yahd' ('Park your car in Harvard Yard').

Interestingly, Conception Bay North post-vocalic /r/-deletion (particularly in such salient environments as following a low vowel, as in *yarn* or *yard*) enjoys negative rather than positive evaluations on the part of Newfoundlanders and Labradorians. A recent Canadian Federal Cabinet minister whose accent maintained close ties to his Conception Bay North roots was mocked mercilessly by both the local and national press for his 'quirky' pronunciations. Their caricatures included reference not only to his post-vocalic /r/-deletion, but also to his supposed pronunciation of pre-vocalic /r/ as *w* (e.g. 'cwisis' for *crisis*, 'wetie-uh' for *retire*) – a feature that, funnily enough, was often known in Britain as 'upper class' /r/. Hampson (1982a) found that speakers from the Conception Bay North area evaluated local non-rhotic speakers as somewhat less smart, wealthy and successful than local speakers whose varieties preserved post-vocalic /r/. Sociolinguistic studies that have examined post-vocalic /r/-deletion in Conception Bay – Reid (1981) for the town of Bay de Verde at the northern extremity of the bay, and Lawlor (1986) for two small communities on the outskirts of St. John's

– have found that the area is becoming increasingly '*r*-ful'. *R*-deletion is much less frequent among younger speakers in these communities than among older speakers; yet, in general, it occurs almost as often in careful as in casual speech.

A second enclave of /r/-lessness is somewhat more geographically remote. It is located near the southern tip of the Irish-settled Avalon, in the community of Branch, where older speakers at least display post-vocalic /r/-deletion. However, this is a twentieth-century phenom-enon. Late nineteenth-century descriptions of the area note a highly marked /r/ pronunciation. Though portrayed by a visiting sportsman in the late nineteenth-century (Kennedy 1885) as a 'rolled' French *r*, it was probably more accurately a uvular [ʁ] – a pronunciation which continues to exist, though recessively, in parts of eastern Ireland, and which in former days characterised the Waterford area, where many Irish Newfoundland migrants originated (see e.g. Hickey 2002). (Some support for Kennedy's observation, however, is provided by the use of a tapped intervocalic /r/ in words like *Mary* in recordings from the 1960s of several highly conservative NLE speakers with Irish and Scottish backgrounds.) In the Branch region, one outcome of early twentieth-century change in the direction of loss of marked local features was deletion of post-vocalic /r/ in syllable-final position (as in *car*) as well as pre-consonantally (as in *card*).

Outside these two enclave areas on the Avalon Peninsula, post-vocalic /r/-deletion is also found in a number of rural coastal com-munities scattered throughout both the island and Labrador. In fact, the majority of traditional speakers who appear in Chapter 7 exhibit this feature to a small degree. However, its distribution is considerably more restricted: it tends to be limited to unstressed /ɚ/, as in *cheaper* (Speaker 4) or *trousers* (Speaker 7, from Labrador), along with a few unstressed function words and adverbials, such as *for*, *there('s)* or *their* (Speakers 1, 6 and 7). In addition, /r/ is deleted in many areas of the province when it precedes an alveolar or, especially, an alveopalatal consonant, so that *marsh* may be pronounced 'mesh' (or 'mish'), and *partridge*, 'patridge'. This represents a sound change which began as early as the fourteenth century in English, and which has resulted in such lexical outcomes as 'cuss' (*curse*) and 'bust' (*burst*) in much of the English-speaking world.

In many post-vocalic /r/-deleting varieties – standard British English (RP) in particular – /r/ is not deleted word-finally when the next word begins with a vowel, as in a phrase like *near and far*. Seary et al. (1968) suggest that this 'linking /r/' is used occasionally in the Port-de-Grave area, while Reid (1981) and Lawlor (1986) – who document Avalon Peninsula communities with fairly extensive traditional /r/-deletion

– appear to show contrary results. The /r/ pronunciation patterns of Speaker 5, however – who maintains /r/ before vowels, in *our ah coats* and *for us* – suggest that linking /r/ may have been the traditional norm in the Port-de-Grave area. Yet there is no indication that /r/-deleting varieties of NLE regularly insert a non-etymological or 'intrusive' /r/ across word boundaries, as is the case for RP, to separate vowel sequences, as in a phrase like *law-r and order*. That said, the Conception Bay North variety described above does sporadically display the tendency referred to by Wells (1982) as 'hyper-rhoticity', a tendency also attested in West Country English. In these varieties, intrusive /r/ may occur after an unstressed vowel, as in the final syllable of words like *tuna* or *Diana*, pronounced with [ɚ] ('tuner', 'Dianer'). Intrusive /r/ may also be found in unstressed final syllables written -*ow* or -*o* (as in *window, fellow, tomorrow, piano, yellow*, pronounced 'winder', etc.), where the standard English [oʊ]-like realisation is in any case a spelling pronunciation (Upton and Widdowson 2006). (An alternative though even more recessive pronunciation of the final syllable of such words in NBE is tense /iː/, as in 'folly' or 'piany' rather than *follow* or *piano*.) While intrusive /r/ in both of these contexts is infrequent today, it is more common in stressed syllables in several other lexical items, most obviously *Chica(r)go* and *wa(r)sh*, where it may occur even among non-/r/-deleting speakers of SNLE.

Though /r/-deletion is most in evidence in post-vocalic position, it may also occur in unstressed syllables where /r/ is the second element of a syllable-initial cluster, as in *pretend* or *from*. This feature characterises traditional NBE throughout the province, and may have been facilitated by metathesis, a process which reorders adjacent sounds for ease of pronunciation. In conservative NBE, /r/ in such clusters was frequently metathesised, as in *children* pronounced 'chil(d)ern', *hundred* pronounced 'hunnerd', *apron* pronounced 'apern', along with *presume* pronounced 'persume' on the part of (NBE) Speaker 2 (7.1.2). Metathesis also occasionally occurred in stressed syllables, as in *pretty* pronounced 'purty'. NBE metathesis is an inherited feature, since it follows patterns attested in southwest British English, where it has been in evidence since at least the Middle English period (Wakelin 1988).

2.3.5 Processes affecting stops

Several developments affect stops in NLE, particularly when they occur in non-syllable-initial position. These processes are largely inherited from source varieties in southwest England and southeast Ireland. They include voicing, fricativisation and glottalisation. While these tendencies apply primarily to non-initial /t/, they may also affect the voiceless stops /p/ and /k/. In addition, both /t/ and /d/ are frequently deleted in word-final consonant clusters.

2.3.5.1 Voicing

> This **Tutor**-style 2 storey home with double . . . garage has over 5000 sq. ft. of executive living. (Home Buyers Guide, *The Telegram*, St. John's, NL, 29 November 2008, p. 30)

The use of *Tutor* instead of *Tudor* in the above advertisement suggests 'confusion' of *t* and *d*. In contemporary SNLE, as in North American English in general, in post-tonic (that is, post-primary stress) position the consonant /t/ is typically articulated as a voiced [d] or a flapped [ɾ], a flap being a voiced [d]-like sound produced with a single quick tap of the tongue tip against the roof of the mouth. Flapping is the casual speech norm when /t/ occurs between a stressed and an unstressed syllable (as in *dotted*, *bottom* and *butter*), provided the latter does not consist of syllabic /n/ (as in *cotton*). Yet while many NLE speakers make no distinction between words like *shutter* and *shudder* in their casual styles, the *t/d* opposition is often restored – particularly among older speakers – in more formal styles.

Just as in SNLE, the voiced or flapped variant is a frequent realisation of post-tonic /t/ in rural southwest English-settled areas of the province. The traditional NBE speakers in Chapter 7 use both the flap and a voiceless [t] pronunciation (contrast Speaker 6's flapped realisation of *gotta* with her lack of flapping in *Batteau*; 7.4.1). Since flapping is also found in traditional West Country English (e.g. Widén 1949; Rogers 1979), it was presumably imported to Newfoundland in the speech of original settlers from southwest England. Voicing also occurs sporadically in NBE – as it does in southwest England – for the post-tonic voiceless stops /p/ and /k/. Thus a word like *pepper* may be pronounced [pʰɛbɚ] 'pebber' by conservative NBE speakers and *picket*, as 'piggott'. The *DNE* contains such variants as *stribbins* for the local word *strippings* 'dried tree boughs', *clumber* for *clumper* 'small iceberg', and *cobby* for *copy* 'jump from one pan of ice to another'.

Before /r/, as noted earlier in 2.3.1, word-initial voiceless /θ/ (*th*) may undergo affrication. An alternative realisation in NBE – which is also typical of West Country English – is voicing (and stopping), resulting in the initial sequence [dr]. As the *DNE* indicates, this process results in such traditional lexical items as *drash* (< *thrash*) 'a heavy shower', *drong/drung* (< *thrang*) 'a narrow lane or passage' and *drashel* 'threshold'. Despite these fossilised pronunciations, voicing in pre-/r/ position is no longer an active process in NBE. (The same is true of the rare cases of initial stop voicing before other sonorants, as in the word *clam* pronounced 'glam'.)

In word-final position, the opposite tendency may occur in traditional NLE, whether British or Irish in origin. Here, especially after the sonorants /n/, /r/ and /l/, voiced final /d/ may undergo devoicing to [t], so that *diamond* is pronounced 'diamont', *husband* becomes 'husbant', and *hunnerd* (< *hundred*, by metathesis) may be pronounced 'hunnert'. This tendency is perhaps most noticeable throughout the province in the lexical item *hold*, commonly heard in phrases such as *get (h)olt to, get him (h)olt.*

2.3.5.2 Fricativisation

While a voiced or flapped realisation is the most common pronuncia-tion of post-tonic /t/, a competing variant is found on the Irish-settled southern Avalon Peninsula, including the area of the capital, St. John's. This is the alveolar slit fricative [ṭ] pronunciation, which also occurs in Irish English (cf. Wells 1982; Hickey 2007). This sound is produced with a relatively flat tongue shape and wide mouth aperture, similar to the articulatory setting involved in the production of a fricative such as the initial /θ/ of *thin*, rather than the grooved tongue shape and smaller lip aperture used to articulate a sibilant fricative like /s/ or /z/. Slit fricative pronunciations may be heard in (NIE) Speaker 4 (7.2.2), in words like *water*. While the slit fricative is a salient feature to those from outside the area, it tends to pass relatively unnoticed on the Irish-settled Avalon. Clarke (1986) found that in St. John's speech the slit fricative, unlike most local features, was associated more with women than with men, and particularly with older women; and unlike most local features, its use did not diminish in formal styles.

The slit fricative realisation is found not only in post-tonic position, as in *better, putting* or *fitted*, but also in word-final position following a vowel or a sonorant, as in *but, benefit, felt* and *start*. In certain lexical items – notably the word *Saturday*, along with, occasionally, *(I) think* – the /t/ may simply be articulated as the voiceless glottal fricative [h]. Alveolar /t/ is not the only stop to display fricative variants in NLE. As in Irish English, fricativisation of velar /k/ occasionally occurs in Irish-influenced NLE in the same syllable-final environments in which slit fricative /t/ is found (as, for example, in *speak, ticket* and *working*).

2.3.5.3 Glottalisation

In present-day British English there is an increasing tendency for post-vocalic /t/ in words like *better* and *get it* to be deleted or, more accurately, heard as a slight pause. This may take the form of full replacement of the consonant by a glottal stop (noted [ʔ]), produced by a brief interruption of the airstream at the level of the glottis, as for example between the two syllables of *uh-oh*. The alternative is pre-glottalisation (glottal reinforcement), where the /t/ is retained, but preceded by glottal closure. While glottalisation in such environments does not typically occur in North American varieties – at least, outside of a syllabic /n/ context, as in *cotton* – NLE, and particularly NBE, occupy an intermediate position between Britain and North America with respect to this feature.

In NBE, including southwest English-influenced SNLE as spoken by older generations at least, a glottal variant of /t/ is often found before syllabic /l/, as in *bottle*, *mortal* and *mental*. A glottal(ised) variant may also occur in NBE in syllable-final position, whether before a consonant (as in *football*, *bootleg*, *catnap*, *Gatwick*, *salt pork*) or a pause (*foot*, *salt*). Glottalisation likewise occurs in syllable-initial position between sonorants, in words like *country*. Traditional speakers of NBE may use a glottal(ised) /t/ before syllabic /r/ (*glitter*) and /m/ (*captain*, pronounced [kʰæpʔəm]); this variant may be heard in the realisation of *winter* and *pattern* by Speaker 5 (7.3). Perhaps less frequently, glottalisation occurs in intervocalic position across word boundaries, as in *it (h)appened (this year)* or *what (h)e's gonna need* from Speaker 1 (7.1.1), and in *quite a (difference)* from Speaker 5. Yet /t/ glottalisation in this environment remains a feature of younger speech in at least some rural English-settled communities of the island, as is shown by Speaker 9 (7.5.2), who uses it in *(the Grey River) accent is* and *but I (can't really think)*. Alveolar stops are not the only ones to display glottalisation; less frequently, velars (as in *hook*) and labials (as in *top*) are glottalised in conservative NBE. Noseworthy (1971) notes a glottal pronunciation of /k/ in the NBE of the south coast community of Grand Bank in such sequences as *picking up* and *marked out*.

Increasingly, however, glottals are associated with older and traditional speakers, as many younger speakers opt for flapped variants in such words as *bottle*. With respect to glottalisation, then, NLE appears to be becoming more like the rest of North America.

2.3.5.4 Cluster simplification: final /t, d/-deletion

Though we noted in section 2.3.5.1 that /d/ in some syllable-final consonant clusters may be devoiced to [t] in NLE, the much more usual outcome is consonant cluster reduction. In vernacular NLE, as has been noted for many varieties of English, final /t/ and /d/ are frequently deleted when they occur word- or syllable-finally after another consonant, that is, in words such as *build*, *happened*, *first* and *draft*. Less frequently, other stops may be affected, as when *desk* is pronounced [dɛs].

Also commonplace in vernacular NLE, as in other varieties, is the deletion of /t/ before a following /s/ or /z/ across a morpheme boundary, as in *it's* [ɪz] and *that's* [dæs]. In English generally (though by no means categorically), reduced final consonant clusters tend to display phonetic similarity in terms of place of articulation and voicing; /d/ is particularly susceptible to deletion after the alveolar sonorants /l/ (as in *child, told*) and /n/ (as in *grind, found*).

Final /t, d/-deletion is a process that has been studied extensively in English, in terms of the various linguistic factors (constraints) that affect it. Though this process has not been subject to detailed investigation in NLE, what is striking in traditional and vernacular varieties is the frequency with which it occurs. Many traditional NLE speakers display extremely high rates of /t, d/-deletion, even when these segments carry a grammatical 'past' meaning (as does the -*ed* (/d/) morpheme in words like *sailed, fastened* and *moved*), and even, to at least some degree, when the past morpheme occurs before a following vowel (as in *moved it*). The perceptual effect is often that of an unmarked past tense which, to the untrained ear, sounds identical to the present tense form (*sail, move*, etc.). In this way, vernacular NLE resembles such varieties as African American English, as well as Caribbean English. In addition, while final /t, d/-deletion is commonplace in the speech samples provided in Chapter 7, Speaker 1, from the northwest coast of the island, offers an interesting apparent re-analysis of the verb *band*. While in standard English verbs ending in /d/ and /t/ add an extra syllable, pronounced [əd], to form their past tense (resulting in *banded*), deletion of morpheme-final /d/ in *band* by this speaker results in a single-syllable past form, pronounced 'banned'. For this speaker, that is, the verb *band* may have been re-analysed as 'ban'.

As is also found in African American English, final stop deletion after /s/ may result in such plurals as [dɛs] for *desks* and [nɛs] for *nests* (with or without lengthened final /s/), along with such verb forms as 'assin' for *asking* and 'twissin' for *twisting*. This suggests that for some traditional NLE speakers the underlying forms of such words do not include the final stop. For other conservative speakers, however, disyllabic plurals such as 'deskes' and 'nestes' indicate that the final segment is maintained in underlying mental representation. This is the case for the plural 'postes', as used by Speaker 6 from southern Labrador (7.4.1).

Despite extensive /t, d/-deletion, the opposite phenomenon – final /t, d/-insertion – has occasionally been observed in conservative NLE in a number of lexical items. These include 'clift' for *cliff*, 'skift' for *skiff*, 'townd' for *town* and 'cord' for (*apple*) *core*, along with 'cousind' and 'gownd' in NIE. This may be the effect of hypercorrection, though the phenomenon is not unique to NLE; it is reported for both southwest England and Ireland. Intrusive [d] is also occasionally found in other than word-final position, most notably in the pronunciation of *weren't* as 'weredn'(t)', as well as the more recent analogical creation 'dodn't' for *don't*.

2.3.6 Fricatives in NLE

2.3.6.1 Fricative voicing

One of the best-known features of the traditional dialects of southwest England is the tendency to voice word- and syllable-initial fricatives, so that a word like *fault* is pronounced with [v] ('vault') rather than standard voiceless [f], and *sip*, with [z] ('zip') rather than [s]. This tendency was brought to NL by settlers from the West Country and continued to characterise conservative NBE speakers born prior to the First World War.

Today, however, initial fricative voicing has all but disappeared. Its lexical effects remain in two well-known local words: *junk* (from 'chunk', a piece of wood used for burning) and *vir/var* (from 'fir'). Yet a more general effect remains in parts of the northeast coast of the island, where hypercorrection has been observed for this highly salient feature of pronunciation. In these areas, a generalised devoicing rule may apply to all lexical items pronounced locally with syllable-initial voiced fricatives: this results in 'correct' pronunciations with initial *f* in words like *fault* or *fur*, and initial *s* in *same* and *sin*, but also overgeneralised devoicings such as 'falley' for *valley* and 'sone' for *zone*. This devoicing trend may be longstanding, as attested by such *DNE* entries as *fegary*, a variant of *vagary* ('excessive ornamentation'), as well as its appearance in late nineteenth-century Devon speech (Hewett 1892), where a word like *very* could be pronounced with initial *f*. Along the northeast coast, devoicing also applies to environments other than word-initial. Thus Speaker 2 (7.1.2), representing conservative NBE from this area, exhibits fricative devoicing in word-internal position (as in *exactly* pronounced with [ks] rather than the usual [gz], along with *dessert* pronounced with [s] rather than [z]), as well as word-finally (*roses, potatoes*).

In NLE varieties of southern Irish origin, an unrelated devoicing tendency is also longstanding, and remains in common use today. This is the tendency to fully or partially devoice word- and syllable-final fricatives and affricates: thus words like *move*, *leave* and *twelve* may be articulated with final [f]; *suppose, was* and *years*, with final [s], and *judge*, with final [ʧ]. Speaker 3 (7.2.1), a conservative speaker from St. John's, illustrates this tendency in his pronunciation of *houses*, in which both the word-internal and word-final fricatives are devoiced to [s]. In NLE as well, the plural of such lexical items as *leaf* may be 'leafs' rather than standard 'leaves'. The generalisation of the singular to the plural form in such items is, however, also characteristic of vernacular NBE, as in plurals like *wolfs* (for 'wolves'), *hoofs, wharfs, midwifes* and *ourselfs*.

2.3.6.2 Metathesis and assimilation of fricatives

As we saw, syllable-final clusters consisting of /s/ + stop are frequently subject to reduction in vernacular NLE, resulting in pronunciations like [lɪs(s)] for *list*, and [æs(s)] for *ask*. In traditional NBE, however, as in southwest England, /sp/ and /sk/ may also be subject to reordering or metathesis. This process affects a handful of lexical items. Among them are *(h)asp* 'latch, snap fastener' pronounced 'apse'; *aspen* pronounced '(h)apse(n)'; *crispy* 'brittle' as 'cripsy'; *lispy* as 'lipsy'; and *wasp* pronounced 'waps'. This last item may undergo re-analysis in NBE, in that final *-s* may be interpreted as a plural, yielding a singular form *wop* or *wap*.

A feature that is not uncommon in present-day vernacular NLE – though increasingly infrequent – involves the partial assimilation of sibilants to a following syllabic nasal. In NLE, this process is restricted to negative forms of the verb *be*, where the /z/ of *is* and *was* is realised as [d]: thus *it isn't* may be heard as '*tidden*' [tɪdn̩] and *it wasn't*, as '*twudden*' [twʌdn̩]. The same lexical restrictions also applied in both major source areas of NLE, southwest England (see Troike 1986) and southeast Ireland (Hickey 2002). Once again, NLE demonstrates its conservative nature: unlike parts of the southern US, NLE has not generalised the sibilant assimilation rule to affect all lexical items in which /z/ is followed by a nasal consonant. Thus, in NLE, *doesn't* and *business* are generally pronounced with standard [z], though they may occur with [d] in southern American English.

A somewhat parallel assimilation of a fricative to a following stop occurs in traditional NBE and is much less in evidence today. This involves sequences where /v/ is followed by syllabic /n/, in words like *seven, eleven* and *heaven*. Here, the labiodental /v/ assimilates the stop feature of the following nasal, resulting in the bilabial stop [b]; and, in turn, the syllabic nasal /n/ may assume the bilabial articulation of the preceding segment, and become [m]. The result, which may also involve lowering of the stressed vowel, yields such pronunciations as 'sebm' or 'sabm' for *seven*. Again, this is an inherited feature, since it also occurs in the source varieties of NLE.

2.3.6.3 Initial /hw/ and /hj/

NLE does not distinguish words with initial *wh*, as in *whale* (a voiceless fricative represented phonetically as either /hw/ or /ʍ/) from those with initial *w*, as in *wail*. This opposition is also increasingly infrequent in much of mainland North America, as any child who has struggled with the spelling of a sequence like 'Which witch is which?' could well attest. This does not mean, however, that the [ʍ] pronunciation is entirely absent from NLE: since this realisation continues to carry connotations of correctness and elegance, it is at times consciously incorporated into the formal speech styles of some residents of the province. Cases of hypercorrection also occur, as with a recent St. John's television weather forecaster who often pronounced *southwest* – which historically contains a /w/ – as it if were 'southwhest' [sɐʊθʍɛst].

As to the initial cluster /hj/, represented by the *h* in words like *human* or *huge*, a similar process of reduction occurs in much of NLE. This results in pronunciations with simple initial [j] – thus 'hyoo-man' is pronounced 'yoo-man'. Though the historical [hj] pronunciation is generally retained in CE, usage in SNLE is divided. For many standard speakers in the province, the pronunciation of initial [h] in such words would be a feature only of formal (and for many, conscious) style.

2.3.6.4 Unusual fricative features

While the fricative features outlined above are now in decline, many enjoyed a relatively wide regional distribution within NLE in earlier days. Some features, however, appear always to have been geographically restricted.

2.3.6.4.1 /s, ʃ, tʃ/

In several small communities on the remote western south coast of the island – an area settled largely by migrants from West Country England and the Channel Islands – the palatal affricate /tʃ/ may be realised as the corresponding palatal fricative /ʃ/, so that a phrase like *chicken and chips* sounds like 'shicken and ships' (Newhook 2002). Newhook documented this feature for the community of Burnt Islands/Isles aux Morts, some twenty-five km to the east of Port-aux-Basques, at the southwestern extremity of the island. As Speaker 9 (7.5.2) notes, it also exists in the tiny coastal community of Grey River, approximately 160 km further east, though unconnected by road. Substitution of the fricative for the affricate occurs only in word-initial position, so that words like *teach* and *stretcher* are never realised as 'teash' [tʰiːʃ] and 'stresher' [stɹɛʃɚ]. The fricative realisation is highly salient in the local area and, according to Newhook, people who use it are teased about this pronunciation, which is becoming increasingly rare among younger speakers. Though its origin in Newfoundland is not fully clear, this feature was noted by Matthews (1939) as having existed several centuries ago in southwest England.

A second feature observed for parts of the southwest coast involves consonant clusters of which /s/ is the first segment (e.g. *star*, *scream* and *sleeve*). In such clusters, /s/ may be palatalised to [ʃ], so that a word like *strange* is pronounced as 'shtrange' (as exemplified by Speaker 9). The same feature occurs occasionally on parts of Newfoundland's west coast, as well as coastal Labrador, but its full geographical range has not as yet been investigated.

2.3.6.4.2 *w and v 'confusion'*

In the English-speaking world, the 'confusion' of *v* and *w* is perhaps best known via the Cockney character Samuel Weller in Charles Dickens' 1837 novel *Pickwick Papers*. In the following trial scene from Chapter 34 of the novel, though Sam indicates that his surname is spelled with a *v*, his father (the voice in the gallery) declares it to be spelled with a 'we', while at the same time pronouncing his son's name with a *v* ('*Samivel*'):

> 'What's your name, sir?' inquired the judge.
> 'Sam Weller, my lord,' replied that gentleman.
> 'Do you spell it with a "V" or with a "W"?'
> 'That depends upon the taste and fancy of the speller,' replied Sam; 'I never had occasion to spell it more than once or twice in my life, but I spells it with a "V".'
> Here a voice in the gallery exclaimed, 'Quite right too, Samivel. Put it down a we, my lord, put it down a we.'

As Wells (1982) points out, the *w/v* overlap may have been virtually obsolete in London working-class speech even in Dickens' day. Outside of parallels in Celtic Englishes, this overlap occurs today only in a small number of conservative transported overseas varieties. These include Caribbean and Tristan da Cunha English, along with the traditional dialect of Lunenburg, Nova Scotia (Wilson 1975); all of these cases, however, involve contact with other languages, and may not represent the preservation of *v/w* 'confusion' in southern British English.

On the island of Newfoundland, an overlap between labiodental *v* and the bilabials *w* as well as *b* has been documented, though rarely. NBE speakers born in the late 1800s have been known to articulate the labiodental fricatives /f/ and /v/ as bilabial stops or fricatives, and vice versa (so that *bed* may sound like [vɛd]). A few entries in the *DNE* also display *v/b* alternation, among them *bavin/babben* 'piece of wood used as kindling', and *barvel/barbel* 'apron'. In parts of southern Labrador, however, an overlap between standard English /v/ and /w/ (as well as /b/) is a clear feature of traditional speech, though it is disappearing among younger generations. Thus in the communities of North West

River and Mud Lake, near the town of Goose Bay, initial /w/ may be heard as *v*, as in words like *west*. The same is true of initial /b/ words: for example, *bedlamer* 'young seal' may be pronounced 'vellamer'. Even more common is the reverse phenomenon, whereby *vine* is pronounced like 'wine', and *vegetable*, as 'wegetable'. This tendency is not restricted to word-initial position, since it also occurs in words like *evening*.

To the untrained ear, southern Labrador speakers appear to be 'confusing' *v* and *w*, much like Dickens' Sam Weller. Closer listening, however, suggests that, in Labrador, words containing standard English /w/, /b/ and /v/ are frequently articulated with an intermediate pro-nunciation, in the form of the voiced bilabial fricative [ß] (similar to the sound heard in Spanish in words like *lava* 'lava' or *iba* 's/he was going'). Why this feature is most prevalent in the traditional speech of southern Labrador rather than the island of Newfoundland may have to do not only with European settler origins, but also language contact. A number of the early European settlers in the North West River area came from mainland Scotland as well as the Orkneys; in Scottish and Irish Gaelic, there is no simple phonemic opposition between labiodental /v/ and bilabial /b/ or /w/, as there is in English. The same is true in at least one aboriginal language of Labrador: in Innu-aimun, the *v* sound is unknown. Thus *v/w* 'confusion' in southern Labrador may have been reinforced by the aboriginal language substrate.

2.3.7 Glides in NLE: deletion, coalescence and insertion

... can you trust one of our own CBC [Canadian Broadcasting Corporation] announcers who says stoodents and opportoonidy? Certainly not ... You know that here is a brain but one evolutionary spin away from the cave (Landsberg 1980, cited in Chambers 1998)

Like most North American varieties, NLE is characterised by the general deletion of the palatal glide ('yod') when historical /juː/ follows the stops /t, d, n/ in stressed syllables, as in words like *tune, duke, new* and *student* (e.g. both traditional speakers of NIE in 7.2 – Speakers 3 and 4 – display glideless pronunciations in the word *new*). Yet as the above quote from *Toronto Star* newspaper columnist Michelle Landsberg indicates, glideless pronunciations in CE tend to be evaluated less positively than British-like glide-retaining variants, which continue to carry connotations of elegance and erudition (on this, see Clarke 2006a). As a result, pronunciations containing the glide are more usual in formal than casual styles, particularly among older generations, though Speaker 8's pronunciation of *knew* (7.5.1) indicates that the glide has by no means disappeared among younger residents of the province. For those who are particularly sensitive to the social meanings indexed by glide retention, a yod occasionally surfaces in both CE and SNLE after /s/ (as in *suit* pronounced 'syoot') and /l/ (*solution, luminous*), though this is quite rare and undoubtedly consciously done.

An alternative pronunciation for words involving /t/ and /d/ may be found in vernacular NLE. This is 'yod-coalescence', or the fusion of the stop and glide into the corresponding palatal affricates [ʧ] and [ʤ]. Thus *tune* may sound like 'choon' and *dune*, like 'June'. While the affricated pronunciation is reasonably common in contemporary British and Irish English, it is much less frequent in North America; in stressed syllables in CE, it tends to be limited to a small number of words, among them *Tuesday* and *opportunity*. In NLE, however, it represents an alternative variant in the full set of /t, d, st/ + /juː/ words, as exemplified by the pronunciation of *during* on the part of Speaker 6 (7.4.1), a traditional speaker from coastal Labrador. The affricate does, however, appear to be on the decline in the speech of younger generations.

Yod-coalescence is not the only glide feature that differentiates NLE varieties from their mainland counterparts. Conservative NBE speakers born before 1900 displayed a glide insertion and deletion tendency inherited from West Country English (cf. Wakelin 1986; Jones and Dillon 1987). Thus words beginning with a vowel or *h* – for example, *ear* / (*h*)*ere* and *other* – could be pronounced with an intrusive initial yod, to sound like 'year' and 'yuther'. At the same time, an inherited syllable-initial yod was subject to deletion, so that a word like *yeast* could sound like 'east'. This suggests that for such speakers, initial yod may have played a sandhi or liaison role similar to that described for initial *h* in section 2.3.2. Parallels are found for syllable-initial /w/ before a back rounded vowel: /w/ could undergo deletion in words like *wool* or *wood* (e.g. Noseworthy 1971), and could be inserted before /o/ or /ɔ/ following an initial consonant, as in the pronunciation of *coil* to sound like 'kwoil'. Though this process of glide insertion and deletion is no longer active in NBE, it has left lexical relics: thus *swoil/swile* 'seal' displays /w/-insertion, and words like *livyer* ('liver', in the sense of 'permanent settler') and *lovyer* 'lover' may display the addition of non-historical yod.

2.4 Sound segments in contact: deletion, insertion, assimilation

To non-Newfoundlanders, speakers of Newfoundland English may seem to speak faster than speakers of General Canadian. (http://en.wikipedia.org/wiki/Newfoundland_English)

It is probably safe to say that vernacular NLE undergoes such processes as segment deletion and assimilation to a considerably greater degree than does vernacular CE. Since outsiders often remark on the fast speech rate of many Newfoundlanders, speech tempo may well play a role here. Whatever the reason, these processes undoubtedly contribute to the difficulty experienced by many outsiders in understanding vernacular, and particularly traditional, varieties of NLE.

In section 2.3.5.4, we suggested that final consonant cluster simplification occurs in NLE with higher frequency than in most English varieties. Likewise, unstressed vowels are subject to high rates of deletion, whatever their position in the word. The narrators in the traditional folktales published by Halpert and Widdowson (1996), for example, often delete initial schwa in such words as *accordin'*, *alongside*, *another*, *appeared*, *away* and *electric*, and even the full initial unstressed syllable in words like *between*, *indeed*, *suppose* and *toward*. Word-medial unstressed vowels may also be elided, especially before sonorants, as in *partic'lar*, *lit'rate*, *bar'l* ('barrel') and *for'n* ('foreign').

Unstressed grammatical (function) words are not exempt. Prepositions are frequently deleted in traditional NLE, as in sequences like *down the store* ('down to, down at') or *bring it up d'ouse* ('up to the house'). As the last example shows, the definite article *the* is also affected. While in SNLE *the* is frequently pronounced with final [iː] before vowel-initial words, as is the norm in contemporary standard English, an alternative option in vernacular NLE is vowel elision. Given the tendency for the interdental fricatives to be pronounced as stops, this results in pronunciations like 'd'apple' [dæpl] ('the apple'), 'd'orange' [dɔɹəndʒ] ('the orange'), along with 'd' needle', as illustrated by traditional (NBE) Speaker 5 (7.3). A second alternative is a glottal stop (as in Speaker 7's pronunciation of *the island*, 7.4.2), which is often found even in SNLE for the sequence *the* + vowel. As Speaker 9's pronunciation of *the* as [dəʔ] in *the all-grade school* and *the island* (7.5.2) demonstrates, the glottal remains an option among younger speakers, just as it does in the case of the indefinite article *a* (as in Speaker 9's realisation of *a* [əʔ] *elementary school*). Contemporary NLE speakers, that is, also have an alternative to the standard English form *an* before words beginning with a vowel.

Another obvious difference involves the sequence *it* + verb *be*. While in present-day varieties of English it is the verb that undergoes contraction (e.g. *It's cold today*), conservative NLE (particularly NBE) preserves the historically earlier pattern, in which contraction affects the pronoun rather than the verb. This results in the form *'tis* rather than *it's*, along with *'twas* ('it was'), *'twill* ('it will') and *'twould* ('it would'). Today, however, these pronominal contractions are becoming increasingly less frequent.

Despite the tendency towards deletion of unstressed vowels in NLE, a schwa vowel may be inserted in certain consonant sequences for ease of pronunciation. The most obvious of these is /l/ + /m/, as in *elm* pronounced 'ellum', or *film* pronounced 'fillum'. A schwa is also inserted in conservative NIE between /r/ + /m/, as in *worm* and *barm* ('yeast') pronounced as disyllables, that is, as 'worrum' and 'barrum' (see Dillon 1968). Schwa insertion after /l/ is also found before stops, as in the pronunciation of *kelp* as 'kellup' by traditional Speaker 6 from Labrador (7.4.1), as well as in the local word *killick/kelleck* 'a stone anchor', which derives from *kelk*, a regional British English word meaning 'stone'.

Vernacular NLE also stands out in terms of consonant assimilation. By way of example, nasals frequently assume the place of articulation of a following consonant, as when *by 'n' by* 'by and by' is pronounced [bʌɪmbʌɪ], or the *m* of *I'm* is assimilated to [n], as in *I'm not* [ɐɪnnɐt], as well as in Speaker 1's pronunciation of *I'm concerned* (7.1.1). As we saw earlier, in NBE the /v/ of words like *eleven* may partially assimilate to the following nasal stop, and become articulated as a labial stop ([b]), just as in West Country English.

2.5 Prosodic features

Thus far, we have outlined the chief characteristics of individual sound segments (vowels and consonants) in NLE. The study of prosodic features (also known as suprasegmentals) involves those aspects of speech production that span individual segments, including rhythm, tempo, stress, intonation, along with voice quality and vocal tract setting. For most varieties of English, this general area of sound production is not well investigated. In fact, for NLE, there are no empirical studies of suprasegmental features.

That said, a number of impressionistic observations may be made. As previously noted, speech tempo in NLE is often perceived as being faster than in mainland Canadian varieties, though this has not been formally investigated. Some lexical items exhibit stress patterns in traditional NIE that are different from those of standard English, as well as from NBE. The NIE tendency, inherited from Irish English, is to accentuate final or next-to-final syllables in words like *appreciATE, interESTed* or *opeRAtor* (cf. Hickey 2007); this may be heard in the pronunciation *experiMENTin'* by Speaker 4, who represents traditional NIE (7.2.2). NIE and NBE, likewise, exhibit differences in their intonational patterns, though these have yet to be explored. As to vocal tract setting, it appears that speakers of NIE have a generally more fronted tongue position than speakers of NBE: the effects are seen not only in a number of vowel articulations, but also in the NIE 'clear' vs. NBE 'dark' or velarised realisation of post-vocalic /l/.

In parts of the province where local varieties of English have come into contact with minority languages, suprasegmental transfer effects have been informally observed. In the French-settled Port-au-Port area of the island's west coast, some traditional speakers of French ancestry display a degree of syllable-timed rhythm, in which syllables are of fairly equal duration, rather than the stress-timing that characterises most varieties of English, where stressed syllables have greater duration and intensity than unstressed ones. In coastal Labrador communities with mixed Inuit–European populations, the English of the resulting 'Métis' groups may differ in rhythm and intonation patterns from that of more southerly coastal Labrador communities where less interethnic contact has occurred. Speaker 7 (7.4.2) constitutes an example of this mixed variety; contrast his speech with that of Speaker 6, whose suprasegmental (and segmental) patterns more closely resemble those of the traditional NBE varieties spoken in the island portion of the province. And in the Labrador Innu communities of Sheshatshit and Natuashish, where Innu-aimun still remains the home language of most residents, the varieties of English which have emerged bear obvious contact effects at both the segmental and suprasegmental levels.

One prosodic feature of NLE has been described in some detail (e.g. Paddock 1981; Shorrocks 2003). This is the feature of pulmonic ingressive articulation, which involves the production of sounds while breathing in, rather than breathing out, as is the norm. In NLE, ingressively articulated speech has several functions (e.g. speech disguise in certain types of traditional folk performance), but today is most associated with the articulation of the discourse particles *yeah*, *no* and *mm*. Ingressive particles may be heard in several of the speakers in Chapter 7, but are most frequently used by traditional NBE female Speaker 6 (7.4.1). Clarke and Melchers (2005) trace the areal diffusion of ingressively articulated discourse particles across the North Atlantic, from northern Europe through parts of Britain and Ireland, and thence to North America, where they occur today not only in Newfoundland, but also in the Atlantic provinces and the Ottawa Valley of Canada, as well as parts of New England. Clarke and Melchers also show that ingressive particles – generally associated more with female than male speech – carry a special pragmatic meaning, namely, confirmation of already shared information or knowledge on the part of speaker and addressee.

2.6 A final note

The overview of pronunciation patterns given in this chapter attests to the remarkable degree of phonetic diversity found in the spoken English of the province. As we observed in Chapter 1, the geographic, demographic and socioeconomic situation of Newfoundland and Labrador provided ideal conditions for preservation of linguistic features brought to the area by European founder populations. Today, much phonetic change is occurring within the province, as younger generations increasingly adopt features that characterise the speech of mainland North America. Aspects of this change are discussed in Chapter 5. Yet despite the fact that younger, urban and upwardly mobile Newfoundlanders and Labradorians are coming to sound more like their peers in such mainland Canadian cities as Toronto and Ottawa, characteristic local accents are in no danger of disappearing from the province in the foreseeable future.

Additional references (phonology, and phonetic change, in Canadian English)

Boberg, Charles (2008), 'Regional phonetic differentiation in Standard Canadian English', *Journal of English Linguistics* 36.2: 129–54. (A good overview of recent developments in standard CE in all areas of the country, including Newfoundland)

Kinloch, A. M. (1983), 'The phonology of Central/Prairie Canadian English', *American Speech* 58.1: 31–5. (An earlier treatment of standard CE from Ontario to the western provinces)

Web resources (phonetic terminology)

Many descriptions of phonetics and sound production may be found online. These include:
<http://en.wikipedia.org/wiki/List_of_phonetics_topics>
<http://ell.phil.tu-chemnitz.de/phon/phon.html>

3 Morphosyntax

3.1 Introduction

Contemporary varieties of standard English differ to a much greater degree in terms of accent and sound system than they do with respect to their grammatical patterns. Though certain differences relating to word structure (morphology) and sentence structure (syntax) are evident if, say, standard Newfoundland or Canadian English is compared to standard British English, on the whole, standard varieties of English throughout the world display shared grammatical features. Likewise, English varieties spoken by those towards the lower end of the socio-economic spectrum share a number of grammatical features which are judged non-standard, no matter where in the English-speaking world they are found. These include forms such as *she don't go there* (rather than *she doesn't go there*), *they seen it* (rather than *they saw it*) and *we don't want no favours* (instead of . . . *any favours*).

What is unusual about the English of present-day NL (Newfoundland and Labrador), however, is the rich array of non-standard morphosyntactic patterns that it displays. These extend well beyond the type of features just cited, labelled 'mainstream non-standard' by Hay et al. (2008). They include many grammatical patterns inherited from source areas in the British Isles and Ireland. A small number of these – including the Irish *after*-perfect form, as in *I'm just after doing it*, meaning 'I've just done it' – also occur in contemporary Standard Newfoundland and Labrador English (SNLE). As in the case of inherited sound patterns examined in Chapter 2, some of these grammatical features continue to distinguish the vernacular speech of the Irish-settled (NIE) and southwest English-settled (NBE) areas of the province to this day.

Illustrative examples provided in this chapter are drawn from a range of sources. The chief of these, involving tape-recorded collections of regional speech within the province, are listed in Table

Table 3.1 Sources of recorded materials cited in Chapter 3

Source name	Abbreviation used	Details
Newfoundland and Labrador Feature Catalogue	NLFC (community location, and community name, provided in brackets)	A catalogue of local features of pronunciation and grammar, assembled by the author in the late 1970s from existing recorded holdings, in particular MUNFLA (see below)
Lanari tape corpus	Lanari (1994) (speaker initials appear in brackets)	Interview recordings by Catherine Lanari for 1994 MA thesis, in a mixed south coast Irish–English-settled area (greater Burin)
Newhook tape corpus	Newhook (2002)	Interview recordings by Amanda Newhook for 2002 MA thesis, in the western south coast English-settled community of Burnt Islands
Memorial University of Newfoundland Folklore and Language Archive	MUNFLA (+ speaker identification number; the C prefix represents the Card Collection)	Archival repository of NL recorded materials collected largely over the past fifty years. For information, see http://www.mun.ca/folklore/munfla/

3.1. The second column of the table provides the abbreviated form by which these sources are identified throughout the chapter. The nine speech samples given in Chapter 7 also provide a source of local grammatical features. In addition, illustrations are drawn from various printed sources which document traditional speech. These include Noseworthy (1971) and Harris (2006), who describe regional varieties of NBE as spoken in English-settled areas of the island (the south coast and Bonavista Bay, respectively); Dillon (1968), who deals with the NIE of the Irish-settled southern Avalon Peninsula; and Paddock (1981), whose data were collected around 1965 in Carbonear, a northern Conception Bay town with a mixed English–Irish population. A very important source of conservative rural speech from various parts of the island is to be found in Halpert and Widdowson (1996), a collection of folktales transcribed from sound recordings made in the 1960s and 1970s with speakers many of whom were born prior to 1900.

In all examples cited from print sources, the spelling conventions of the original have been retained. Otherwise, standard spellings are used in this chapter, despite the fact that speakers would have displayed many of the local phonetic features described in Chapter 2. The only exceptions are the use of -*in'* rather than -*ing* (as in I'm *leavin'*), and the occasional representation of consonant deletion, such as absence of the final /t/ of *wouldn't*, or of initial *h* particularly in unstressed syllables (notably in the object pronoun '*en*, where *h* is never pronounced; see section 3.3.2.3).

This chapter does not attempt to cover a number of the grammatical features that NLE shares with many spoken varieties of English elsewhere in the world. These include the use of 'singular' indefinite *they*/*them*/*their* (*everyone should give their thanks*); doubly marked comparatives and superlatives (*more richer*, *most crappiest*); and *that* instead of *who* as a subject non-restrictive relative pronoun (*a friend that took me there*). Other such features include the use of *would have* (often heard as and written 'would of' or 'woulda') rather than *had* in sentences of the type *I wish you would have done that*; and general avoidance of the modals *shall* (cf. NLE *Will I* (i.e. 'Do you want me to') *open the window?*), as well as *must* with a 'necessity' meaning (as in *You really must do it*). That said, several syntactic features that NLE shares with other vernacular varieties are treated in section 3.5. In addition, one local feature, possibly inherited from Irish English, is not further mentioned because of its apparently rare occurrence – or, at least, its rare attestation. This is the '*had to* + bare verb' structure, used to represent unrealised events in conditional (*if*) clauses, as in *If she had to be* (i.e. 'had been') *where she was three seconds earlier, we would have had to take her to the hospital* (*The Telegram*, St. John's, NL, 1 June 2009, A2).

Since the verb system in traditional NLE differs in many ways from that of standard English, it is dealt with first and is followed by a description of elements of the noun phrase; NLE pronouns in particular display a range of forms which are infrequent in contemporary world Englishes. The chapter concludes with a look at connectives (prepositions and conjunctions), as well as several non-standard syntactic patterns (among them sentence embedding and negation) that continue to characterise vernacular NLE.

3.2 The verb

3.2.1 Past forms

> I think the Government *did* the right thing, after they *done* a serious analysis, and what they *did*, they absolutely had to. (Male speaker from Grand Falls, NL, interviewed on 'Here and Now', CBC NL TV, 16 December 2008)

From its Germanic roots, English inherited a regular ('weak') past formation pattern involving the suffix *-ed* (contrast non-past *I wish* with past tense *I wished* and the perfect form (see 3.2.5 below) *I've wished*). It also inherited a host of 'strong' or irregular patterns. Most of these involve vowel change (for example, non-past *(I) ring*, past *(I) rang*, perfect *(I) have rung*); some require an additional *-(e)n* suffix in the past participle, as in the case of the verb *choose*, which has a past tense *chose*, but a past participle (*have) chosen*. In contemporary English, each irregular verb has to be learned individually, as the vowel of the non-past or 'bare' form does not indicate which pattern of vowel change it adheres to. Contrast, for example, past tense/past participle forms of three irregular verbs in standard English, all of which in their non-past form contain the 'long i' or /aɪ/ vowel: *fly (flew, have flown)*; *drive (drove, have driven)*; *fight (fought, have fought)*.

Over the centuries, some irregular verbs (e.g. *help, glide*) have become fully regularised in standard varieties, through loss of vowel change and adoption of the *-ed* past suffix. In popular speech, partial regularisation has affected other verbs, such that either the past tense or the past participle assumes the role of a single past form. This latter tendency may also occur in the more casual styles of standard speakers, in forms like *I should've ate* (rather than *eaten*), *we could've rang* (rather than *rung*), and *they might've went* (rather then *gone*).

In traditional and vernacular NLE, these regularising tendencies are considerably more advanced, as they are in many vernacular varieties throughout the English-speaking world. Table 3.2 presents a partial listing of verbs so affected. Note that the same verbs may undergo more than one regularisation process, depending on the speaker or the region. For example, on the part of traditional NLE speakers, the verbs *see* and *come* may be fully regularised via the addition of the regular past suffix *-(e)d* (*seed, comed*); the more common forms, however, are *seen* and *come* (see II in the table), just as in most vernacular varieties. Not included are verbs for which a single past form results simply from the loss of the *-(e)n* suffix in the past participle, as in (*they've/they should have) broke (it), forgot, spoke (up), stole (it), tore (it up)*, or *wore (it before)*.

Table 3.2 Non-standard past formation in traditional and vernacular NLE

Process	Examples
I. Full verbal regularisation via addition of past suffix -ed, with no vowel change	[*They/ They've*]: *blowed, buyed, catched/ cotched, creeped, choosed, comed, dealed, digged, drinked, drawed, eated, falled (down), flied, freezed (up), goed, growed, heared, hided, keeped, knowed, leaved, lied (down), losed, maked, meaned, rised, runned, seed, shined, sleeped, swimmed, teached, throwed, winned* cf. also [*She*] *borned* (*the baby*), [*They*] *were borned*
II. Partial regularisation, through extension of the vowel of the past participle to the past tense, creating a single past form [The verbs in (ii) represent cases where the resulting vowel is also identical with that of the non-past or bare form]	(i) [*They/ They've*]: *begun, done, riz* ('rose') (*up*), *rung, seen, swum* (ii) [*They/ They've*]: *become (sick), come (here), eat (it already), give (it up already)*
III. Partial regularisation, through extension of the (vowel of the) past tense to the past participle, creating a single past form	[*They/ They've*]: *did (it), drank (it all), drove (here before), fell (down), ran, rode, took (it already), went (there already), wrote (it)*
IV. Creation of new irregular verbs by analogy with existing strong verb patterns	[*They*]: *brang/have brung, scrope* ('scraped'), *sove* ('saved'), *wove* ('waved')
V. Preservation of original irregular past form in cases where standard English favours the regularised -ed form	[*They*]: *hove* ('heaved') (*it down*) (cf. *dove* and *snuck*, as also found in CE)

As Table 3.2 also suggests, vernacular NLE is occasionally less regular than are current standard varieties of English. Thus, by analogy with strong verb vowel change patterns, the past form *scrope* may be found in NLE, along with *sove* and *wove*; standard English retains the historically regular forms *scraped*, *saved* and *waved*. And as in CE in general, *dove* is often used in NLE rather than *dived*, and *snuck* rather than *sneaked*. A handful of verbs preserve the historically earlier vowel change pattern in NLE, whereas they have become fully regularised in standard varieties: the past form *hove* rather than *heaved* represents one such example. In addition, some irregular verbs display past forms in vernacular and traditional NLE that differ from those found in standard varieties: these include *sot* rather than *sat* (e.g. *They sot down*); and *upsot*, *bet* and *med* [mɛd] as the past forms of, respectively, *upset*, *beat* and *make*. While many of these forms are often encountered in contemporary NLE, some are much less frequent: this is the case, for example, of the past participle *frore* ('frozen'), which was commonplace among NBE speakers several generations ago. Two other features are even more recessive today:

(i)   the retention of the prefix *a-* before past participles, as in (*they've*) *a-come, a-seen, a-put* and *a-sold* (see section 3.2.5);

(ii)   realisation of the regular past suffix [əd] with a tense vowel ([iːd]), giving rise to such past forms as *fittied, loadied, wan(t)ied, mattied* and (as produced by Speaker 7 (7.4.2) from coastal Labrador), *floatied*.

As we saw in Chapter 2, phonetic processes in connected speech often lead to the deletion of the past suffix *-ed*. This is even the case when the verb stem ends in /t/ or /d/, which in standard English would require the addition of the past tense suffix /əd/, pronounced as a separate syllable. Thus, instead of disyllabic forms such as *shifted, wanted* or *haunted*, the past form may appear to be articulated as a single syllable, which to the untrained ear may be perceived as identical to the non-past or bare form. The following examples illustrate this for the verbs *start, want* and *land*:

1.

(a)   And I **start** to sew when I was 12 year old (Harris 2006: 97).

(b)   The woman **want** me ten years longer and I wouldn' stay (MUNFLA 305, northeast coast).

(c)   and they **land**[ed] on the island – **land**[ed] on the- to boil up I guess (Speaker 7, northern Labrador; see 7.4.2).

As (c) above (*land*[*ed*]) illustrates, however, the past suffixes of such verbs may continue to exhibit a small phonetic trace. At the same time, some verbs may be doubly marked as pasts, whether through hypercorrective regularisation or because the past marker (as in *drowned, owned*) is re-analysed as the final element of the verb stem. This results in such past forms as *beated, builded, bursted, drownded, hurted* and *ownded*. Yet for some traditional NBE speakers, verbs with stems ending in a sonorant followed by /d/, which in standard varieties mark their past forms by changing final /d/ to /t/ – among them *build, send* and *spend* – display past forms ending in [d] that appear identical to their non-past forms (Harris 2006: 97).

3.2.2 Agreement in lexical verbs

In standard English varieties, the simple non-past (the so-called 'present') tense is marked with a suffix (-*s*) only in the third-person singular, that is, with *he/she/it* subjects: contrast *s/he goes* with *I/you/we go*. In some regional varieties of English – in particular, Scottish, Scots-Irish and northern British – the verbal -*s* suffix also occurs with plural noun subjects (though not normally with adjacent personal pronoun subjects), as in the following example from earlier Scottish English:

2. The burds **cums** an' **pæcks** them ('The birds comes and pecks them') (Murray 1873: 212).

In vernacular NLE, however, the -*s* suffix serves as a generalised non-past tense marker with all subjects of lexical (full) verbs. The following examples, from traditional NLE (Clarke 1997a, drawn from Lanari's 1994 corpus) illustrate the use of verbal -*s* in cases involving pronominal subjects adjacent to their verbs:

3.
(a) They ('dragger fishermen') **comes** home long enough to get their clothes packed and go again.
(b) I always **calls** him Joseph, see.
(c) You **looks** like Sarah.
(d) I **wants** to go down if you **goes** down 'cause I **wants** to get a case of drinks.

As Clarke (1997a) shows, the -*s* suffix is employed most frequently to represent habitual events (as in 3(a) and (b) above), though it occurs readily with other event types (as in 3(c) and (d)). The use of the -*s* suffix throughout the present paradigm is extremely robust in contemporary NLE and shows few signs of diminishing in the casual speech styles of many residents of the province, particularly those in rural areas. As a highly salient grammatical marker, it forms part of the local feature repertoire when, for whatever purpose – identity, regional solidarity, caricature – speakers engage in 'performance style' (Van Herk et al. 2008). Among urban middle-class speakers, however, along with the upwardly mobile, it is largely absent outside of such contexts.

While the verb *be* constitutes a special case (see section 3.2.3 and 3.2.4), a similar levelling occurs in NLE in past tense forms of *be*, just as it does in many vernacular varieties. The past form *was* – which in standard English is associated only with third-person singular (that is, *he/she/it* subjects – is frequently generalised to all grammatical subjects in vernacular NLE, as the following examples (from Harris 2006: 100) illustrate:

4.
(a) What you **was** eating was good.
(b) They **was** a bit higher up.

While *was*-generalisation is not a feature of SNLE, it nevertheless occurs in one context in which it is also frequently found in standard varieties of English worldwide: the case of a plural subject introduced by *there*. In this context, *there was*, along with its present-tense analog, *there is*, are typical:

5.
(a) **There was** no horses to do the work (Harris 2006: 100).
(b) **There's** not too many people around here knows much about it (Lanari 1994/AM).

In British regional dialects, regularisation of past *be* may involve the generalisation of the form *were* throughout the paradigm, via extension to both first-person singular (*I*) and third-person singular (*s/he, it*) subjects (Anderwald 2001). In some British varieties, along with a handful of their North American descendants, the *were* form has become associated primarily with negative contexts, as in the US Outer Banks variety described by Wolfram et al. (1999: 98), from which the following example is drawn:

6.   Of course, when she got it, it **weren't** worth anything . . .

In NLE, first and third singular *were* is occasionally attested in traditional varieties of both NBE (7(a) and (b)) and NIE (7(c) and (d)). Most cases, however, involve affirmatives (positives) rather than negatives:

7.
(a) When I **were** twelve years old . . . He **were** a good doctor (Harris 2006: 102).
(b) I **weren't** there (MUNFLA C1221, Conception Bay).
(c) They ('there') **were** an old woman . . . lived upalong (MUNFLA C6880, Irish Avalon Peninsula; cf. also section 3.3.2.3 below).
(d) There **were** no such thing as any help from the government (MUNFLA C42, Irish Avalon Peninsula).

In conservative NLE, in short, *were*-generalisation represented a minority regional feature. In contemporary vernacular NLE it has all but disappeared in favour of the generalisation of *was* throughout the past tense.

3.2.3 Forms of do, have and be

The verbs *do, have* and *be* – which in English serve as auxiliaries as well as full (lexical) verbs – stand apart from other verbs in vernacular NLE. *Do* and *have* display a dual set of forms, correlating with their auxiliary vs. full verb function; as to *be*, it has retained a number of regional non-standard forms, particularly from its southwest British source varieties. As the examples in 8 below indicate, when *do* and *have* are used as full (that is, stand-alone) verbs in the present tense, they typically take the suffix *-s* in vernacular NLE with all subject types – that is, they behave just like other lexical verbs:

8.
(a) 'You can't tell nothing what I **does**, 'tis no odds ('it doesn't matter') what I **does**', he said . . . (Halpert and Widdowson 1996: 535).
(b) They **does** it four or five nights through 'til Christmas (MUNFLA C121, Scottish-settled southern west coast).
(c) An' they **haves** two pigs about ten feet away from the house (Halpert and Widdowson 1996: 666).
(d) . . . they **haves** seal pelt for their pillows (Recorded in Nain, Labrador, 2002).
(e) or – anything that **haves** – that kind of a stopper onto it (Speaker 2, northeast coast; see 7.1.2).

When used with a purely grammatical function as auxiliary or 'helping' verbs, however, *do* and *have* take a zero suffix, even with *he/she/it* subjects:

9.
(a) No, she **haven't been** nowhere the ('this') summer (Lanari 1994/FL).
(b) . . . and she ('horse') **haven't got** her coat back (Speaker 6, Labrador; 7.4.1).
(c) B. **wants** me, do she? (MUNFLA C404, northeast coast).
(d) . . . you know if the net **don't tangle** too much in the rocks; it **don't cost** the fishermen no money (Speaker 4, Irish Avalon, section 7.2.2).

The above pattern prevails in NBE and is still frequently encountered in the speech of all age groups. In full verb usage, the variant *has* occurs alongside *haves*; in more traditional speech *does* may be pronounced 'doos' [duːz]. Though the *-s* suffix may also be heard today in Irish-settled areas, it appears that NIE did not originally share this pattern; in conservative NIE an absence of *-s* suffix has been noted not only for third-person singular auxiliary usage of *have* and *do*, but also when these are used as lexical verbs, as in:

Table 3.3 Present-tense forms of (non-habitual) *be* in conservative NLE

Grammatical subject	
First-person singular (I)	I's ('I is'), *I be*, negative I ain't [ɛnt/ eɪnt]
First-person plural (we)	we'm ('we am'), we's, *we be*
Second-person singular ('ee < thee)	*'ee bis* [bɪs]; negative *'ee bain't* [bɛnt]; is 'ee (e.g. 'Where'<u>s</u> 'ee goin?', Noseworthy 1971: 66)
Second-person (singular and plural) (you)	you'm, you's, *you be*
Third-person singular (he, she, it)	he'm/she'm, *he/she/it be*
Third-person plural (they)	they'm, they's, *they be*

10. There's hardly a day but he **have** a different complaint (Dillon 1968: 140).

While the verb *be* does not display a differentiation of form between auxiliary and lexical verb usage, it exhibits a range of non-standard forms in the present tense. These are summarised in Table 3.3 (apart from forms representing habitual *be*, which are discussed in section 3.2.4). As can be seen, these forms largely involve the generalisation of first-person singular *am*, or third-person singular *is*, to other subjects. While these variants were quite common in the speech of earlier generations, they are much rarer today, with the exception of *ain't* (which also occurs in mainstream non-standard English). Note that the table also contains forms of *be* used with the second person singular subject *'ee* (< *thee/dee*); these have largely – though not totally – disappeared from contemporary NLE, though are known to have characterised NBE speakers born prior to 1900. It also contains the unmarked non-habitual form *be* – inherited from southwest British English – which was very rare even among NBE speakers born in the late nineteenth century. These last mentioned unusual or virtually defunct forms are italicised in the table.

3.2.4 Habitual aspect and the verb be

As noted in 3.2.2, the suffixation of -*s* to present (non-past) lexical verbs for all grammatical subjects tends to favour habitual readings. When it comes to the verb *be*, the same process is in evidence. In NBE, the invariable form *bees* (as used by Speaker 1, section 7.1.1) occurs with all grammatical subjects to represent habitual (i.e. regularly occurring) events. Contrast the habitual representations in example 11:

11.
(a) I **bees** home all the time.
(b) I never **bees** sick (Noseworthy 1971: 66, 67).

with the corresponding single-event examples in example 12:

12.
(a) I'**m** home at the moment.
(b) I'**m** sick today.

In NIE, habitual representation for the verb *be* takes another form: unstressed *do* [də] *be*, as in

13. I **do be** so hungry I don't know what I'm at (Dillon 1968: 131).

While affirmative (unstressed) *do be* is rare today, habitual *bees* is still heard in the vernacular styles of rural speakers, though it is a highly salient feature. More common still in both NIE and NBE (and even occasionally among standard NLE speakers) are negatives and interrogatives of the type:

14.
(a) There **don't be** no weather lights (NLFC, northeast coast (Twillingate)).
(b) People **don't be** afraid anymore (MUNFLA C1223, Irish Avalon Peninsula).
(c) ... because **I don't be** on the go that much (female from Happy Valley – Goose Bay, Labrador, interview CBC TV 'Here and Now', October 2008).
(d) **Do** [duᵘ] **I be** sick all the time? (Noseworthy 1971: 67–8).

Here, the auxiliary *do* combines with the stem *be* to represent not only habitual events, but also durative ones, depicting ongoing or general states of affairs. In SNLE, as in other standard varieties, such events would normally be represented by simple forms of the verb *be* ('There aren't any weather lights' or 'Am I sick all the time?').

A somewhat different construction involving *do be* occurs in negative admonitions of the type

15.
(a) **Don't be talkin!**' (Glossed as 'You don't say!' under the entry *be* in the *Dictionary of Newfoundland English*)
(b) **Don't be sayin'** stuff now (NLFC, northeast coast (Bonavista)).

Here, where the reference is to a single (punctual) event, the verb form is progressive ('**be** talk**in**', '**be** say**in**') rather than the standard simple form ('talk, say').

This structure, found throughout the province, originates in Irish English, and may also occur with such verbs as *go* (16(a)), as well as in statements rather than commands, and with auxiliaries other than *do* (16(b)):

16.
(a) I could hear 'em sayin' '**Don't you go makin**' that maid ("girl") do more of that . . .' (Newhook 2002).
(b) I **can't be doin**' that now (overheard from a St. John's male in response to whether he had done a particular task, 2 December 2003).

The overall discourse meaning conveyed by this construction is difficult to pinpoint, though the use of the progressive – which typically represents an ongoing rather than a completed event – seems to carry such connotations as greater involvement on the part of the grammatical subject, or the idea that the event in question (talking, saying or making someone do something) is not fully terminated (e.g. for 15(a), 'what you say is true, but I could tell you more/top your story'). We might add that traditional speakers of NIE also exhibit the Irish tendency to use progressives in cases where simple infinitives would be used in most English varieties, as in the following example, regarding the elderly male speaker's tendency to watch a particular television programme:

17. Oh yes. I like **to be lookin**' at it, you know (MUNFLA C6880, Irish Avalon).

3.2.5 The perfect and its equivalents

NLE is characterised by an abundance of forms that represent perfect aspect – that is, events which, though begun prior to the point of temporal reference (generally, the present), are not yet completed or have ongoing consequences. In standard varieties of English, including SNLE, perfect events are typically represented via the combination of a form of the auxiliary *have* plus the past participle of a lexical verb, as in:

18.
(a) I've just **seen** him.
(b) I **haven't seen** him yet (i.e. he's presumably still around).
(c) I **hadn't seen** him (at the point of temporal reference in the past).

Given the number of perfect equivalents available in NLE, the standard English perfect form is rarely used by some vernacular speakers, at least outside of negative and question forms.

Like other varieties, particularly those spoken in North America, NLE may employ a simple past rather than the perfect form, as in the following vernacular equivalent of 18(b):

19. I never **seen** 'en ('him') yet (Newhook 2002).

However, NLE differs from North American varieties in its use of the *after*-perfect form, consisting of *be* + *after* + the present participle (*-ing*) form of the verb, as in the following 18(a) equivalent:

20. I'm just **after seeing** him.

The *after*-perfect is inherited from Irish (and Highland Scottish) English, and was originally confined to Irish- and Scottish-settled areas of the province. Over the past half-century, however, it has been increasingly adopted in other regions, as well as among standard speakers. While 20 above might suggest that its grammatical meaning is restricted to an extremely recent ('hot news') event, the NLE *after* form actually covers a full range of perfect meanings. 21(a) and (b) below refer to events that occurred considerably prior to the speaker's description of them; 21(c), from a male speaker born in 1871, represents an event (gradual loss of his ability to speak Gaelic) which progressed over a fairly lengthy period; and 21(d) represents a still ongoing state of affairs, since the speaker continues to want the item in question:

21.
(a) No, I made one of them, too. I'm **after makin'** three or four (Lanari 1994/AM).
(b) The fire's **after burnin'** all the woods up this way (MUNFLA C6880, Irish Avalon).
(c) Anyhow, yes, I'm **after losin'** it ('the Gaelic'), losin' it fast, too (MUNFLA C121, Scottish-settled southern west coast).
(d) I'm **after wanting** that so bad, Sharon (Lanari 1994/MJA).

For some contemporary speakers, the *after*-perfect is used most frequently to depict negative outcomes, or else the importance that the speaker attributes to the event, as in

22. ... you're **after gainin'** weight since you come to Marystown (Lanari 1994/WR).

Three other forms also serve as perfect equivalents in contemporary NLE. The first – often referred to as the 'extended present', since it consists of a present tense form, almost always, through not exclusively, a simple form of the verb *be* as in example 23(a) and (b) – is restricted to the representation of ongoing events, and is largely confined to Irish-settled areas, along with the Scottish-settled southern west coast:

23.
(a) But, eh, Jim **is** ('has been') there a nice little while [now], isn't he? (Lanari 1994/WCM).
(b) I'**m** here since May (MUNFLA C121, southern west coast).
(c) I'**m** ('I've been') lookin' for a man the ('this') whole spring (male speaker from Irish Avalon, recorded St. John's August 1979).
(d) Sure she **got** ('she's had') the diarrhea the whole week (Lanari 1994/FL).
(e) ... we **have** it ('salmon trap') out since Monday now (Speaker 4, Irish Avalon, section 7.2.2).

The second and third types, both of which represent forms that were in more general use in earlier periods of English, occur frequently not only in NBE and NIE, but also SNLE. Intransitive change of state verbs (among them *change, come, drown, go, grow, move, shift* 'move', etc.) frequently take the auxiliary *be* rather than *have*, as in:

24.
(a) And when '**twas stopped** ('it had stopped') she lugged 'em into the house (Halpert and Widdowson 1996: 351).
(b) And I **wasn't left** very long before ... it got very dark (Halpert and Widdowson 1996: 660).
(c) ... but his helmet **was fell** ('had fallen') off (Lanari 1994/MWC).

As to transitive verbs, a 'medial-object perfect' is an option in cases where the grammatical object undergoes a change of state. This form differs from the present-day English perfect in that the object is situated before rather than after the past participle; in NLE, it typically co-occurs with the auxiliary *got* rather than *have*, when temporal reference is to the present, as in 25(a) and (b):

25.
(a) '... she **got everything bought** ('she's bought everything') for a boy [baby]', I said, 'she sure looks like she's havin' a girl' (Lanari 1994/AM).
(b) I **got her outlived** ('I've outlived her') by a good many years (Harris 2006: 109).

(c) If I **had a book wrote** ('If I'd written a book') now what I done ...
    nobody wouldn't believe it (Harris 2006: 108).

(d) That's as I **had the rosary said** ('That's just after I said the rosary')
    (MUNFLA C1200, Irish Avalon).

While all of the above forms are in regular use today, this is not the
case for two other perfect forms. The first is identical to the standard
perfect, apart from the fact that the past participle carries the prefix *a-*,
a remnant of the Old English prefix *ge*, as in:

26.
(a) You can't imagine how much change **we've a-seen** in our life (Harris
    2006: 109).
(b) (I've) **a-brought, a-drove, a-eat, a-heard, a-nailed** (Noseworthy
    1971: 72).

While the *a*-prefixed participle was in use by NBE speakers born prior
to about 1920, it has all but disappeared today. The same is true of *a*-
prefixed present participle forms, such as (*I'm*) *a-loading, she was a-watchin'
us*, which seem to have been less frequent in NLE than prefixed past
participles. Nonetheless, an apparent example, *they're a-watchin'*, is used
by Speaker 1, from the island's northwest coast (see 7.1.1).

The final NLE perfect form to be mentioned is not only infrequent;
it is also quite geographically restricted, as it has been attested only in
traditional NBE from parts of the south coast of the island. This form
consists of the combination of past participle (with or without the *a*-
prefix) and auxiliary *been* (pronounced [bɨn]):

27.
(a) I **been heard** it (Noseworthy 1971: 69).
(b) Dad **bin a-pulled** his weight (NLFC, Burin Peninsula).

This '*bin*-perfect' is highly unusual in world Englishes, since it is otherwise documented only for African American English. There, as in NBE,
it appears to designate an event that is relatively remote or removed
from the point of temporal reference, the present. Noseworthy (1971:
69) also provides examples of the combination of *been* + past participle
with the auxiliary *have* (along with its negative form *ain't*), as in:

28.
(a) **Have 'ee been eat?** ('Have you [singular] eaten?')
(b) I **ain't been done** it ('I haven't done it').

Such examples suggest that the affirmative *bin* form in traditional NLE
might have resulted from a more complex form consisting of *have/'ve*

+ *bin* + past participle, with ensuing loss of contracted *have* via phonological attrition (cf. section 2.4). This offers an interesting insight into a possible parallel origin for the affirmative *bin* form in African American English.

3.3 Nouns, pronouns and determiners

As we have seen, the verb in vernacular NLE possesses an especially rich morphology. Yet NLE nouns and related lexical categories also contain a number of features which are no longer widespread in contemporary English. While such features are most in evidence with respect to pronouns, they are also found among nouns, as well as determiners (among the latter, the use of *the*, *a(n)* and equivalents). One adjective feature should also be noted. In earlier English, the suffix *-en* was frequent in adjective formation (as in *woollen* 'made of wool', *wooden* 'made of wood'). Traditional NBE contains a number of adjectives of this type, among them *boarden, glassen* and *tinnen* (Noseworthy 1971; see also Halpert and Widdowson 1996). The *-en* suffix designating 'made of X', however, is no longer productive in NLE.

3.3.1 Nouns

Several noun-related features in NLE are worthy of note. The first is shared with many vernacular English varieties throughout the world: the variable omission of plural *-s* in phrases of measure which involve a specified numeral, such as *four* or *five*. These include measures of volume (*three gallon of berries*), distance (*ten mile from here*), time (29a) and weight (29b):

29.
(a) And that's **sixteen year** I (al)low ('I'd say') (MUNFLA C305, northeast coast).
(b) We had **five or six hundred pound** ('of fish') (Speaker 4, Irish Avalon; 7.2.2).

A second feature is more restricted in world Englishes: in addition to NLE, it has been noted in some regional British varieties, as well as African American English. This is the 'associative plural', used to represent an unspecified group of habitual associates, often family or close friends. It normally takes the form *and them* [n̩dɛm], but as the examples below indicate, it has an additional variant *and they*, along with a possessive form *and their* [n̩dəɹ]:

30.

(a) **Margie and them** were tryin' to say that you were over thirty-five (Lanari 1994/FL).

(b) Of course, even Scrooge didn't insist that **Cratchet and them** have mandatory drug testing (local actress Mary Walsh's 'reading' of Dickens' *Christmas Carol*, *The Telegram*, St. John's, NL, 29 November 2000).

(c) And **her brother and they** lived down there (MUNFLA C305, northeast coast).

(d) I called the plant this morning to see what was goin' on [on] **Phonse and their** boat (Lanari 1994/FL).

Though the first element of an associative plural noun phrase is normally a proper noun designating a particular individual, it also may represent the name of a group or, as in 31, a community (where 'Eastport and they' refers to residents of Eastport and neighbouring communities):

31. **Eastport and they** would come up (Harris 2006: 123).

A non-animate associative plural equivalent, *and that* [ndæt], is also found. In example 32(a), the reference is to traps and other fishing gear; in the second, a St. John's security guard describes a physical attack, in which he sustained various facial injuries; and in the third, the reference is to a house and surrounding area:

32.

(a) They used it ('shed') for mending **their traps and that** (NLFC, northeast coast (Tilting)).

(b) **Me teeth and that** was drove through me lips (CBC TV evening news, St. John's, NL, 19 January 1998).

(c) [We] cleared up **the house and that** (MUNFLA F25229, Makkovik, Labrador).

And that corresponds to indeterminates like *and everything* or *and stuff* in many contemporary varieties of English. Among the nine speakers transcribed in Chapter 7, the two younger ones (Speakers 8 and 9) use *and stuff (like that)/and things like that* exclusively, while *and that* is associated with more traditional and older speakers (such as Speaker 5 and Speaker 3, who also uses *and stuff like that*). All of these indeterminate phrases, often used as sentence-final tags, can apply to more than nouns, and thus function as more than simple associative plurals. Though no examples of this discourse function appear in the Chapter 7 data, younger speakers of NLE may produce sentences like *I go out with my friends and that* (alternatively, *and stuff/and everything*), which indicates that the speaker also engages in activities other than 'going out' with his or her friends.

3.3.2 Pronouns

Traditional and contemporary vernacular NLE display many regional pronominal features, affecting particularly, but by no means exclusively, the personal pronoun system. These are outlined in the following sections.

3.3.2.1 Pronoun exchange

didum Used by some [Newfoundland Irish] English speakers as a derisive term for English speakers of West Country origin who frequently formulated their questions with 'didem' ['did they'], as in 'Didem have blows, and didem have smacks?' (Kirwin and Story 2008)

In contemporary standard English, including SNLE, it is commonplace for subject-like pronouns to be used as grammatical objects in conjoined noun phrases (that is, after the conjunction *and*). Thus in example 33(a), *he* is used in rather than the 'grammatically correct' *him* after the preposition *for*, and *she* rather than *her* occurs as the indirect object in 33(b):

33.
(a)   He ('John McCain') said it was important for **he** and Senator Obama to debate the financial crisis (CBC radio news, St. John's, NL, 26 September 2008).
(b)   We gave **she** and her husband a tour of the place this morning (CBC NL radio interview with male resident of St. John's, May 2008).

Traditional NBE inherited a similar tendency towards 'pronoun exchange' from southwest England. Here, however, subject-like forms are used as objects whenever they bear word-stress, rather than when they are conjoined:

34.
(a)   There was a lot of **they** around (NLFC, south coast (Burgeo)).
(b)   I'll always remember **he** (Harris 2006: 115).
(c)   He load [ed] **she** ('boat') full of slabs (Harris 2006: 113).

The pronoun exchange rule is still in active use today in many small rural southwest English-settled communities. It does not occur, however, on the Irish-settled Avalon, where sentences like those above might well provoke mirth (yet cf. 58(b) below, from an Irish enclave community in northern Newfoundland).

The opposite tendency, likewise inherited from southwest England, also occurs in traditional NBE, though to a considerably lesser degree. This is the use of an object-like pronoun instead of subject forms in cases where grammatical subjects are unstressed. This usage appears confined to questions, including tag questions, as in:

35.
(a) Is **'em** ('them') goin' to get any? (Noseworthy 1971: 78).
(b) And Sam said, 'Where's **us** goin', he said, 'Eric?' (MUNFLA C296, northeast coast).
(c) We lived up on a hill, didn't **us**? (Harris 2006: 113).
(d) Where's **'en** ('him') got to? ('Where's he gone'?) (Strowbridge 2008: 43).

3.3.2.2 Grammatical gender in inanimates

Standard English the world over represents inanimate objects by means of the pronoun *it*. Yet in many varieties, including CE and SNLE, *she* is often used as the referential pronoun for mobile objects, in particular the vehicle class (cars, boats, trains, etc.). The pronoun *she* may also be found in North America, as well as Australia and New Zealand, for a number of other reference types (see Wagner 2003 for a detailed treatment), including 'non-referential' uses, where what is designated is abstract or difficult to identify. In such cases, the reference may simply be to an ongoing state of affairs or the situation at hand. A recent Canadian example occurs in the phrase *Steady as she goes*, as used by the national media to describe the Conservative Party's economic policy in the October 2008 Canadian general election.

A very different gender assignment system is to be found in those areas of NL settled by migrants from southwest England (see Paddock 1991; Wagner 2003, 2004, 2005). There the default option for inanimate count nouns (that is, nouns that can be pluralised) is a masculine referential pronoun (*he, his, him*). Thus entities ranging from buildings to tools, clothing, food, body parts, plants and beyond (see 36(f) below) were traditionally referred to as *he* rather than *it*.

36.
(a) The more barrels is under, see, the higher [h]e'd ('house') float up (Harris 2006: 117).
(b) .. me children['d] carry **he** ('keg') up on a bar[row] (MUNFLA C305, northeast coast).
(c) But what was this wooden machine, . . . what was [h]e called? (Speaker 6, Labrador, section 7.2.1, referring to an object used to bail water out of boats).
(d) And **he** ('suitcase') had a lot o' . . . newspapers into 'en ('in it'), see (Halpert and Widdowson 1996: 535).

(e)   ….. and **he's** ('finger') bad; that little bit of Bandaid come off (MUNFLA C305, northeast coast).

(f)   I'll tell ya a trick was played on me one time, and **he** was a good one (MUNFLA T84–64, northeast coast).

In conservative NBE, there are two exceptions to masculine pronoun representation for non-animates. The pronoun *it* is reserved for non-count or mass nouns, such as *weather, rain, frost, flour, truth* and *beauty*. The pronoun *she* (along with *her* and *hers*) is used to designate mobile and self-propelled entities, and is applied particularly to boats and land vehicles (including non-motorised ones, such as sleds). Though in traditional West Country English they would have been represented by masculine pronominals (Wagner 2003, 2004, 2005), objects that are 'semi-animate' – capable of wreaking destruction, producing sound or noise, and so on – also at times appear with feminine referential pronouns in NBE. These include radios, sound recorders, engines, tides from a tidal wave (as in 37(a)), guns (b), and even a burning barn (c):

37.

(a)   In **she** come again. That time **she** never come up so far. **She** went out again, an' next time **she** come in, **she** come in like **she** was before, level, ya know (C5116, southwest coast).

(b)   'Well … I had a little gun,' he said, 'an' I shoved **her** in through the hole in the door' (Halpert and Widdowson 1996: 61).

(c)   I ran down to the barn and **she** was all ablaze (*The Telegram*, St. John's, NL, 4 June 2008, A1).

In contemporary vernacular NLE throughout the province, however, – as in NIE and, occasionally, NBE – *she/her* is applied more extensively, much as it is elsewhere in North America. This is illustrated by the first two examples in 38(a) and (b) (where the reference is, respectively, to the Great Depression of the 1930s and to a Labrador City restaurant), as well as the non-specific reference uses represented in 38(c) and (d):

38.

(a)   Depression, whatever you might call 'er (MUNFLA C5116, southwest coast).

(b)   We finally decided that we would have to shut 'er down (CBC TV 2008 'Here and Now' feature 'Booming Lab West', part 1).

(c)   Every now and then I gets out and lets 'er go, right, when I get there (Lanari 1994; said of nights spent out drinking).

(d)   They'd sing 'er up (MUNFLA C6880, Irish Avalon) (cf. *put 'er up*, meaning 'make a racket').

In 38(c) and (d), *her* has a more general reference to the ongoing situation or the context at hand.

The use of *she* in present-day vernacular NLE is, however, by no means identical to its use in mainland North America. NLE possesses a number of well-known expressions which are not shared with mainland varieties, other than in parts of the Maritime provinces of Canada. These include the greetings *How's she goin?* and the Irish-inherited *How's she cuttin?*, as well as such expressions as *she's gone, boy, she's gone* (where *she* might refer to the old way of life, the economic situation, etc.). These expressions have come to take on an emblematic or iconic status, amusingly illustrated by the skit 'She's awful bad' from the Newfoundland comedy group Buddy Wasisname and the Other Fellers (available at www.buddywasisname.com/l_awful.htm). As markers of solidarity or local identity, or in a playful way, they may also be interjected into conversation by speakers of SNLE.

3.3.2.3 Third-person singular forms ('en, existential it/they)

In addition to its use of grammatical gender, traditional NBE displays another inherited feature affecting third-person singular pronouns. As in southwest England, the object form of the masculine pronoun is not the standard *him*, but rather [ən], a form that is generally assumed to have originated in the historical direct object form (cf. Old English *hine*) rather than the indirect object *him*. Since, as we have seen, non-mobile count nouns are typically masculine in NBE, the *'en* object form is used not simply to designate humans (as in 39(a)) and animals, but also inanimates (39(b) and (c)):

39.
(a) We held meetings and explained to 'en (Speaker 1, northwest coast; 7.1.1).
(b) And he ('suitcase') had a lot o' ... newspapers into 'en ('in it'), see (Halpert and Widdowson 1996: 535).
(c) I didn't realize the lamp chimney was hot, [I] just grabbed 'en off for to clean 'en (Newhook 2002).

The use of *'en* distinguishes NBE from NIE; Irish-settled areas use the standard object forms *him* and *it*, except for a small number of cases where dialect transfer of the *'en* form has occurred.

Both traditional dialect types, however, share another third-person singular pronominal feature, again fairly infrequent today. This is the use of *it* rather than standard English 'existential' or 'expletive' *there* – that is, in cases where *there* is non-referential, but simply represents a place-holder before the verb (generally a form of *be*), as in:

40. **There are** two people outside the window.

As can be seen from examples 41(a)–(d), existential *it* occurs in NLE not simply in main clauses, but also in tags (as in 41(d)):

41.
(a) He said, 'Oh, **it's** no need to stand up' (NLFC, northern Newfoundland (St. Anthony)).
(b) I couldn't say **it was** anything to it (NLFC, northeast coast (Carmanville)).
(c) **It's** people out there for probably ten or twenty years [who] still gets [sea]sick (Lanari 1994/JP).
(d) Lot of guys through here this year, **is it**? (MUNFLA C5431, west coast).

Even more rarely, *they* ('dey') occurs as an existential form in NIE, as well as in some areas of southwestern Newfoundland. Examples include 7(c) (***They** were an old woman . . .*), along with Speaker 3 (the conservative St. John's speaker of 7.2.1, as in *And then on the corner of Springdale Street **they** were – Goobie's grocery store*), who also employs both *it* and *there* as existential pronouns. Whether this form originates in the third-person plural pronoun *they*, or whether it represents an *r*-deleted variant of existential *there*, is unclear. However, the general persistence of post-vocalic /r/ among the majority of NIE speakers (including Speaker 3) may constitute evidence in favour of the former origin. Montgomery (2006) attributes the existential *they* form, which also occurs in Appalachian English, to an Ulster and ultimately Scottish historical source: To account for its appearance on the Avalon Peninsula, this construction in all likelihood also had a southern Irish origin.

3.3.2.4 You forms
In standard spoken English, the historical second-person distinction between singular (grammatical subject form *thou*, object *thee*) and plural (subject form *ye*, object form *you*) had disappeared by the mid-eighteenth century. Such was not the case, however, for conservative and vernacular NLE. Conservative rural speakers of NBE born up to around the First Word War maintained this distinction via use of a singular form *thee* (pronounced as either *dee* or, more usually, *'ee*), and a plural form *you* (much more rarely, *ye*). Examples 42(a) and (b) were recorded from rural males on the northeast coast of Newfoundland, born in 1874 and 1883, respectively:

42.
(a) That's so ('as') much, Bob, as I can tell **'ee** into ('in', i.e. 'of') that story (NLFC, Bonavista).

(b) **Thee's** [di:z] got a young jar ('seal'), that's what **thee's** got (MUNFLA C299).

Though it may still be heard in some rural areas, the singular (*d*)*ee* form is highly recessive in contemporary NBE. However, the singular/ plural distinction remains alive in some parts of southwest English-settled Newfoundland through use of a special plural form, *yous* ([juːz], unstressed form [jəz], 'yiz'), as in the following example:

43. Did **yous** go mummering when **yous** was young? (Newhook 2002).

Whether or not the *yous* plural form was imported to Newfoundland or developed independently via the analogical extension of plural -*s* is unclear. Whatever its origin, this form has existed in Newfoundland for some time, since it is attested among NBE speakers from the south and northwest coasts of the island who were born in the last decades of the nineteenth century (see Halpert and Widdowson 1996).

In Irish-settled areas both on and off the Avalon Peninsula, neither (*d*)*ee* nor *yous* is the norm. There, the singular/plural distinction was traditionally maintained through use of *ye* [jiː] as a plural form (as in example 44, from the community of Flatrock, near St. John's), and *you* (when unstressed, *ya* [jə]) as the singular:

44. How long are **ye** here? (Halpert and Widdowson 1996: 564).

The *ye* plural remains in regular use today in the casual styles of younger speakers in NIE areas, including standard speakers, as does its possessive form *yeer*. Among younger speakers, however, it is increasingly coming into competition with imported North American forms, in particular the plural *you guys*, used to refer to both males and females.

In some areas at least, the tendency to maintain a singular/plural distinction in the second person has given rise to a considerable range of forms among traditional speakers. For the south coast NBE community of Grand Bank, with a population of only 4,000, Noseworthy (1971) noted more than half a dozen constructions representing plural *you*. These included *yous, all yous, ye all, y'all* and *'ee all*.

3.3.2.5 Other pronominal features

Traditional and vernacular NLE – whether southwest British or southeast Irish in origin – shares a number of pronominal features with many other vernacular varieties. These include the first-person singular (unstressed) possessive adjectival form *me* rather than *my* (as in *me book*;

see section 2.2.3.1), along with reflexive pronouns based on the posses-sive form (*meself, hisself, theirself/ theirselves*). Likewise, as in many varie-ties, *what* can be used as a relative pronoun in NLE. Though infrequent today, it occurred in traditional NBE to refer to both things (as in 45(a)) and people (as in 45(b) and (c)):

45.
(a) **Everything what** she had (NLFC, northeast coast (Twillingate)).
(b) ... the other **woman** now **what** Jack was livin' with (Halpert and Widdowson 1996: 770).
(c) ... them men **what** was doin' the work (MUNFLA C3122, Big Bay, Labrador).

Vernacular NLE also shares with many vernacular varieties the use of pronominal *them* as a demonstrative in place of standard *those* (as in 45(c) above, where it occurs as a determiner, or in *All them were tore down* from Speaker 3; see 7.2.1). This usage is most frequent in phrases designating past time, notably the phrase *them days* ('in days gone by' or, in contemporary North American English, 'back in the day') and its equivalent *them times*, as used by Speaker 5 (see 7.3). Note that in NBE the rule of pronoun exchange (section 3.3.2.1) may also apply here, resulting in the form *they*, as in

46. ... for to lanch ('launch') one of **they** schooners (MUNFLA C305, northeast coast).

Two final pronominal features of NLE were inherited from Irish English. On the Irish Avalon, 'untriggered' reflexives are occasionally found, as in *Himself wants to speak to you*. Slightly more widespread and more common is the use in requests of (plural) *us* to mean (singular) *me*, as in *Give us a nickel, missus* (Story 1982: 64).

3.3.3 Determiners: articles and quantifiers

Traditional NLE differs from standard varieties of English with respect to its use of the definite article (*the*), as well as the indefinite quantifiers *either* and *neither*, which often correspond to simple indefinite articles (*a/ an*) in other varieties.

When reference is general – that is, to a class of objects rather than a specific object – contemporary standard English frequently uses no article at all, though *the* with the meaning 'any/a' may be found in such phrases as *on (the) plane/train, in/to (the) hospital, in (the) summer/winter*. In traditional NLE, however, the definite article is used with non-specific

reference for a much wider range of nouns, among them the following
(the examples in 47(a) represent traditional sayings):

47.
(a) black as **the tar**; to be like **the bun** (' to be simple-minded'; Strowbridge
    2008: 20); clean as **the whistle** (Speaker 4, Irish Avalon; 7.2.2).
(b) And she a-lyin' there **in the bed** (Recorded in Nain, Labrador, 2002); I
    don't be **in the bed** two minutes and I'm asleep (Recorded in St. John's,
    July 2008).
(c) (I) used to make **the lye** ... with **the wood ashes** (NLFC, Avalon
    Peninsula (Ferryland)).
(d) He was very fond of **the gun** (Halpert and Widdowson 1996: 173).

The definite article also occurs in NLE in two other contexts in
which it would not be found in standard English. The first, however,
occurs in many vernacular varieties: use of the definite article, rather
than possessive *my*, in a handful of idiomatic phrases (notably *the
wife, the woman*). The second is less common in world Englishes and
involves the use of *the* rather than a demonstrative ('this') or adjective
('next, last') with nouns designating specified periods of time (e.g. *the
week, the year*). It frequently occurs with names of seasons, as in 48(a)
and (b):

48.
(a) No, she haven't been nowhere **the summer** ('this past/last/current
    summer') (Lanari 1994/FL).
(b) I'm going there **the fall** ('this coming/next fall').

Whether or not the origin of this use of *the* is the definite article or the
preposition *to* (as in *tomorrow, today*) remains unclear (see section 2.3.1 for
a possible parallel with the NLE time phrase *the once*).

As to the expression of indefinites, traditional NLE is unusual in that
it has generalised the forms *either* and *neither*, which in standard varieties
– at least, according to prescriptivists – are restricted to the representation of only two entities (as in 'neither one of the two'). *Either* (and its
reduced form *e'er* or *a'r*), along with *neither* (*ne'er, na'r*), are used in both
NBE and NIE with the general sense of 'any' and 'no/none'. As the
following examples show, they frequently appear in contexts in which
standard English would be more likely to use the indefinite article *a(n)*,
or *any*:

49.
(a) You don't see **either** old washing tub ('any old washing tubs') out on a
    fence today ((MUNFLA C6880, Irish Avalon).

(b) He hasn't got **either** ('a') hammer (NLFC, St. John's area (Petty Harbour)).

(c) You wouldn't have **neither** ('a') drop of milk (Harris 2006: 128).

(d) I never had **na'r** gun ('I didn't have a gun') (MUNFLA C299, northeast coast).

(e) I wrote off a hundred and six now from memory. I never took **neither one** ('any') of 'em out of a book (*DNE* Supplement (1990), citation under the *neither* entry).

Several other frequent NLE noun quantifiers or intensifiers are used in ways that are either unusual or no longer current in world Englishes. These include *scattered* (with the meaning of 'occasional'), *all, every bit* and *a nice bit*:

50.

(a) ... a **scattered** feed o' meat (Widdowson 1964: 45); a **scattered** feller asked me (NLFC, northeast coast (Bonavista)).

(b) ... when we was growin' up, sir, we had to drink **all** ('nothing but/only') molasses (MUNFLA 305, northeast coast).

(c) 'Twas **every bit** ('totally/completely') fresh butter (MUNFLA 305, northeast coast).

(d) ... **a nice bit** of time ('quite a while') (NLFC, northeast coast (Bonavista)).

3.4 Other lexical categories

As described below, the categories of adverbials, prepositions and conjunctions are also of interest in NLE in that they may be used differently than in contemporary standard English.

3.4.1 Adverbs

Apart from a few forms (such as *very good, fast asleep, quite bad*), adverbial intensifiers (or 'adverbs of degree') are marked in standard English with the suffix -*ly* (*really bad, terribly good*). These adverbs no longer retain their literal meaning, but simply serve to intensify or reinforce the quality designated by a following adjective or adverb. While in earlier English adjectives and adverbs were often indistinguishable in form, the formation of adverbs from adjectives through the addition of the -*ly* suffix became the norm in the eighteenth and nineteenth centuries. In popular speech, however, many of these intensifiers continue to display bare adjective-like forms, as in *real bad* or *awful quick*(*ly*).

Vernacular NLE is characterised by a number of adjective-like adverbial intensifiers that may not be typical in the casual styles of contemporary speakers elsewhere in the English-speaking world. In addition to *terrible* (as in *terrible bad*), these include *shocking* (*shockin' good*), *pure* (*pure miserable*), *ugly* (*ugly fine*) – a form most frequently encountered in Labrador – as well as *wonderful*, as in the name of a well-known Newfoundland music group, *The Wonderful Grand Band*, who had they come from elsewhere might simply have been called 'The Really Great Band'. Less usual, and more common in Irish-settled areas, is the intensifier *cruel*, as in a *cruel stormy day*, documented by Dillon (1968: 135). Some of these adverbials can modify both adjectives and (verbal) participles, but at least one, *fair*, tends to be associated almost exclusively with participles: (*I'm*) *fair gone* ('really tired out/almost totally exhausted'); *fair poppin'* ('almost bursting with too much food'; Strowbridge (2008: 168)). The intensifier *handy* (as in (*I'm*) *handy gone*) may also behave in the same way.

The best known of the NLE adverbial intensifiers, however, is *some* (example 51(a)) which also occurs in parts of Nova Scotia and the New England state of Maine. Another frequently-used intensifier (*right* in 51(b)) has undergone decline in much of the English-speaking world, though it is maintained in a number of vernacular varieties in locations that include the north of England (Ito and Tagliamonte 2003) as well as Atlantic Canada.

51.
(a) 'Tis **some hot** today (Paddock 1981: 15).
(b) It's not too far at all, it's just ... **right handy** ('really near/close by') (MUNFLA F25229, Makkovik, Labrador).

Both *some* and *right* readily co-occur with other intensifiers (e.g. *some shockin' good*), though not with each other.

In NLE, these adverbial intensifiers tend to occur more frequently in traditional speech rather than the vernacular speech of adolescents and young adults; the latter tend to favour a range of newer intensifiers (see section 5.5). None of these forms, that is, has been recycled by younger generations in NL, and thereby taken on new and 'trendy' connotations, as has happened in at least two cases elsewhere. Stenström et al. (2002) show that the *right* intensifier has recently begun to re-emerge in the teenage speech of London. And Macaulay (2006) documents the recent rise of *pure* as an intensifier among teenagers in Glasgow.

While adverbial intensifiers stand out in NLE, several other adverb uses merit mention. It is not uncommon for *after* to be used in contemporary NLE as an adverb, with a meaning that somewhat, but not fully, approximates standard English 'afterwards'. In the conversational examples below, both from St. John's, the speaker in 52(a) is referring to her situation after surgery, while the second speaker's query relates to the activities of the addressee after the speaker had left her the previous day:

52.
(a) I was losin' a lot of blood and that **after** ('as it turned out'; 10 December 2008).
(b) Where did you go, **after**? (15 July 2007).

Also common is the use of the adverb *so* in the denial *It is so!*, which contrasts with *It is too!* in much of North America, and which may be of Irish origin. Likewise fairly common is the use of the traditional verb phrase *had (a)like to* with the meaning of 'almost', as in:

53. I **had alike to** finish ('I almost finished') the job (Strowbridge 2008: 43).

Finally, though it has virtually disappeared today, conservative speakers of Irish and Scottish origin used the adverb *yet* where contemporary standard English would use *still*, as in:

54.
(a) Dan talks the Gaelic **yet**?
(b) I can remember **yet**, I was tryin' to learn to talk English (both from MUNFLA C-121, Scottish-settled southwest coast).

3.4.2 Prepositions

In vernacular NLE, locational and directional prepositions are often found in combination, as opposed to their single prepositional equivalent in standard varieties. *Off* frequently combines with *of*, as in *That come off of* (prounounced 'offa') *the roof.* The combination *out of* occurs in such examples as in *I went on home out of it* (suggesting a person's voluntary relocation from an undesirable situation) or *Get on out of it!* Directional ('dynamic') *to* often co-occurs with a more specific directional preposition (*down, up, over* or *out*) to yield prepositional phrases such as (*I walked) down to the store/over to the seniors' home/up to the mall* or *out to Topsail* (cf. Harris 2006: 124). Greater specification is also apparent in traditional NBE in the use of the noun phrases *spring of the year* and *fall of the year*, rather than simply 'spring' and 'fall' as names of seasons; this usage is inherited from southwest England. This tendency can also take the form of over-specification, as in *a meal of food* or *a job of work*. In addition, in all traditional varieties, preposition-like words are used as particles in some verb + particle combinations that are not the norm in standard

English. These include *kill up* ('kill'); *come in* ('be introduced, start'), as in *when the draggers first come in*; and *go out* ('cease to exist, disappear'), as in *six or seven year I guess the bands (h)ave been gone out*, from Speaker 1 (7.1.1), where *gone out* is equivalent to *gone* (cf. also the use of *gone out* by Speaker 3).

What is probably most striking to outsiders, however, is Newfoundlanders' and Labradorians' use of the dynamic prepositions *to*, *into* and *onto* with stative (that is, non-dynamic) meaning. Thus NLE *to/into* may correspond to standard *at* or *in* or, quite frequently, to no preposition at all, while *onto* is the equivalent of *on*. All of the following examples are drawn from traditional NLE speakers, particularly speakers of NBE:

55.
(a) working **to** Grand Falls; out where I was **to** (NLFC, northeast coast (Twillingate)).
(b) Where did you see the woman **to**? (NLFC, Irish Avalon (Ferryland)).
(c) I was there **to** the meetin'; livin' down **to** Pike's Arm (NLFC, northeast coast (Lewisporte)).
(d) like over (h)ere **to** the Grenfell Mission (Speaker 6, Labrador; 7.4.1).
(e) a bottom **into** ('in') it; whatever was **into** ('in') the board (NLFC, northeast coast (Carmanville)).
(f) And also there's a can opener **onto** ('on') it (Speaker 2, northeast coast; 7.1.2).

In fact, stative *to* and its counterpart, stative *at*, figure in one of the most widely-known stereotypical expressions associated with NLE:

56. Stay where you're **at** (alternatively, 'where you're to') and I'll come where you're **to** (alternatively, 'where you're at').

Stative *to* remains common in contemporary NLE, even among young standard speakers. The following example occurred in a recent television interview with a newly graduated male student of a St. John's community college:

57. I'd like to live in Europe some day, or here – wherever the money's **to** (CBC TV 'Here and Now', St. John's, NL, week of 1 September 2008).

Also common in present-day NLE is is the Irish-like use of *on* to signify the negative impact of an event on the speaker (the Irish English 'dative of disadvantage', noted by Kallen 1995; Filppula 1999). This is illustrated in 58 below. 58(b) comes from the Irish enclave community of

Conche, towards the northern extremity of the island of Newfoundland, an area otherwise settled by the southwest English:

58.
(a)   It broke **on me** (overheard in St. John's, 2003).
(b)   ... the squalls was that ('so') hard she ('boat') blowed around twice **on he** (MUNFLA C3354).

Other prepositional-like phrases which characterised traditional NLE, however, have not fared as well among younger generations. Among these are *clear of*, along with *outside of*, with the meaning of 'except (for)', and *handy to/handy about*, with the meaning of 'close to' or 'like':

59.
(a)   That was all **clear o'** Gander (Harris 2006: 126).
(b)   nothing **handy to** it (NLFC, northern Newfoundland (Conche)).

3.4.3 Conjunctions

Vernacular and traditional NLE are characterised by a number of conjunctions not found in current standard English. Today, many of these are quite old-fashioned, though are still heard in the casual styles of some speakers. As illustrated in example 60, they include (*as*) *according* [kɐɹdɪn] *as* ('when, while, in the order in which, in proportion to'); (*a*)*fraid* ('for fear that'); and *till* and *where* [wəɹ], both used in clauses of purpose with the meaning 'so that, in order that' (the former, *till*, apparently of Irish origin). Two further forms, *without* (meaning 'unless') and (*a*)*gain* ([gɪn] 'against'), function as prepositions in contemporary standard English:

60.
(a)   ... she said 'Step on every step **'cording as** you comes down' (Halpert and Widdowson 1996: 152).
(b)   You cooked **according as** they came in (*The Telegram*, St. John's NL, 2 May 2009, E2).
(c)   And she got to keep her eye on him **'fraid** he's going to go off ... and fall down ... (Paddock 1981: 16).
(d)   Bake me [a] cake mother ... **till** I goes off to see where Tom is (Halpert and Widdowson 1996: 7).
(e)   The woman got to watch her steps **where** she won't go down between and break her leg (Paddock 1981: 16).
(f)   ... **without** there was no crooked one (NLFC, Conception Bay (Bell

Island)); you wouldn't touch that **widout** you had to (Harris 2006: 127).

(g) ... **(a)gain** they come ('against their coming') (Widdowson 1964: 45).

One conjunction identified as new in Canadian (Toronto) English (Chambers 1987) may, however, be long-standing in NLE. This is the conjunction *(ex)cep(t) for* (represented by Chambers as *'cep' fer*, which accurately notes its pronunciation), as in the following example, recorded in 1984 from an eleven-year-old speaker in the small south coast Burin Peninsula community of St. Bernard's:

61. Well then it sounds [the] same as – baseball, **except for** like you got to kick the ball.

In comparative clauses (and phrases), standard English *as ... as* often corresponds to *so ... as* in traditional NLE. This is illustrated by the following examples 62(a) and (c):

62.
(a) just **so plain as** daylight (NLFC, northeast coast (Twillingate)).
(b) that's **so much as** I can give (NLFC, northeast coast (Bonavista)).
(c) it wasn't **so prosperous** then as it is today (Speaker 5, Conception Bay; see section 7.3).

A vernacular alternative to *so ... as* is the use of *that* as an intensifier, as in example 58(b).

3.5 Non-standard syntactic features

Many of the sentence-level features of vernacular NLE are shared with mainstream non-standard varieties. These include negation patterns, verb order in embedded questions and subject relative pronoun deletion (sections 3.5.1–3.5.3). Others are nowadays largely archaic elsewhere in the English-speaking world (among them *for to* usage, outlined in section 3.5.4), or else highly regionally restricted (subordinating *and*, in section 3.5.5). While not dealt with in this section, traditional NLE also exhibited word orders that are unusual in contemporary standard English, such as the placement of the adverb *ever* as in *She give me the first little cake of yeast ever I seen* ('I ever saw') *in my life*, from a northeast coast NBE speaker born in the 1870s (MUNFLA C305). Nor does this section include features like the use of the noun phrases *no odds* and *what odds* where in standard English an entire clause ('it doesn't/didn't matter') would be required, as in *No odds how simple the thing was that you'd get in your stocking then, outside of a few candy* (MUNFLA 6775, Irish Avalon Peninsula).

3.5.1 Negation

The normal sentence negator in standard English is *not* and its contracted variant, *n't*; the negator *never* applies to a general stretch of time (as in 63(a) below), rather than to a single point. Yet in NLE, as in many varieties of English, *never* can also have punctual reference (63(b) and (c)), even among fairly standard speakers:

63.
- (a) I **never** did see her, while she was here.
- (b) Sorry I **never** emailed you this morning (email message to author, 24 September 2008).
- (c) That was Friday; I **never** had 'im ('my baby') till the following Sunday night. (Lanari 1994/FL).

Like many vernacular varieties of English, vernacular NLE also displays negative concord or the tendency for more than one negative morpheme to appear within a negative clause or sentence. This typically involves an indefinite (*nobody, no one, nothing, neither/na'r, no*) along with a verbal negator (*not, n't, never*). As the following examples show, negative concord can affect subject + verb (as in a to c) along with the more usual verb + object, etc.:

64.
- (a) **No one don't** know what anyone goes through (Lanari 1994/FL).
- (b) **Nobody couldn't** stay into ('in') it; **didn't** say **nothing**; **never** said **na'r** word; **no** other man'll **never** live here (Halpert and Widdowson 1996: 685).
- (c) There's **no one** got **none** of that stuff I **don't** guess today (MUNFLA C5421, south coast).
- (d) I **don't** have **no** breakfast when I **ain't** got **none** ('cereal') (MUNFLA 305, northeast coast).

As seen above, as well as in Chapter 2, traditional NLE displays a number of now unusual negative forms: *'tidden'*, corresponding to standard 'it isn't'; *'twudden'* ('it wasn't'); *weredn'(t)* ('weren't'); *dodn't* ('don't'); and *neither/ne'er/na'r* as a generalised indefinite ('a(n), any').

3.5.2 Embedded question formation

In standard English, a direct question of the type *She asked me, 'Do you go there often?'* corresponds to the indirect or embedded form *She asked me whether/if I went there often.* That is, in standard English embedded questions introduced by *whether* or *if* contain the usual non-question word order of subject followed by verb (as in *I go there often*). In vernacular varieties, however, word order in an embedded question (after main verb *ask, wonder, see*, etc.) is often reversed, just as in a direct main clause question, and *whether/if* are absent. Vernacular NLE is no exception:

65.
(a) (he) asked her **did she mind** ('whether she remembered') the time when ... (recorded Cartwright, Labrador, 1978).
(b) ... he asked Jack **was he any good** to rob ... (Halpert and Widdowson 1996: 235).
(c) I phoned Leonard's wife too then this morning to see **did Leonard hear** anything (Lanari 1994/FL).

3.5.3 Subject relative pronoun deletion

In standard English, relative pronouns are often deleted when they function as grammatical objects: thus *the man whom I saw yesterday* becomes *the man I saw yesterday*. In vernacular English, however, relative pronouns may also be deleted when they function as subjects; this is frequently the case in vernacular and traditional varieties of NLE, as examples 66(a) and (b) indicate (cf. also 41(c)):

66.
(a) There's **no one got** none of that stuff (MUNFLA C5421, Burin Peninsula, south coast).
(b) **Couple of fellas got** ... their boats wrecked up in Cow (H)ead is here (MUNFLA C5431, west coast).

In both of the above, the relative clause (beginning with *got*) does not contain the relative pronoun *who* or *that*, as it would in standard English (that is, 'There's no one who has ...', 'Couple of fellows who had ...').

3.5.4 For to complements

In contemporary standard English, infinitive clauses with a meaning of purpose or intent ('in order to') are typically constructed with a *to*-infinitive (*I came to see you, they did it to help*), just like other types of infinitival complements (*I wanted to see her, they like to do it*). Such was not the case in Middle English, where such complements were often introduced by *for to*. Though long gone from standard English, the *for to* complementiser continues to exist in a number of regional varieties. In vernacular NLE, *for to* (usually pronounced [fəɹdə]) is still a feature of the speech of many younger rural residents of the province. Its usual meaning is purposive (i.e., 'in order to'; see also 39(c)), as in:

67.
(a) So, when he put his hand up **for to** open the porch door (MUNFLA 79-633, south coast).
(b) Got to wait till I goes in **for to** get the plastic (Lanari 1994/FL).
(c) I leaved **for to** go down to where I lived (NLFC, northeast coast (Bonavista)).

However, the *for to* infinitive can also occur in contexts in which the purposive meaning is either absent or less apparent:

68.
(a) The music wasn't loud enough **for to go** all over the hall (NLFC, south coast (Harbour Buffett)).
(b) ... a few women **for to come up** for to help (NLFC, Conception Bay (Bell Island)).
(c) ... no beds **for to** sleep on (NLFC, south coast (Harbour Breton)).
(d) I managed/wanted/tried **for to do** it (examples collected from Memorial University students from the Burin Peninsula and south coast, 1990s).
(e) He asked me **for to** use it ('whether he could use it') (Informal conversation, 86-year-old female speaker, St. John's, 21 December 2008).

3.5.5 The 'subordinating and' construction

Irish English is known for its use of constructions involving *and* + present participle (e.g. *the size of er and she barking*; Kallen 1995: 179). In this structure, *and* does not serve as a coordinating conjunction as it does in standard English. Rather, it introduces a subordinate clause, generally with either a concessive meaning ('though the dog was small, she was barking') or else a temporal one, equivalent to a standard English *when*-clause.

The same construction appears in the NIE of the Avalon Peninsula, along with other Irish enclaves in the province; it also occurs in some NBE speech (Wagner 2006–7). Both the following examples were uttered by a fisherman from Conche, an Irish-settled community in northern Newfoundland (MUNFLA C3354). As the first example indicates, the structure in question does not require the presence of initial *and*:

69.
(a) **We comin' out along [the] shore**, the squalls was that ('so') hard she ('boat') blowed around twice on he.

(b)   And the seas my son, the great big lops, **an' (th)ey rollin' right down on us**.

Irish English is also well known for its topicalisation or clefting constructions. Apart from the mention of a few examples – such as *It's sorry you will be* ('You'll be sorry'; Story 1982: 64) – this feature has not been generally noted in the traditional dialects of Irish-settled areas in Newfoundland.

3.6 Concluding remarks

Despite the general observation that varieties of English differ from one another considerably more in their phonological than in their grammatical systems, this chapter has shown that NLE possesses an extremely rich morphosyntax relative to standard varieties of English. As Chapter 4 demonstrates, the lexicon of NLE likewise sets it considerably apart from mainstream English.

4 Vocabulary and discourse features

> The Newfoundland seal-hunters always speak of 'seals' as 'swiles', and for our word 'carry' they say 'spell'. A school-master, who had been listening to a seal-hunter's story, said sneeringly: 'Swiles! How do you spell swiles?' 'We don't spell 'em', replied the hunter; 'we most generally hauls 'em!' (From the *Dictionary of Newfoundland English*, under the entry *spell*)

As the previous two chapters have shown, NLE constitutes a distinct North American variety with respect to both its pronunciation and its grammatical features. The same is true in the case of the regional lexicon of the province, as is well illustrated in the above citation, taken from an American children's magazine of 1895. In fact, the vocabulary of NLE is sufficiently distinct to have merited its own dictionary, the well-known *Dictionary of Newfoundland English (DNE)* (Story et al. 1990 [1982], available online at http://www.heritage.nf.ca/dictionary). As is the case for its phonological and grammatical systems, the lexicon of NLE exhibits a high degree of linguistic conservatism, as well as internal diversity.

NLE is characterised by the retention of many words and meanings that have either disappeared or are now archaic elsewhere, as well as by the preservation of a host of more localised regional items that were brought to the area from southwest England and southern Ireland. Most of the latter originate in Irish Gaelic. At the same time, a number of these words and phrases have undergone subsequent change, whether in meaning or in form. In addition, new lexical items have emerged in the local context.

As a glance at the *DNE* will confirm, the lexicon of NLE reflects the central role of the fisheries and the sea in the province's history. Also abundant are terms representing the natural environment, traditional activities such as logging and sealing, and domestic life. NLE lexicon also reflects a small amount of borrowing from other languages with which the English and Irish settlers of the region came into contact, notably local aboriginal languages.

This chapter outlines the lexicon of NLE in terms of the major themes mentioned above: conservatism; West Country English and southern Irish inputs; the effects of the maritime context; borrowings from other languages; lexical and semantic change; and regional variation. It concludes with a brief look at lexical loss in contemporary NLE.

4.1 The conservative nature of NLE lexicon

In 1863, a visiting English clergyman, the Reverend Julian Moreton, noted the obsolete nature of many of the words he encountered on the northeast coast of Newfoundland. More than 100 years later, the folklorist and linguist J. D. A. Widdowson echoed this observation:

> During my own fieldwork and research in the Province over the past twenty-five years I have been repeatedly struck by the survival into the late twentieth century of many words and phrases which were once part of Standard English but have now become archaic or disappeared altogether in everyday usage in England. Whereas the erosion of regional lexis in the old country has had a devastating effect, especially in the thirty years since fieldwork was undertaken for the Survey of English Dialects, the Newfoundland lexicon as yet shows little sign of such loss, though change will of course inevitably take place in the fairly near future. (Widdowson 1991: 246)

The phenomenon noted by both Moreton and Widdowson can be attributed to Newfoundland's geographical and social situation: the existence of many small coastal fishing communities whose links to the outside world were relatively sparse provided optimal conditions for the preservation of lexical items transplanted to the region by its original European settlers. Thus the *DNE* contains many items which are noted as archaic or even obsolete in the English-speaking world. The following list presents a small sampling of these. In several cases (*empt* for 'empty', *souther* for 'southern') it is the phonetic form of the word that is now archaic. In addition, some of the items listed below may always have been regionally restricted within the United Kingdom (cf. section 4.2).

barm	'yeast'
bide	'remain, stay'
boo-beggar (< obsolete *bull-beggar*)	'imaginary figure used to terrify children'
dout (< *do* + *out*)	'put out, extinguish'
easter, wester, norther, souther	'eastern, easterly', etc.
emmet / immit	'ant'

empt	'empty, pour out'
firk	'to move about aimlessly', (of fowl and birds) 'to scratch, dig'
flashet	'pool, marshy place'
funk	'strong smell'
gentles	'people of high status'
hurt	'blueberry'
maid	'woman, girl'
more	'large tree root'
piss-a-bed	'dandelion'
pismire	'ant'
puncheon	'large wooden cask'
scull	'school' (of fish; obsolete variant, but used in NLE in, for example, 'caplin scull')
slice	'flat wooden utensil used for stirring'
sparable	'short nail used to stud sole and heel of boot, to prevent slipping'
sprong	'prong or fork used for manure, fish, etc.'
tallywacking	'spanking' (cf. obsolete *talliwap* 'blow')
yarry/yary	'wary, energetic'

Many lexical items in NLE have retained meanings that are now largely archaic. Take for example the following sentence from Dillon (1968: 134):

70. Some animals, girl, are as **cute** as a **Christian**.

Here, *cute* has the older meaning of 'acute' or 'shrewd', while *Christian* retains the meaning of 'human as opposed to animal'. While these senses may also survive in other regional dialects, they are no longer found in standard English. Table 4.1 documents a number of other common items which have preserved an earlier meaning in NLE. Again, these meanings are not necessarily unique to NLE: thus the 'remember' meaning of *mind* occurs in a number of regional varieties, while the older meanings of *allow* and *proud* have been retained, for example, in the southern and midwestern US. *Spell* with some of the meanings listed in Table 4.1 is also found in Australian English.

The conservative nature of NLE lexicon is also evident in its preservation of a large number of words and phrases from southwest England, along with a smaller number of Irish origin. Much specialised lexicon relating to seafaring and the fishery – some of which developed locally several centuries ago – has likewise been preserved. These sources are discussed in the following sections.

Table 4.1 Semantic retention in NLE

Word	Meaning	Example
abroad	'apart, in pieces'	My shoe came abroad
allow (usually pronounced *'low*)	'say, think, declare'	He's gone, I (al)low
clever(-looking)	'good-looking, in good health, fine (of weather)'	It's a clever(-looking) day
condemn	'judge unfit for use, and discard'	They condemned the door
fig; figgy	'raisin; containing raisins'	We had figgy pudding for dinner
handy	'nearby, close; almost'	They live handy to here; I'm handy gone
lunch	'small meal, snack'	We had a lunch before we went to bed
mind	'remember'	Do you mind the time we did that?
pitch	'land, alight'	The plane pitched
proud	'pleased'	I'm some proud to see you
spell	(noun) 'a rest period'; (verb) 'to give a rest period to', 'to carry on one's shoulders, stopping from time to time to rest'	They took a spell; They spelled the wood home on their backs

4.2 The southwest English contribution

Outside the Avalon Peninsula, the West Country English were the dominant settler group in much of the island, as well as southern Labrador. Consequently, it is not surprising that a great number of lexical items that can be traced to the southwest of England have survived in NLE. Table 4.2 contains a representative sample of these words, some of which have all but disappeared in their southwest English homeland. As Table 4.2 shows these by and large relate to aspects of everyday life, along with the natural environment.

Table 4.2 Some NLE words of southwest English origin

General semantic category	Examples
Flora and fauna	*dumbledore* 'bumble-bee'; *gillcup* (also *dillcup*) 'buttercup'; *horse-stinger* 'dragonfly'; *stout* 'deerfly'; *wrinkle* 'periwinkle'; *yess* 'earthworm'
Natural environment	*conkerbill/conkerbell* 'icicle'; *crunnick/crannick* 'dead tree root, or parts used as firewood'; *droke* 'valley with steep sides'; *duckish* 'twilight'; *dwy* (also, *scad*) 'flurry, squall'; *nuddick* 'small bare rounded hill'; *tolt* (cf. West Country *towte, toot*) 'prominent rounded hill'
Human activities	*breeze (down)* 'press down on'; *c(r)oochy/coopy/quat down* 'squat down'; *glutch* ' to swallow, to gulp down'; *mooch* 'to play truant from school'; *stog* 'to fill (in), to be stuck (in snow or boggy ground)'; *toll/tow (away)* 'to entice, allure'
Human appearance and characteristics	*bazzom* (said of flesh) 'blue or discoloured'(with cold); *bivver* 'shiver, quiver of the lips'; *clit* 'tangle, knot' (as in hair); *crousty* 'cantankerous'; *daps* 'likeness, image' (as in 'the very daps of someone'); *nish/nesh* 'soft, delicate, brittle'; *scrammed* 'numb' (with cold); *stun(ned)* 'foolish, stupid'; *vamp* 'short woolen oversock worn as a slipper'
House and environs, household	*bavin* 'piece of kindling wood'; *cotterall* 'notched metal bar on which pots are hung in fireplace'; *drung/drang* (< 'thrang') 'narrow lane or passage'; *dunch* 'soggy, doughy, stiff'; *flanker* 'live spark from a wood fire'; *forel/farrell/furl* 'bookcover'; *fousty* 'mouldy, musty'; *(h)apse* (< *hasp*) 'latch, (snap) fastener'; *linn(e)y* 'storage shed, or room attached to back of dwelling'; *pook* 'haycock, to place hay in a stack'; *st(r)outer* 'supporting post in wharf, fence post'; *yaffle* 'armful' (of wood, fish, etc.)
Other	*plim* 'to expand from absorption of water'; *scroop* 'to squeak'; *spudgel* 'small wooden bucket with long handle used for bailing'; *suant* 'straight, smooth, graceful'

4.3 The Irish contribution

The Irish language has also left its mark on NLE lexicon, though perhaps to a surprisingly small degree, given that the southern Irish constituted the majority of early settlers in much of the southern Avalon

Peninsula and that a number of these would have had Irish Gaelic as their first if not only language. A search of the *DNE* reveals fewer than 200 lexical items of Irish origin, out of more than 5, 000 entries.

Table 4.3 represents a partial listing of borrowings from Irish Gaelic that have been attested in NLE; definitions are for the most part adopted from the *DNE*. Table 4.3 does not include Irish borrowings which have found their way into general English, such as a word like *smithereens*. As Table 4.3 indicates, many of these items depict human beings, particularly in terms of undesirable characteristics. Others represent the natural landscape, farming, and such aspects of daily life as food and clothing. While many of these words would have been known on the Avalon Peninsula a generation or two ago, few have passed into more general usage; Kirwin (1993) estimates that no more than a couple of dozen remain in active use today. Younger present-day residents of St. John's would probably recognise very few, apart from *gig* (as in *not a gig in 'er*, said of a car engine); *streel* (as in *You look like a streel*); *hang-ashore* and *sleeveen*, both of which figure in representations of traditional Newfoundland 'characters'; and possibly also *scrob* 'scratch' and *smatter* 'smash' (as in *smatter to smithereens*).

Table 4.3 does not include lexical items of Irish English origin which represent direct translations from Irish Gaelic. The most obvious of these is *after*, which in the combination *be* + *after* + verbal *-ing* (as in *I'm after doing it already*) functions as a grammatical perfect form (see section 3.2.5). Other direct translations include the frequently used *be poisoned* ('be upset, disgusted'); the discourse tag *my son* (as in *Yes, my son!*), from the Irish *amhic* (Kirwin 1993); the adjectives *soft* in *soft day* 'a day with gentle rain' and *grand* (as in *How are you? I'm grand*); and the interjection *Go 'way (with you)!*, which expresses surprise or disbelief on the part of the speaker.

A number of words of Irish Gaelic origin have undergone change of meaning within NLE. These often attest to the importance of the fishery and the sea in local life. Thus the word *bawn*, which in Ireland originally referred to an enclosure in which cattle could be kept, then an enclosed grassy land or meadow, became applied in NLE to include a flat rocky area, usually a beach, on which cod was dried and salted. In Ireland, the word *múrach* (the origin of NLE *moryeen*) referred to mud from the seashore used for manure; in Newfoundland, its meaning is, according to the *DNE*, 'fertiliser prepared from fish offal mixed with peat'. Most residents of the province understand *slob (ice)* to mean slushy, densely packed sea ice; however, this term comes from Irish *slab* 'mud'. But perhaps the most striking transformation occurs in the well-known NLE word *(h)angashore*, which originates in Irish Gaelic *aindeiseoir*, 'an

Table 4.3 Words of Irish Gaelic origin in NLE: a partial listing [Irish source words – generally, as provided by the *DNE* – appear within parentheses, in non-italicised font]

General semantic category	Examples
Types of people (generally, negative characteristics)	*(h)angashore* (aindeiseoir) 'a lazy, worthless or sickly person'; *bostoon* (bastún) 'clumsy, stupid person'; *buckaloon* (cf. púicirliún), also *bucko* 'guy, fellow'; *ga(w) mogue* (gamóg) 'silly, mischievous person or action'; *glauvaun* (glámhán) 'habitual complainer, complaint'; *gom, gommel* (gamal) 'stupid person'; *kenat* (cnat) 'sly youth'; *maneen* 'bold boy'; *omadhaun* (amadán) 'foolish or stupid person'; *omaloor* (amalóir) 'clumsy or simple-minded person'; *ownshook* (óinseach) 'foolish ignorant person, Christmas mummer'; *slawmeen* (slimín) 'dirty, untidy person'; *sleeveen* (slighbhín) 'sly or mean person, rascal'; *stookawn* (stuacán)' stupid or lazy person'; *streel* (s(t)raoille) 'dirty, slovenly person, especially a woman'; *teak* (tadhg, 'Irishman') 'Christmas prankster'
Human behaviour	*bogger(s)* (bagar) 'activity in which children try to outdo one another'; *carawat* (carabhat) 'to gossip, argue'; *clobber* (clábar) 'untidy state'; *in a crit* (cruit) 'stooped, bent over'; *croost* (crústa) 'to pelt, throw stones at'; *cugger* (cf. cograim 'I whisper') 'whisper, converse'; *have the dawnies* (donaidhe) 'be tired, hung-over'; *flahoolach* (flaitheamhlach) 'generous, wasteful'; *gatch* (gaisch) 'swaggering behaviour, strut'; *glaum* (glám) 'to snatch, make a grabbing motion'; *pishogue(s)/fizoge* (piseog) 'foolish talk, complaint'; *plaumaush* (plámás) 'flattery'; *poltogue* (palltóg/falltóg) 'a smack, kick'; *ramlatch* 'foolishness, nonsense'; *ree-raw* (rí-rá) 'uproar, racket, confusion'; *rompse/rampse* (ramsach) 'to fight playfully, to skylark'; *scrawm* (cf. scramaim) 'to reach for, grope'; *scrob* (scrábaim) 'to scratch'; *sharoosed* (searbhas) 'disgusted, surprised'; *shaugraun* (seachrán) 'drifting/vagabond state, drinking spree'; *shebeen* (síbín) 'unlicensed place where illicit liquor is sold'; *slommocky* (cf. slaimice) 'untidy in appearance'; *stalky/stalkish* (stailceach) 'stubborn' (of person, horse); *smatter* (smeadar) 'to dirty, to smash'; *whis(h)t* 'be quiet'
Clothing	*caubeen* (caíbhín) 'cap, hat'; *pampooty* (pampúta) 'sock or soft shoe'; *teeveen* (taoibhín) 'patch on a shoe or boot'

Table 4.3 (continued)

General semantic category	Examples
Animals	*boneen* (banbh, bainbhín), *bonnive* 'young pig'; *booshy* 'louse'; *brackety* (cf. breachtach) 'spotted, speckled' (of domestic animals); *puckawn* (pocán) 'goat'
The landscape	*bawn* (badhún) 'grassy land, or rocks on which fish are spread to dry'; *bresna/bresney* (brosna); 'bundle of firewood or dry twigs'; *briss* (brus) 'dry conifer needles'; *cosh/coish* (cos 'leg, foot') 'estuary, riverhead'; *crump* (crompa) 'small twisted tree or trunk'; *kippin* (cipín) 'piece of kindling, insignificant item'; *moryeen* (múrach) 'fertiliser made of fish offal and peat'; *starrigan/stalligan/stattigan* (stairricín) 'small (dead) tree, stump'
Food and tobacco	*colcannon* (cf. cál ceannfhionn) 'vegetable/cabbage hash'; *crubeen* (crúibín) 'pickled pig's foot'; *dudeen* (dúidín)' short-stemmed tobacco pipe'; *gombeen* (gaimbin) 'small lump of tobacco, often used as stakes in a card game'; *pratie* (práta, préata) 'potato'; *sadogue* (sodóg) 'soggy cake or bread'; *sulick* 'liquid from cooking meat or fish'
Miscellaneous	*gig* [gɪg] (giog), *joog* (diúg) 'slight sign of life' (said, for example, of an engine); *pick* (pioc) 'small bit or amount'; *puck* (poc) 'blow, butt'; *scow-ways/scowish* (sceabha) 'askew, untidy'; *staneen* (stanna) 'makeshift keg for fresh water'; *stiel* (cf. stiallaim) 'rip, tear, slash'; *tayscaun* (taoscán) 'small amount'; *tilly* (tuilleadh) 'small amount given as gift, above the amount purchased'; *weigh-de-buckedy, buckety-board* (cf. bacaideach, bogadaich 'undulating, moving') 'see-saw, teeter-totter'

unfortunate person or thing'. Folk etymology, or the attempt to make an unknown word more familiar, has resulted in the re-interpretation of this word as 'hang-ashore' – that is, a person too lazy to go out fishing, and hence one who remains onshore.

4.4 Fishery and maritime-related vocabulary

Over the more than five centuries of European presence in the region, its settlement and economy have been closely linked to the inshore cod fishery. The result is a wealth of fishery-related vocabulary, along with many lexical items depicting weather and sea conditions. A specialised vocabulary has likewise developed around subsistence activities pursued by fishermen and their families, among them the annual seal hunt, the hunting of land mammals and seabirds, and the gathering of such necessities of life as firewood and berries.

Until the mid-twentieth century, the lifestyle of many rural NL outports was not substantially different from that of previous centuries. Likewise, much of the vocabulary relating to the fishery and other activities remained fairly stable. Thus a glossary compiled in the late eighteenth century by George Cartwright (Cartwright 1792), an Englishman who spent some sixteen years in coastal Labrador, contains many lexical items that would still be known today by rural residents of the province; all appear in the *DNE*. Most of the items documented by Cartwright pertain to the fishery and the ocean environment, including names of fish, sea mammals and seabirds. Table 4.4 provides a sampling of these, along with Cartwright's definitions. Editorial additions made by Townsend in his 1911 edition of Cartwright are enclosed within square brackets.

That an abundance of fishery and maritime terms continued to exist into the late twentieth century is evident from the results of an ongoing project the aim of which is the production of an online Dialect Atlas of Newfoundland and Labrador English (DANL). The lexical component of this project is based on a questionnaire administered under the direction of the linguist Harold Paddock in the 1980s, in representative communities throughout the island as well as in Labrador. By way of illustration, respondents to DANL provided more than a dozen words for 'non-poisonous jellyfish', including *bonnie-clobbers, sea-dabs, squid dabs, squid squalls, squid squash, soldiers* and *sun-fish*. When asked what word they would use to describe mild and damp weather, respondents offered some two dozen terms, including *logy, mauzy, miggy, misky, mudgy, muggy, murky, sluggish, smuggy* and *stucky*. As to various types of sea rocks (those visible at low tide, visible in a heavy sea or dangerous to navigation), a multitude of terms were again offered, including *brandies, breakers, sunkers, ground(er)s, mad rocks, man-of-war rocks, shoals* and *washrocks*. DANL has also yielded more than two dozen words or phrases for seals, which depict different seal types at various life stages. New-born harp seal pups are referred to as *white-coats* or *cats/kits* (or, if undernourished, as *bleaters, nog-heads* or *screechers*); once capable of taking to the water, they become *beaters*; once they lose their white coats, they become *ragged-jackets* or *raggy jacks*; when migrating northward in their first year, they may be referred to as *quinters*. Seals in their second year are

Table 4.4 Selected lexical items from Cartwright's 1792 *Glossary*

Semantic area	
Fish and the fishery	*Bulk of fish.* A quantity of fish salted one upon another *Caplin.* A fish 'Salmo Archeus' Pennant [*Mallotus villosus*] *Dillroom.* The well in a boat *Flakes.* Sets of beams, which are supported on posts and shores, and covered with boughs. They are used to dry fish upon. *Gigger or jigger.* A pair of large hooks fixed back to back with some lead run upon the shanks, in the shape of a fish *Killick.* A wooden anchor *Lance.* A small fish. The Sand-eel [*Ammodytes americanus*] *Slink.* A salmon which has spawned, and has not yet recovered itself by returning into the sea; till which time, it never will. [*Salmo salar*] *Water-horse.* Newly washed codfish, which are laid upon each other to drain before they are spread to dry
Ice conditions	*Barricado.* That ice which is formed upon the shore above low-water mark *Lolly.* Soft ice, or congealed snow floating in the water when it first begins to freeze *Pan of ice.* A piece of flat ice of no determined size, but not very large *Raftering of ice.* Ice is said to rafter, when, by being stopped in its passage, one piece is forced under another, until the uppermost ones rise to a great height.
Names of birds	*Auntsary.* A bird of the wading genus, resembling a redshank [greater yellow-legs, *Totanus melanoleucus*] *Bull.* A small seabird [dovekie or little auk, *Alle alle*] *Hound.* A water-fowl rather larger than a teal . . . [old-squaw, *Harelda hyemalis*] *Lord.* A water-fowl of the teal kind [male harlequin duck, *Histrionicus histrionicus*] *Shellbird.* A water-fowl . . . [sheldrake, red-breasted merganser, *Mergus serrator*] *Tinker.* A sea fowl, 'Razorbill' [razor-billed auk, *Alca torda*] *Whabby.* A water-fowl of the diving genus [red-throated loon, *Gavia stellata*]

called *bedlamers*; in their third year, they are termed *turners* (reflecting the change in the colour of their coat), *rusties*, *smutties* and occasionally *jinnies* or *jennies*. Young hood seals are referred to as *blue(back)s* and *hopper hoods*. Other terms elicited include *square flippers*, *blackbacks* and *saddlers*, while old male seals are referred to as *dog harps* or *dog hoods*. As to bay and harbour seals, those in their first year are called *jars*; in their second year, they become *dotards* (generally pronounced 'doters' or 'daughters'); and in their third year, they are *rangers*.

The importance of the sea and the fishery in local life is also highlighted by the existence of many expressions that are nautically-based. A century and a half ago, the Reverend Julian Moreton (Moreton 1863: 40) remarked that nautical phrases were in general use, and listed such examples as:

to get to windward of someone	'to gain advantage over'
to be going to leeward	'to be in declining circumstances'
to make headway	'to prosper'
to get under way	'to get any work or business in order'
to go very near the wind	'to live meanly and parsimoniously'

While such expressions may not be as predominant today, they have by no means disappeared. For example, the verb *go aboard*, with the meaning of 'verbally attack or criticise' (as in *he went aboard them*) remains commonplace. The same is true of *caplin weather*, designating a period of wet and foggy weather which typically occurs in early summer, when caplin, a small, smelt-like saltwater fish (see below), come inshore to spawn.

Not all local lexicon pertaining to the sea and the fishery is exclusive to NLE. A portion is shared with the Maritime provinces of Canada, particularly Nova Scotia and Prince Edward Island (for the latter, see Pratt 1988), along with parts of New England. Similarities in settlement history play a role in this, but perhaps even more so the regular contact associated with sea trade and the fisheries. In their examination of local lexicon found in Nova Scotia's Cape Breton Island, which also occurs on Prince Edward Island and in Newfoundland, Davey and McKinnon (2002) note that, of eighty-five shared terms, fully one third refer to the fishery and another 15 per cent refer to types of ice, weather and coastal features. Not included in their list are such traditional items which were known by seamen throughout the Atlantic provinces and New England as: *switchel* (*tea*) 'molasses-sweetened weak tea, drunk especially while at sea'; *callibogus* 'a drink made of rum, molasses and spruce beer'; *lobscouse*, defined by Cartwright (1792) as a 'sea dish' composed of minced, salted beef, crumbled 'sea biscuit', potatoes, onions, etc.; and the still well-known weather term *silver thaw*, glossed by Cartwright as 'when it rains and freezes at the same time'. At least one lexical item, *tomal-ley*, which refers to the edible green liver of a lobster, originated in the Caribbean; salt fish from Newfoundland was regularly exported by ship to the islands of the Caribbean ('the West Indies'), in return for sugar, molasses and rum.

4.5 New words and meanings in NLE

Despite its general conservatism, the NLE lexicon contains much which was not inherited from source varieties in the British Isles and Ireland. New words arose through language contact, as well as through new coinages to represent local items and activities. In addition, existing words developed new local applications through the process of semantic change.

4.5.1 Lexical borrowing

Outside the Avalon Peninsula, speakers of English would have come into contact with speakers of languages other than Irish Gaelic. Acadian French and Scottish Gaelic speakers settled pockets of the southern west coast of the island (see Chapter 1 for details), and small numbers of Mi'kmaq speakers were scattered throughout the island, though principally in southern and western sections. For the most part, small populations, along with social and ethnic barriers, led to little early intergroup contact on the island of Newfoundland, apart from the emergence of a mixed (i.e. Métis) French and Mi'kmaq group traditionally referred to as *jackatars* or *jackie tars* (and occasionally as *brunet(te)s*). In Labrador, the small European settler group came into much closer contact with speakers of Inuktitut and Innu-aimun, as described in Chapter 1.

The overall effect of this linguistic contact on the NLE lexicon, however, has not been great. Its most important legacy lies in the numerous place names that originate in aboriginal languages as well as French (though many of the latter date to the pre-European settlement period; see Chapter 1). As Hewson (1978) points out, the Mi'kmaq language contained several hundred names for lakes, rivers, portages and land features on the island of Newfoundland. Many of these places carry English names today, though some Mi'kmaq terms remain. These include the *Annieopsquotch* Mountains (literally, 'terrible rocks') on the west coast; *Meddonegannix* Lake ('down to the shore portage'); *Meelpaeg* Lake 'lake with many bays and coves'; and *Noneduck* Lake (Mi'kmaq *nanetek*). In Labrador, aboriginal names for land features abound, from Inuktitut *Torngat* (Mountains), *Saglek* (Bay) and *Okak* (Islands) to the

Innu-aimun lake names *Minipi* (< *minai-nipi*, 'burbot lake'), *Michikamau* (< *meshikamau*) and *Mistinippi* (<*mishta-nipi*), both meaning 'big lake'.

Apart from place names, the French legacy lives on in NLE in a handful of borrowings. These include *barachois* (pronounced 'barasway', reflecting the French pronunciation of the period), with the meaning of an estuary sheltered from the sea; *caplin* [kʰeɪplɳ], a fish name probably borrowed from Spanish or Portuguese, but ultimately from Provençal (see Kirwin 2001); *capillaire* 'creeping strawberry'; *labry/lavry* (from French *l'abri*; see the *DNE* entry); and *soirée* [s(w)ɘriː] 'a party, community gathering', best known via the title of a traditional Newfoundland folksong, 'The Kelligrews' Soiree'.

As to the aboriginal languages of the province, they too have had a small input to local lexicon. The handful of words borrowed from Labrador Innu-aimun (formerly known as Montagnais and Naskapi), Labrador Inuktitut and Mi'kmaq include names for fish and sea mammals, clothing and means of transportation. Table 4.5 provides a listing of most of these, along with their source language. Apart from the words *komatik*, *babbish* (*babiche*) and *ulu*, which occur elsewhere in Canada, these items are little known outside Labrador. Not appearing in Table 4.5 are two lexical borrowings which have been incorporated into English in general, as well as local varieties. The first, *caribou*, representing an eastern North American reindeer, comes from a Mi'kmaq word meaning 'snow-shoveller', from the animal's habit of pawing the snow to get at the mosses underneath. The second, *husky*, has a uniquely NL origin. *Husky* comes from the local European pronunciation of the word Eskimo, as *huskimaw*, via *h*-insertion (see section 2.3.2). Abbreviated to *husky*, and used as a derogatory epithet for Inuit people, it also became associated with the sled dogs used by the Inuit. It is this latter meaning that has passed into general English usage.

4.5.2 Neologisms

Despite the generally conservative nature of NLE lexicon, the origin of many local words has resisted documentation. Items such as *damperdog* and *bangbelly* – both of which designate common food items in earlier times (either a pork bun or a pieced of bread dough fried in fat) – are in all likelihood neologisms, or new lexical items, that were created locally. Other local words may possibly be inherited, yet cannot be traced to any definitive source. This group includes the frequently encountered *toutin* [tʰɐʊtɳ] with the same meanings as *damperdog* and *bangbelly*; *chovy* 'shaved wood used to kindle a fire'; *coady* 'boiled sauce, generally molasses, served with pudding'; *janny*

Table 4.5 A selection of NLE borrowings from local aboriginal languages (Source: *DNE*)

Lexical item	Source	Meaning
adikey	Inuktitut *atigik*	'cloth or skin parka'
babbish/babeesh	Mi'kmaq *apapitsh*, cf. *babiche*, via Canadian French	'strips of rawhide used as laces, thread, etc. in snowshoes'
komatik	Inuktitut *qamutiq*	'long sled for winter travel, hauled by dogs'
naluyuk, nalajuk	Inuktitut	'Christmas mummer'
pipsi	Inuktitut *pitsik*	'dried fish'
poegie [pʊ.dʒɪ]	Inuktitut *puijik*	'seal'
ounaniche	Innu-aimun *unaniss* (diminutive of *unan*), via Canadian French	'landlocked Atlantic salmon'
sina	Inuktitut *sina*	'edge of landfast ice'
tabanask	Innu-aimun *utapanashkᵘ*	'native sled' (with flat bottom rather than runners)
tibbage/tibeesh	Innu-aimun *atipish*	'fine strips of animal hide plaited in ends of snowshoe'
ulu	Inuktitut	'Inuit knife with semicircular blade, typically used by women to scrape skins'
oo-isht/twet *aw* *auk/ouk* *ra/urrah*	*huit* 'go' *aa* *auk* *hara* (Inuktitut commands to dog teams)	'go on' 'stop' 'turn right' 'turn left'

'Christmas mummer'; *moldow* (generally with final syllable stress) and *mollyfodge*, designating beard-moss and lichen, respectively; *turr*, the local name for the seabird known elsewhere as the *murre*; *twack*, with the meaning of shopping but not buying; *tickle* 'narrow strait or channel', also known in the neighbouring Maritime provinces; and the apparently newer and possibly onomatopoeic word *barmp* ('blow', as in *barmp your horn*).

One NLE neologism which has passed into general English is unlikely to be recognised as having a Newfoundland source. This is the word *penguin*, which was first reported from Newfoundland in a letter of 1578, to designate a now extinct flightless bird, the great auk. One possible source of the word are early Breton fishermen, since a similar phrase meaning 'white head' exists in several Celtic languages, including Breton. An alternative though equally unproven source lies in the word's supposedly original pronunciation, 'pin-wing'; this might relate to the bird's rudimentary wings and would clarify why this term was ensuingly applied to similar birds in the Antarctic.

A number of NLE neologisms have emerged from already existing words or morphemes. For example, *tuckamore/tuckenmore* 'low stunted vegetation, scrub' appears to originate in the combination of *more*, an older word for root, and *tucking*, which may come from the now obsolete verb *tuck* 'pull, pluck'. The addition of the agentive suffix -*er* (as in *farmer, runner*) to other parts of speech has resulted in new words and meanings, including:

empter	small berry container emptied frequently (< *empt* 'to empty')
growler	piece of floating ice, small iceberg
longer/lunger	long pole used in building floors, fences, etc.
nipper	mosquito; hand covering worn while fishing by line
sinker/sunker (also, *grounder*)	rock over which the sea breaks, often hazardous to vessels
stouter	heavy vertical post in wharf or fence (cf. southwest English *strouter* 'support in a wagon')

New adjectives have been created from the addition of the adjectival suffix -*y* [iː] to inherited lexical items, as in *lundy* ('sheltered', from *lun(d)*, 'a sheltered location'), and *dunchy* ('thick and soggy', from *dunch*; see Noseworthy 1971). This suffix may also be added to borrowed words, as in *plauma(u)shy* 'obsequious' from Irish Gaelic *plaumaush* 'flattery'. New compounds have resulted from the addition of prepositions to existing nouns and verbs, as in *mug-up* and *boil-up* ('a mug/cup of tea and a snack', the latter usually referring to a small meal eaten out of doors), along with *fit-out* and *rig-out* ('outfit, clothing'). The combination of noun +

preposition is also attested in *pourdown,* which corresponds to standard English *downpour.*

Other neologisms are the results of folk etymology (that is, the attempt to make sense of an unknown word by relating it to words that are known). The first element in *ose egg* 'sea urchin' may come from the Latin *ursena*; but the term is often pronounced and written *whore's egg.* The French word *capillaire,* designating a type of berry on a low creeping plant, has been reinterpreted as *caterpillar* in the earlier mentioned DANL online atlas project. The day preceding Christmas Eve may be called *Tipp's Eve* in NL; originally *Tibb's* (<*St. Tibba's*) *Eve,* the phrase seems to have been reshaped through a presumed connection with *tipsy,* since the Christmas period was among the few times of the year that alcoholic beverages were generally sanctioned (see Kirwin 1982 for further information on folk etymology in NLE).

Likewise, many new pronunciations have arisen for borrowed lexical items, making their origins often obscure. The Spanish or Portuguese loanword *barricado* (see Table 4.4) is realised in a multitude of ways; among those listed by the *DNE* are *ballicatter, batticatter, belly-catter, belly-carder, ballicabber, ballicanter* and even *cattibatter.* Many toponyms have also been transformed. Thus *Bay d'Espoir* ('Bay of Hope'), on the south coast of the island, was borrowed with the French pronunciation of the time, and continues to be pronounced 'Bay Despair'. French *l'Anse/Ance Arb(r)e* has become *Hant's Harbour.* Portuguese or Spanish *Capo de Espera/ Cabo de la Spera* ('Cape of Hope') just south of the capital, St. John's, is now *Cape Spear.* And the Notre Dame Bay community of *Twillingate,* a French fishing station until 1713, was originally named after *Pointe de Toulinguet,* at the entrance to Brest Harbour (Hamilton 1996). Phonetic transformation also affects many inherited, non-borrowed lexical items: for example, the word *copy,* which in NLE refers to the children's game of 'copying' a leader when jumping from ice pan to ice pan (see the *DNE* entry) is also attested in such forms as *cobby, cockey, conky, coody* and *coony.*

4.5.3 Semantic change

Innovations in NLE involve not only changes in word form, but also changes in meaning. In the local context, many words come to take on new meanings, which often relate to the local environment. Thus the word *steady* in NLE has undergone a semantic change from 'something that is steady' to 'a stretch of still water in a river' or 'a small pond'. The regional southwest English word *nuddick* has changed in meaning from 'head, skull' to 'a small bare rounded hill'. The term *glitter*, which in West Country England referred to any frosted or glazed surface, has taken on a more specialised weather-related meaning in NLE ('the coating of ice deposited by freezing rain'). Specialisation of meaning has also affected the regional British word *cracky*, meaning 'a little person or thing', since in NLE its most common meaning is 'a small mongrel dog'.

By far the greatest number of semantic changes, however, involves the fishery and the ocean. On the one hand, many NLE words have undergone a narrowing of meaning and have taken on a primarily or exclusively maritime association. A listing of some of these follows; the original meaning of the word appears in the second column, while the NLE-specific meaning appears to its right:

barrow	two-wheeled cart or frame used to transport various items	flat wooden frame used to transport fish
beater	bold, aggressive person	harp seal just past the whitecoat stage
bedlamer	lunatic > troublesome person or animal	immature seal approaching breeding age
brewis [bruːz]	bread soaked in hot water or broth	sea-biscuit (hard-tack), soaked and boiled, served with fish (*fish and brewis*)
chitlins (< *chitterlings*)	intestines of animals, used as food	part of internal portion of codfish, cooked and eaten as a delicacy
clumper, *clumpet*	lump, mass, clod of earth (British regional dialect form)	small iceberg or floating pan of ice
daddle	hand (British regional dialect)	hind flipper of a seal
faggot	bundle of sticks for burning	stack of split and salted codfish
killick, kellick	cf. *kelk* (a large stone)	anchor made of a stone encased in pieces of wood
lolly	thick gruel (*loblolly*); broth, soup	loose ice or snow floating in water
quinter	ewe sheep	young migrating harp seal

rafter	to plough land in a certain way	action of sheets of ice buckling, or overriding one another
scrunchins (< *scrunchings*)	scraps or remnants of food, broken meat	small pieces of fried-out fatback pork, served with fish dishes
yaffle	armful, handful	armful of dried and salted codfish, or of wood

The opposite type of meaning shift has also frequently occurred in NLE, whereby a word originally associated exclusively with a nautical or fishery context has taken on a more general meaning. In the following list, the earlier meaning again appears in the middle column, with the more generalised NLE meaning to its right.

barvel / barbel	apron (leather, canvas or oilskin) used when processing fish	homemade domestic apron
bridge	wooden gangway connecting waterfront buildings in a fishing premises	verandah-like wooden platform at the door of a house
clew up	draw up the lower ends of a sail to the mast, ready for securing	finish, complete (any action or task, as in *I clewed up my work*)
fair	smooth, streamlined (said of a boat)	even, straight (as in *Your bangs are fair* – that is, cut straight)
hand	member of a ship's crew	person who performs an activity, usually well (as in *He's a wonderful hand to sing*, meaning 'He's a good singer')
haul	pull (used in nautical contexts, said of nets, ropes, etc.)	pull (used generally, whether a tooth (*haul out*) or a large load is involved)

| *in order* (pronounced 'narder') | 'regionally of high frequency in nautical usage' (*OED*) | ready, prepared |
| *rig/rig-out* | ship's sails, masts and supporting ropes | clothing (as in *That's some nice rig she's wearin'*) |

4.6 Regional variation

Previous chapters have shown the persistence of considerable regional variation in NLE pronunciation and grammatical patterns, much of which correlates with Irish vs. English settlement origins. A similar patterning also occurs for a number of traditional lexical items in NLE. Among these are names designating the insect known in standard English as the *dragonfly*, as mapped by Paddock (1984; see Figure 4.1). Paddock shows that while in traditional varieties spoken in English-settled areas of the island the regional British term *horse-stinger* (in several phonetic manifestations) was predominant, in the Irish-settled southern Avalon Peninsula the usual variant was *devil's darn(ing) needle* or simply *devil's needle*, inherited from Irish English.

As yet unpublished maps of two other lexical items produced by Paddock – terms for 'sap of fir trees' and 'needles of conifers' – suggest further regional divisions within areas of coastal Newfoundland settled predominantly by the southwest English (see Chapter 1). In most of these areas, the word reported for 'sap of fir trees' was *turpentine* (along with phonetic variants like *turkumtine* and *turpentime*) – a word which in contemporary standard English has undergone a meaning change, since it has come to refer to the oil distilled from the resin of trees, rather than to the resin or sap itself. On the Wessex-settled northeast coast, however, the term most frequently reported proved to be *myrrh*, which is generally unknown in standard English outside its biblical reference (*gold, frankincense and myrrh*). As to 'needles of conifers', the entire northeast coast of the island favoured *sprinkle*-type words (among them *sprinkles, prinkles, prickles* and *sprigs*). The English-settled south coast, however, favoured such terms as *brimbles, brambles* and *pin boughs/bough pins*.

Paddock's preliminary findings also point to Labrador as a distinct dialect area. While Labrador has *turpentine* and *myrrh* in common with the English-settled portions of the island, its terms for 'dragonfly' include *mosquito hawk* and *flycatcher*, terms not attested elsewhere in

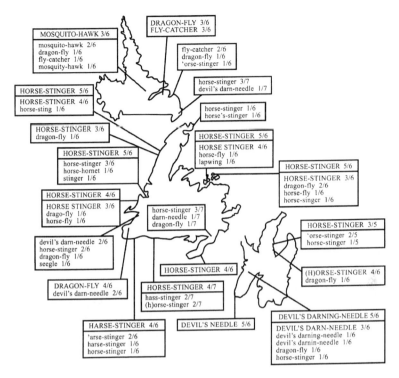

Figure 4.1 Regional distribution of NL terms for *dragonfly* (from Paddock 1984)

Paddock's survey. Yet *mosquito hawk* is known in parts of the southern US, and may well have been brought to southern Labrador by settlers from northern Scotland. Paddock's findings also suggest that the southern west coast portion of the island – the ethnically mixed area whose early settlers included French, Scots and Irish (see Chapter 1) – may stand out lexically from the island's southwest English-settled coastline. There, *devil's darning needle* was reported as a minority variant for 'dragonfly', while *gum* and *balsam*, rather than *turpentine* or *myrrh*, were the terms favoured for 'sap of fir trees'.

Paddock's preliminary lexical findings largely correlate with the settlement patterns reported in Chapter 1. Many lexical items, however, reveal considerably more complexity in their regional distributional patterns. Take, for example, the multitude of terms used to describe a pancake-like piece of homemade bread dough fried in fat, for which the name *toutin* is generally used and recognised throughout the province. Even though in most NL homes today pancakes are no longer made of homemade bread dough, younger generations generally remain aware of traditional local terms for this item. Questionnaires administered in recent years to introductory linguistics students from all areas of the province attending Memorial University in St. John's have yielded a number of responses, in addition to *toutin*, for this item. They include the following (students' home areas appear in brackets):

bangbelly	(south coast)
bannock	(Conception Bay; northeast coast; west coast, including Corner Brook and the Port au Port Peninsula)
damperdog	(Conception Bay; northeast coast; southern west coast; Labrador)
dicky-dough	(single community in Trinity Bay)
flitter	(Conception Bay; northern Newfoundland (Great Northern Peninsula))
flummy	(Labrador)
freezie	(central Newfoundland)
fritter	(Conception Bay; northeast coast; west coast; south coast)
frozie	(Bonavista Bay; southern Labrador)
gandy	(northeast coast; coastal Labrador; St. John's)
posie	(Conception Bay North)
tiffin	(several communities in Bonavista Bay, along with one in Trinity Bay; also noted for Labrador by Flowers 2007)

A recent online survey of approximately 150 residents of Labrador, from all age groups (Flowers 2007), adds still more terms; these include *doughdang, fry bun, slimmer,* along with a number of words which have in all likelihood been borrowed from Labrador Inuktitut, namely, *mappa cake, mukmuk cake, panitsiak* and *sunamajuk*. The listing above shows that, like Labrador, the Wessex-settled northeast coast (Bonavista Bay and points north) also displays a considerable array of terms for this single concept: these include *bannock, gandy, damperdog, flitter, fritter, frozie* and *tiffin*. Some of these terms appear remarkably limited in their regional distribution. *Tiffin*, for example, though carried to Labrador, appears to be localised in a handful of communities in northern Bonavista Bay, yet students from one southern Bonavista Bay community reported this term with the meaning 'small lunch', a meaning which also occurs in regional British as well as Indian English. In addition, the existence of mutated word forms such as *flitter* for *fritter*, and *freezie* plus *posie* alongside *frozie*, suggests the ease with which lexical items may undergo phonetic transformation in NLE.

The ongoing DANL project, which as earlier noted is converting Paddock's unpublished regional lexical findings into an online atlas, confirms that the degree of lexical complexity suggested by the *toutin* example is by no means unusual. One and the same concept may be represented by thirty or forty different terms, as, for example, the case of 'dry dead things that you'd cut down for firewood' or 'types of snow-shoes'. DANL yields still further terms for 'fried bread dough', among them: *cushions* (west coast of the island); *dough cakes/dough dogs* (east coast, southern Labrador); *flapjacks/flatjacks* (east coast); *flatters* (northern peninsula); *johnnycakes* (northern peninsula); *morning buns* (west coast); *stove cakes/stove tops* (northern peninsula and Labrador); and *scones* (southern west coast and Labrador, reflecting the Scottish input to these areas). DANL also confirms the extremely limited geographical spread of many terms (cf. *tiffin*, above). In addition, it points to the distinct status of Labrador: though Labrador shares many lexical items with the island – as would be expected from migration patterns from coastal Newfoundland to coastal Labrador – it displays a number of lexical items which have not been documented elsewhere in the province. In addition to borrowings from Inuktitut, and the *mosquito hawks* and *flummies/flummy dumplings* examples mentioned above, DANL has yielded such Labrador-specific terms as *shoecrop/showcrop/shoal crop/shorecrop* (of unknown origin) to designate the tiny animal known as the *shrew*, and *redberries* to refer to small tart berries resembling wild cranberries, which on the island are called *partridgeberries* (and which are more generally known as *lingonberries*).

4.7 Discourse features

4.7.1 Terms of address and reference

Traditional NLE displays a number of terms that are used both to address people (compare such standard, although formal, English terms as *sir, ma'am, miss*), as well as to refer to them in contexts from which they may be absent. In small coastal outport communities, older individuals were often termed *Aunt* or *Uncle* (e.g. *Aunt Jane, Uncle Charlie*), whether or not they were related to the speaker. Likewise, an older male might be addressed as *skipper*, and the term *the skipper* (as in *I'll have to talk to the skipper*) was used to refer to a male head of household. Again, this reflects the importance of the sea in the traditional NL lifestyle.

Other typical terms of address and reference are also gender-based: *boy* (usually pronounced *b'y* [bɐɪ]), *buddy, girl, maid, missus*, along with the Irish-origin address term *my/me son*. *Missus* may be used to address a mature woman (*Yes, missus*); *the missus* may also represent 'X's wife', as in the title of a 1987 Newfoundland-based movie *John and the Missus*. *Maid*, found in areas of the island settled by the southwest English, is considerably less frequent today than it was a generation ago as a term of address (*Yes, (my/me) maid*), and occurs even less often as a term of reference for younger females, as in the following example from Harris (2006: 133):

71.   The **maids** was home 'bout a hour 'fore we got home.

All of the other terms listed above, however, remain part of the active vocabulary of most residents of the province. *B'y* has taken on iconic status in NLE, with the phrase *Yes b'y!* symbolising Newfoundland identity perhaps like no other. As a discourse tag, *b'y* occurs as a general intensifier, without reference to the gender of the addressee: in phrases like *Yes b'y!, No b'y!, Well b'y!* or simply *B'y!*, it reinforces a range of speaker meanings, including agreement, non-agreement, surprise and disbelief. The same is true of *my/me son*, which tends to occur most often in discourse contexts involving males. *Girl* remains popular in such phrases as *Yes girl!* and *No, girl!*, though also used simply as a discourse tag, it is restricted to cases where the addressee is female. The term *buddy* is used informally for an unknown or unspecified male (*Hey buddy!, and buddy says to me...*).; a less frequent alternative is *chummy*.

Visitors to the province are often surprised at the frequency and range of terms of endearment, which may also serve simply as discourse intensifiers and are used whether the addressee is known or a stranger. These include not only *my/me dear, my/me love* and *honey*, but also *my/me darling, ducky* and *lover*. All of these may turn up in male–female and all-female interaction, but are not generally used solely between males; the exceptions are the now old-fashioned *me old trout* and *me old cock(y)*, the latter of which may be encountered by visitors in the so-called 'screech-in' ceremony which confers on them the title of 'honorary Newfoundlanders' (see section 5.2).

The ideological divide which separates residents of the capital, St. John's, and residents of the smaller outports has resulted in a number of terms which have been in use for some time. Residents of St. John's are referred to, often disparagingly, as *townies* by other residents of the province. Less-known terms for working-class St. John's males are *corner boys*, as well as *cribbies*, the latter originating in the pronunciation of the 'Caribbee (Isles)' as the 'Cribbeys'. In turn, residents of outport communities are referred to as *baymen, baywops* or, less frequently today, *bay noddies*, all of which often carry pejorative connotations when used by urban Newfoundlanders and Labradorians. And to all residents of the province, people from other provinces of Canada (that is, from 'upalong') are referred to as *mainlanders*. Any non-locally-born resident of the province, whatever their origin, may be designated a *CFA*, an abbreviated version of 'come-from-away'.

In traditional NLE, the words *man, woman* and *girl* combined to form referential terms that are not found in standard English. These include *widow man* ('widower'), *widow woman* ('widow'), *carpenter man, labourer man, skipper man, fur man* ('trapper') and *friend girl* ('a female's female friend'), plus combinations like *northern man* 'resident of the northeast coast', and even *Bungay man* 'man named Bungay' (from the south coast of the island; MUNFLA C5116).

4.7.2 Discourse particles

Despite the iconic status of the discourse particle *eh* as a marker of Canadian speech (e.g. Gold 2008), *eh* – which may be realised in NLE with a vowel nucleus ranging from [æ] to [ɛ] to [e] – is also a common discourse tag among traditional speakers, particularly speakers of NBE, that is, from southwest-English-settled areas of NL:

72.
(a) the (A)merican gov'ment ownded it, **eh**? (MUNFLA C5424, northeast coast).
(b) I'm the last in the family and the rest of [the] family were all grown up and they were all married, **eh**? (MUNFLA C1654, northeast coast).
(c) Sometimes we had dog chase(r)s, **eh**? (MUNFLA C580, southern Labrador).

As the traditional speakers from the Irish-settled Avalon Peninsula who appear in Chapter 7 (see 7.2) reveal, however, discourse *eh* is not unknown in NIE. In the Irish-influenced southeast portion of the island, however, the discourse tag *right* is the norm:

73.
(a) And we usta cook them chicken balls and rice and all that kind of stuff, they usta like that, **right**? (Lanari 1994/JP).
(b) ... like Saturday and Sunday there was a lot of boats went out of here, **right**? (CBC NL radio 'Fisheries Broadcast', 27 May 2003, Bay de Verde, Conception Bay).
(c) ... he can't do nothing to bill me, bill me all those arrears, **right** (MUNFLA C6272, Trinity Bay).

As in other parts of Canada (see Tagliamonte 2006), the tag *eh* has declined among younger speakers, though *hey* constitutes perhaps a more contemporary equivalent, as yet uninvestigated as to regional, social and discourse functions. The tag *right*, however, appears to be on the increase: it is used by younger speakers from all areas of the province, including the rural south coast female speaker represented in 7.5.2.

Both *right* and *eh* are used by speakers to ensure listener comprehension and interest, and are typically accompanied by rising intonation. Two other tags function in much the same way in NLE: *look* (usually pronounced [lʌʔ], which does not usually carry rising intonation) and *see*, as in

74.
(a)   ... the other day, **look**, I fell down and cut 'en ('finger'); It was all Father's [that] was there then, **look** (MUNFLA C305, northeast coast).
(b)   His father was skipper, **see**? (Lanari 1994/MK).
(c)   But out on the edge of it, **see**, that's where 'tis to (MUNFLA C2831, south coast).

Of Irish origin is the tag *sure* [ʃɚ], which indicates that a statement should be obvious or self-evident (example 23(d) in Chapter 3 provides an illustration of clause-initial *sure*):

75.   He couldn't eat that, **sure** (MUNFLA C746–7, Irish southern Avalon).

NLE is also characterised by the frequent use of clause-initial *listen*, which often functions as a turn-opener, and may signal the need for the addressee's close attention, given the importance to the speaker of what is to follow (as in *Listen – can you give me a ride home?*).

Almost no published literature exists on the use of discourse particles in NLE, despite the fact that all of the above have existed in NLE for some time. The same is true of discourse *you know*, as evidenced from its use by speakers born in the 1870s and 1880s (though recorded in the 1960s). This discourse tag is favoured by a number of the speakers who appear in Chapter 7, especially the male speakers. Since it is also frequently encountered in the speech of younger residents of the province, further investigation is required to determine whether it is undergoing decline, as is reported for Toronto English by Tagliamonte (2006). In traditional NLE, a competing though much less frequent variant was *do you know* (pronounced in two syllables, as 'd'ya know') as in:

76.
(a)   ... in a barrel, **d'you know**, or a box (MUNFLA F25229, Labrador).
(b)   [we'd] sing it when we used to mill, **d'you know** (MUNFLA C80–134 (French) west coast).

Another infrequently used traditional tag is *I don't know* (*I d'know*), which in Irish-settled areas of the province, at least, could be attached to a question:

77. Is the mail come yet, **I d'know** (Dillon 1968: 146).

As to the use of discourse *like* – that is, the use of *like* with purely contextual or pragmatic meaning rather than actual semantic content, as in 78(a) below, from a young speaker of contemporary NLE – this may be a somewhat more recent phenomenon. A search of many recordings of speakers of traditional NLE born prior to 1920 has yielded almost exclusively instances of non-discourse *like*, whether used as a preposition (e.g. 'like her'), conjunction ('like we did') or adverbial morpheme (e.g. 'fool-like'/'foolish-like' with the meaning of 'foolishly'). Despite ambiguous or intermediate cases (in which *like* could be interpreted as falling somewhere between traditional function-word status and contemporary pragmatic usage, as in 78(b) and (c)), the only clear-cut examples of pragmatic *like* from older traditional speakers revealed by this search appear in 78(d) and (e):

78.
(a) and the school that I went to . . . it was a boys' Catholic school and then it turned into **like** a high school, for **like**, co-ed (Corner Brook female, born 1984, recorded 2006).

(b) I don't know if them Saunders and Howell would – you know **like** that but actually and, you know, some people used to saw lumber up there (MUNFLA C3354, northern peninsula, recorded 1977).

(c) The little soil [that] was there was – **like** rocky soil? (Female speaker from northern peninsula, born 1925, recorded in St. John's, 2003).

(d) . . . know for sure, feel it in your bones **like**, pains, and you know you feel down **like** (MUNFLA C1100, female, southern Avalon Peninsula, born 1892, recorded 1972).

(e) And, before I got to them I'd, you know – **like** the women [who] was there, their cape was rolled up . . . (male speaker from Bonavista Bay, born 1906, recorded 2002).

That said, two of the traditional speakers who appear in Chapter 7 (Speakers 5 and 6, both born prior to 1940) use *like* as a discourse particle (as in *I don't know like, them times we used to appreciate everything* from Speaker 5). Rural speakers born after the Second World War and NL's Confederation with Canada in 1949, however, display considerable use of pragmatic *like*, including, of course, younger Speaker 9 (7.5.2). Example 72(a) comes from a Bonavista Bay resident born around 1950; and 72(b), from a speaker from a mixed English/Irish area on the Burin Peninsula, born almost a decade later:

79.

(a) When you're in bed in the morning **like** you know but when your mother gets up, **like** she['s] makin' breakfast, eh, you [h]ear ... the chairs rattlin' and the stove rattlin' and the kettles rattlin' and the cups rattlin' **like** you know (MUNFLA C1654, recorded 1974).

(b) Dinner's a big thing there ah ... **like** the most would have that ('a food item mentioned earlier') every day, dinnertime (Lanari 1994/JP).

In innovative NLE, *like* is also used as a quotative, in place of *say* (see D'Arcy 2004). This use is discussed in Chapter 5, along with such other recent discourse-related changes as the use of creaky voice and high rising tone.

One final point relates to the pronunciation of the discourse particle *yeah*. As noted in section 2.5, NLE shares with other areas in the North Atlantic an ingressive (or 'in-breathed') pronunciation of this particle, as well as of the particles *no* and *mm*. This suprasegmental feature remains quite obvious in NLE, though is less apparent among younger generations. Traditional NLE (at least, in Labrador, as well as several areas on the island) also displays a disyllabic pronunciation of the particle *yeah* as *e-yeah* or *ayuh* [ejə/ɛjə], a pronunciation which also has been noted by the *Dictionary of American Regional English* (*DARE*, Cassidy and Hall 1985) as characterising earlier speech in New England and the state of New York.

4.8 Recent lexical change and lexical loss

Despite the fact that traditional lexicon has been preserved to a much greater degree in NLE than in its source varieties – and despite the 1991 observation of the folklorist and linguist John Widdowson, cited in Section 4.1 – many of the words presented in this chapter are undergoing rapid obsolescence. Extensive social and economic change in post-Confederation NL has played a major role in this process. Changing technologies in the second half of the twentieth century led to the switch from traditional methods of salt-curing and drying fish to the export of a fresh or frozen product. The collapse of the cod fishery in the 1990s has led to considerable out-migration of younger generations from NL outports – not only to urban areas of the province, but, more frequently, to western Canada, which until the 2008 economic downturn was enjoying a boom. Many rural males who in previous generations would have found their livelihood in the fishery now go to work in the oilfields of Alberta; some leave their families behind and return to the province in their off-time. And, of course, exposure to non-local varieties has increased dramatically through the advent of television, the internet and considerably enhanced opportunities for travel out of the province. The lexical effects of these recent social changes have been immense. Younger people today – even in rural NL – typically do not know such fishery-related terms as *flake* ('a wooden framework for drying fish') or *stage* ('platform where fish are processed and fishing gear stored'), both of which designate items that were fixtures in the landscape of any coastal community just several decades ago. Lexical loss has affected not only fishing vocabulary, along with vocabulary relating to conditions of the sea and the weather, but also the lexicon associated with other aspects of the traditional lifestyle, which included intimate knowledge of the land, gleaned in such places as the 'lumber woods' or the 'berry barrens'.

Yet though lexical loss over the past several decades cannot be denied, NLE retains much that is distinct. Lexical differentiation from mainland North America can readily be found in a number of words that refer to everyday objects and events. As noted in Chapter 1, the Survey of Canadian English (SCE) of almost forty years ago revealed the province to be the most distinct in all of Canada (Warkentyne 1971), and reported lexical differences played an important role in this conclusion. By way of illustration, the SCE showed that rather than the phrase *sick to* (or *sick at, sick in*) *the stomach*, NL residents favoured a form which occurs rarely on the Canadian mainland: *stomach-sick*.

Warkentyne's 1971 observation remains valid today. Boberg (2005) reports on a recent fifty-three-item North American English questionnaire focusing on contemporary vocabulary, ranging from names for 'a small house in the countryside ... where people go on summer weekends' to 'food picked up and taken home to eat', and to 'a device that changes channels on a TV'. Among his conclusions, Boberg noted the degree of lexical separation between NL and the neighbouring province of Nova Scotia to be the greatest of any in English Canada. In NLE, for example, *cabin* was favoured for a seasonal weekend getaway house, while *cottage* was the norm in the rest of eastern Canada. *Bookbag* was selected most frequently by residents of NL for the article that students carry on their backs to hold their books, while *backpack* was the normal Canadian term west of Montreal. *See-saw* proved to be usual option for NL (and Quebec) residents for 'a tilting board on which children play', as opposed to the variant *teeter-totter* for much of the remainder of the country. And *exercise book* was selected by the majority of NL respondents for 'a book of lined paper for school', rather than *scribbler*, the norm in the Maritime provinces – though usual in NLE a few decades ago to designate a notebook containing off-white newsprint-like pages (see the *DNE* entry) – and *notebook*, the American term, which dominated elsewhere in Canada.

Boberg's selection of lexical items is arbitrary, as he acknowledges, and seems geared in some instances towards terms that distinguish Quebec English from the speech of the rest of the country. Had more questions been included, along with more local options from which to select – as, for example, for NLE, *shack* for a weekend retreat, and *weigh-de-buckedy* for a children's tilting board – it is quite possible that NLE would have proved even more distinct than Boberg's study reveals.

Thus despite much lexical loss in traditional areas of vocabulary in recent decades, NLE preserves its distinctive nature within the North American context, not only with respect to its phonology and grammar, but also its vocabulary. Present-day residents of the province still come across *toutin dough* ('frozen bread dough') in their local supermarkets, and use *brin bags* rather than *burlap bags*. Many readily describe a musty or mouldy smell as *fousty*, and a locale or meeting-place that is filled to capacity as *blocked*. If they're excessively cold or upset, they may say *I'm perished* rather than 'I'm freezing' and *I'm poisoned* rather than 'I'm disgusted'. When out camping or in the woods, they may have a *boil-up* to enjoy a cup of tea and a snack. And to get someone's attention, they may *sing out to* or *bawl at* ('shout out to') them. Newfoundlanders and Labradorians continue to refer to deceitful or rascally individuals as *sleeveens*; someone who's cranky or cross will be described as *(some) crooked* (pronounced in two syllables, as [krʊkəd]); a person who's not too bright will be referred to as *stunned*; something that's judged good will be termed *best kind*; and the taunt *sook* [sʊk] or *sooky baby* ('cry-baby') is still frequently used by children.

At the same time, new lexical items are making their way into NLE, some of which are not shared with the Canadian mainland. The following chapter deals with recent change in the English spoken in the province.

Web resources

Section 4.5.1

http://www.innuplaces.ca
http://www.innu-aimun.ca
    Information on Innu place names in Labrador, along with the language of the Labrador Innu

Section 4.7.1

http://www.youtube.com/watch?v=9QlQkw2FCek
http://www.youtube.com/watch?v=chZWmFG5Oxg
Two recent online music videos which amusingly attest to the persistence of the ideological divide between 'townies' and 'baymen'; the first represents Colleen Power's 'New Townie Man', and the second, 'A Bay Man's Wife', Mar Faughten's response from 'the bay'.

5 Language attitudes and language change

5.1 Outsiders' views of Newfoundland and Labrador

On 3 November 2008, NL, for the first time in its fifty-nine-year history as a member of the Canadian Confederation, assumed the economic status of a 'have' rather than 'have-not' province. The province's new revenues from offshore oil meant that it was no longer dependent on the Federal government in Ottawa for annual equalisation payments, designed to produce comparable standards of education, health care and infrastructure throughout the country. At the same time, Canada's most populated province, Ontario – which for many years had driven the Canadian economy – was demoted to the status of 'have-not' province. The irony was not lost on Newfoundlanders and Labradorians. The change represented a much-celebrated development for a province which, over the previous half-century, had been typically seen as the poor cousin of the Canadian Confederation, with all the negative ramifications that such a view entails. This opinion had often found a strong, and official, voice. Thus in the 1980s, the mayor of Canada's then most prosperous city, Calgary, referred to migrant workers from eastern Canada as 'bums and creeps', and residents of the Atlantic provinces were likewise styled as 'welfare bums' by the then premier of Ontario. In the 6 January 2005 edition of Canada's national newspaper, *The Globe and Mail*, the columnist Margaret Wente referred to rural Newfoundland – which in her view was siphoning off an inordinate amount of equalisation funding relative to its small population – as 'probably the most vast and scenic welfare ghetto in the world' and stated:

> And so we send more money so that people can stay in the scenic villages where they were born, even though the fish are gone and there's no more work and never will be, unless they can steal some telemarketing from Bangalore.

However – and despite their continual whining and 'sense of victimhood' – Wente reassured *Globe* readers, 'I like Newfoundlanders, I really do.'

Opinions such as Wente's are by no means new. Almost two centuries ago, a visitor from New England described the area as 'a dark, cold, and benighted region of the earth', and as 'low in the scale of civilisation' (Tucker 1839: viii). Many outsiders have portrayed Newfoundlanders as a friendly and hospitable people, yet at the same time simple, backward and lazy. Visiting Scottish clergyman James Lumsden's (1906: 93) representation of local residents as 'happy, easy-going ... with little apparent regard for the value of time' is by no means unusual. A Newfoundland Royal Commission report (Amulree 1933: 210) concluded that many on the island were 'improvident and happy-go-lucky', given to exhibiting 'a child-like simplicity when confronted with matters outside their immediate horizon'.

When viewed from a socioeconomic perspective, paternalistic opinions such as these are far from surprising. Throughout the long history of the region, its economy has perennially lagged behind, grounded as it was in a small and until recently largely rural population dependent on the vagaries of the fishery, and controlled by a small number of mercantile fishing firms. As a result of the Great Depression, in 1934 NL – which prior to that had been a self-governing British Dominion – was placed under a Commission of Government appointed by Britain in order to stave off imminent default on the public debt. The 1933 Royal Commission report described the majority of Newfoundlanders of the period as impoverished, barely managing to eke out a subsistence living.

While the economy has dramatically improved in the sixty years since its 1949 union with Canada, NL has consistently been the province with the highest unemployment rates and lowest average incomes in the country. Until the recent discovery of offshore oil, the province remained socioeconomically marginalised, with much of its rural population dependent on seasonal employment, often complemented with temporary out-migration to Ontario and, more recently, western Canada. Since 1949 – perhaps more accurately, since the Second World War and its vast though temporary influx of American and Canadian troops into NL, most awaiting transport to Europe – the negative stereotypes associated with the region have, if anything, increased. The 1940s gave rise to the creation of the term 'Newfie' to designate a resident of the area. Though this term is designated 'familiar' by Canadian dictionaries, it is viewed as the equivalent of an ethnic slur by many residents of the province (see King and Clarke 2002). The same period saw the creation of the Newfie joke, involving the stereotype of the 'goofy Newfie'. As Pringle (1985: 186) notes, '[i]n Canadian popular culture, "the Newfie" occupies the role attributed to "Polacks" in American culture at the same level – Polish jokes which find their way to English Canada are recounted as "Newfie jokes"'.

The situation is well summed up by John Fraser, who writes in Canada's national news magazine *Maclean's* (6 October 2008: 23):

> for generations, Newfoundlanders have been the poorest of the poor, the Haitians of North America, the dumb fishermen and brutal swoilers (seal hunters) of old, the butt of national jokes no one outside of Canada ever understood . . . Surveying a national penchant for laughing at 'Newfies', the brilliant and caustic St. John's *Evening Telegram* columnist Ray Guy wrote in 1968: 'Newfoundlanders, what are we? We're slobbering idiots, slack-jawed simpletons, rustic fish billies living in Dogpatch-on-the-rocks, lower than lower Slobovians, the laughing stock and "white trash" of Canada. Why one province of Canada should have become the object of scorn and derision of the other nine is a mystery to us. Do we deserve it? If we do, we'd like our fellow Canadians to tell us why'.

5.2 Attitudes to Newfoundland dialects

> Sure, the Newfoundland dialect is sometimes described as being delightful and colorful and another adjective thrown around much is 'quaint' but that focus would not be on us if it were not for a source of entertainment. (from an editorial in the Gander *Beacon*, 15 December 1982)

Not unexpectedly, outsider attitudes to Newfoundlanders and Labradorians are also reflected in their attitudes to local speech, which, as we have seen from earlier chapters, is highly distinctive within the North American context. Pringle (1985: 186) notes that several salient features (TH-stopping, unrounding of the 'oy' diphthong, as in *boy* pronounced 'b'y', and 'a vague Irish cast to the vowels') are 'sufficient to suggest to English Canadians that the speaker being represented is an uneducated fisherman from a Newfoundland outport'. Studies that have tapped the attitudes of mainland Canadians to NLE varieties confirm that these are largely negative. Edwards and Jacobsen (1987) report that residents of the neighbouring province of Nova Scotia downgraded speakers of NLE not only in terms of their speech characteristics (pronunciation, vocabulary and fluency), but also with respect to social status and education. A more recent study of attitudes towards various regional Canadian accents (McKinnie and Dailey-O'Cain 2002) reveals that NLE was negatively evaluated on both 'correctness' and 'pleasant-ness' ratings by residents of Ontario and Alberta, Canada's wealthiest provinces. NLE was also termed 'drawl', 'Newfie talk' and 'extremely fast lower class [speech]'.

Attitudinal studies carried out on the island of Newfoundland suggest that residents of the province have largely internalised out-sider stereotypes of local speech. Despite the overt claim of many Newfoundlanders to hold positive views of NLE (see Clarke 1982; O'Dwyer 1982), studies using indirect techniques of attitude evaluation (Clarke 1981, 1982; Hampson 1982a, 1982b) show that NL residents downgrade speakers of non-standard local varieties on attitudinal measures relating to perceived social status and general competence. In St. John's and nearby Avalon Peninsula towns (Clarke 1982; Hampson 1982a, 1982b), such speakers were, however, viewed positively in terms of their 'social attractiveness', with respect to such qualities as honesty, friendliness and likeableness. Yet this last view is by no means uniform throughout the province: as Clarke (1981, 1997b) reports, many younger residents of small coastal outport communities may see little positive in symbols designating 'localness', and may downgrade local speakers even on measures of social attractiveness. Sociolinguistic studies conducted in such communities confirm these generally negative views. Of the rural northeast coast area that he investigated, Colbourne (1982a: 90) commented that residents felt they did not speak proper English, and viewed their local variety as 'a sign of ignorance, low class, low educa-tion' and 'poverty'. And for the small community of Burnt Islands near the southwestern extremity of the island, Newhook (2002: 94) noted: 'Most [residents] are aware of their local variety and have either been made fun of themselves or have heard of others who had been teased about their speech.'

Within the Canadian context, Newfoundlanders and Labradorians may, unintentionally or not, have helped to reinforce the negative stereotypes associated with the province and its speech varieties. Newfoundland comedy groups frequently base their humour on the construction of local 'characters', often down-and-outers, who can be readily identified by their thick regional accents. One of the most popular musical and comedy groups within the province and among expatriate Newfoundlanders, Buddy Wasisname and the Other Fellers – a trio containing two former schoolteachers – perform many of their routines and songs (such as 'Gotta get me moose, b'y') in strongly vernacular NLE. A number of talented Newfoundland actors have also taken their humour to the Canadian mainland, where they have proved extremely successful. For more than a quarter-century, national

CBC television has broadcast a weekly series of often satirical comedy programmes written by and featuring Newfoundland actors: 'The Wonderful Grand Band' (1980–83), 'Codco' (1987–92), and 'This Hour has 22 Minutes' (1993–). While 'insiders', including expatriate Newfoundlanders and Labradorians, may identify the intended humour in these portrayals, the situation is complex. Brilliant as some of this often self-deprecating humour may be, it also frequently plays into existing national-level stereotypes of Newfoundlanders as dimwitted, rough-and-ready, working-class individuals.

In an op-ed piece that appeared in the St. John's daily newspaper the *Telegram* ('We should nurture our unique dialect', 27 December 2007, A6), Michael Collins bemoans the fact that the public performance of NLE remains consigned to roles that are in effect caricatures:

One of our great strengths is our ability to laugh at ourselves and to make an intelligent social or political comment while doing so. But ... maybe we need to further demonstrate that a nice, thick Newfoundland dialect is good for more than a laugh. Maybe we need more reminders that the people who speak it are not caricatures. Maybe we need to get more examples of non-comical, heavily accented speech circulating in media ... How about a Newfoundland-written, acted and produced daytime TV drama? ... Nothing eulogizing a lost way of life and a dying culture – that's what we're trying to prevent. Modern, relatable people speaking non-satirical Newfoundland English that is in no way watered down for a mainland audience to understand. Perhaps look to perennially popular *Coronation Street* as a model. If northern England's working class dialects can be a vehicle for relatable melodrama, why can't ours?

We should also note, however, that despite general resentment of 'Newfie' jokes and other perceived insults, the province and its residents have derived economic and other benefits from cultivating the image of the rough-edged, simple, yet good-natured Newfoundlander. This image was clearly behind the Newfoundland government's choice of the marketing slogan 'Canada's Happy Province' in the 1960s and 1970s, a period when the province's tourist industry also produced brochures featuring local folklore, 'figures of speech' and quaint local sayings and place names (e.g. English 1975 [1955]). Today, summer dinner-theatres that cater to the tourist market often involve portrayals of the 'country bumpkin' character, with, of course, a broad local accent. Commodification of local culture can be seen in any tourist shop in the province, from the proliferation of 'Newfie' joke books to other supposedly 'Newfie' paraphernalia, including square rolling pins and mugs with handles on the inside. Visitors are made 'honorary Newfoundlanders' via an invented, non-traditional ceremony, the 'screech-in', which includes drinking rum ('screech') and kissing a cod under the direction of a 'screecher' who uses local vernacular speech (see Byrne 1997; King and Clarke 2002). And in recent years, 'Newfie identity' has increasingly included the image of hard drinking and hard partying. Evidence of this extends from the renown of George Street in downtown St. John's – which styles itself as having the most pubs and bars per square foot of any street in North America – to the proliferation of You-Tube videos with such titles as 'Newfie drinkin'', 'Newfie stomp', 'Newfies gone wild', 'Drunken Newfie debate team' and 'Ain't no party like a Newfie party'.

The image of the hard-living, working-class Newfoundlander is also one recently cultivated in the online performance of a St. John's teenage hip-hop group, Gazeebow Unit, whose rap is characterised by its use of local non-standard phonological, grammatical and lexical features (Clarke and Hiscock 2009). This group garnered considerable attention, since (except for the purpose of comedy, as noted earlier) virtually no NL musicians had previously utilised such broad local dialects; rather, they had tended to sound much like non-Newfoundland performers of their particular musical genre, whether Irish, country and western, or rock. Rather than representing an act of solidarity or an attestation of local identity, however, Gazeebow Unit's choice of local linguistic features turned out to be parody; as middle-class suburban teens whose home language was fairly standard, they were using vernacular speech to mock the image of the tough 'skeets' (see section 5.5) they were purportedly portraying.

Performance of working-class or rural Newfoundland identity on the part of ingroup members is one thing. When, however, this comes from outsiders, it is another matter. This occurred in the autumn of 2006 in national TV advertisement for a newly launched Nissan SUV, the 'Bonavista', named after a Newfoundland community. The commercial featured a car salesman speaking in what appeared to be a very broad Newfoundland accent; his words were accompanied by subtitles designed to convey the general gist of the message, but which aimed to provoke humour. Thus the salesman's greeting of 'How's she gettin' on, me son?' was glossed as 'Hi', and his 'She got de climate control on d'inside' was subtitled 'Automatic climate control'. Ironically, the 'salesman' proved to be an actor from Nova Scotia, whose non-local accent and lexical features – despite his attempt at imitation – were immediately identified as such by Newfoundlanders. According to natives of Bonavista, the actor's speech did not represent theirs: as one noted, 'I had a job to understand any word he said' (http://www.cbc.ca/canada/ newfoundland-labrador/story/2006/09/14/nissan-bonavista.html).

The groundswell of reaction from the province to this ad has been thoroughly documented by King and Wicks (2009). Their analysis shows a range of responses, some of them positive, often along the lines of 'Lighten up, this is fine, we Newfoundlanders are known for our sense of humour'. Much reaction was, however, extremely negative. One online posting noted by King and Wicks observes that had a similar ad been performed in African American vernacular speech, it would have been viewed as racist and pulled from the airwaves.

5.3 Academic and educational perspectives

> Why do you think that we have students in MUN that do whatever it takes to lose their beautiful dialect before they leave the Island or finish school? Why are they felt to feel ashamed of how they speak or w[h]ere they come from?   (http://freenewfoundlandlabrador.blogspot.com/2008/11/new-definition-for-have-and-have-not.html, posted by Calvin, 4 November 2008)

Over the past half-century, the education system has done little to counter the negative stereotypes associated with local varieties. If anything, schools have helped to reinforce the idea that traditional local speech is 'incorrect' and 'ungrammatical'. During the late 1950s and 1960s, the province's sole university (Memorial or MUN) also espoused this idea, by obliging education students from rural areas to enrol in a 'Speech' (i.e. elocution) course designed to reduce their strong local dialects and enable mastery of more standard pronunciation and grammar. A 2007 CBC NL radio documentary, 'My Fair Bayman' (an obvious play on 'My Fair Lady'), presents the attitudes of former students and instructors to this course (for online access, see 'Web resources' at the end of the chapter). As the documentary shows, there are conflicting views surrounding this university course. Some contributors point to its necessity in enabling them to obtain a teaching job and all the other potential benefits that a standard dialect brings; others decry the methods that were used to try to rid them of their traditional language and culture.

So entrenched are attitudes towards local non-standard varieties that scholarly efforts to promote them may be met with public dismay if not outright scorn. This was the case, for example, in two instances in which university academics have been seen to sanction local speech. In the mid-1970s, several MUN professors – in light of the low scholastic performance of rural NL students – advocated that these children should initially learn to read and write via materials produced in their own home varieties, rather than standard English (Walker 1975; Walker et al. 1975). Just as in the case of the more recent Ebonics controversy in the US, which revolved around the incorporation of vernacular African American English language materials into the school system, the idea was to provide a transitional step that would make mastery of standard English easier for such students, and also instil in them a sense of pride in their linguistic and cultural heritage. Yet, just as in the US Ebonics programme, the response from the general public was far from positive. The following is extracted from a letter that appeared in the St. John's *Evening Telegram* in March 1975, written to one of these professors by an outraged parent:

> Dr. Walker, wherever you are:
>
> It's not that I couldn't understand your professional jargon, it's just that I understood it too damn well in spite of my nonstandard English background and limited formal education. So it's Newfie text books next, is it? Well now that should be worthy of a hefty grant. Preserving our culture and dialect is a sure winner. In any case, it seems to be a favourite upalong pasttime – keeping us quaint for their own amusement – and we are just gullible enough to be flattered. I notice there is one thing all of you dialect preservers have in common – a different dialect – which leaves your kids on the safe side of the fence while you 'experiment' with ours. You tell them how 'lovely and fluent' their dialect is but you neglect to add they will have a hard time becoming a professor . . . a teacher, doctor, lawyer or whatever as long as they are saying 'I bees' and 'I sees'. Or don't you think an outport child should have such aspirations? . . .
>
> You know, I'm getting terribly tired of having some Johnny come lately telling me about my culture. I've lived it man! As the umpteenth child in a fishing family, I've known enough cold, sickness and poverty to make a New York welfare recipient look like a Rockefeller. Four to a bed, old coats for covers, a heated birch 'junk' at my feet and a frozen piss pot under the bed – that's culture. But there was a lot of love, togetherness and hope – the hope that someday life would be better and we'd be able to look back with nostalgia at the 'good old days'. Well it would seem I have arrived and just in time to be put up in a bottle by . . . an ever increasing horde of do-gooders to whose advantage it is to preserve me, just as I'm about to get my taste of the good life.

For this commentator, the culture of poverty that local dialects symbolise is something to be left in the past; traditional speech is clearly a liability in the new Newfoundland and Labrador.

A similar opinion emerges from the second example, a reaction from the editor of a regional newspaper, the Gander *Beacon* (15 December 1982), to the newly published *Dictionary of Newfoundland English* (*DNE*), edited by three MUN professors. The dictionary received a great fanfare within the province, and quickly achieved international acclaim. For the *Beacon* editor, however, its potentially negative effects in validating local speech features obviously outweigh its merits:

The dictionary of so-called Newfoundland English has been in for much attention . . . and it will now find a place in the study of the unique culture of Newfoundland. We think the project is, indeed, a worth-while one, particularly from a scholarly point of view and for the sake of history, but we hope, on the other hand, that this dictionary of sorts doesn't serve to entrench people more in the belief that their 'twang' is practical and can present itself as a working language . . . As far as we are concerned the compilation will serve as an enjoyable reminder of our heritage but, apart from that, we are of the opinion it is about time corruption of the English language be put aside and in favor of adopting communication and pronunciation that would be becoming, practical and too long overdue of the Queen's English in Newfoundland.

Probably nothing has done more to make Newfoundlanders down-grading [*sic*] collector items than their dialect. It is not just an accent, either, as many subscribe to, but far from it. The dialect as handed down to us . . . represents a drastic departure from proper English – it is misspelled, illiterate and sloppy . . .

All school students in the province, and at a prime and basic age, should be taught proper English and not something that is corrupted and offends almost every word of grammar when it comes to verbs and the like . . . In the meantime, students can also be taught an appreciation of the dialect of their forefathers and in a fashion as to resort to it at times, if needs be . . . our only aim or wish is that Newfoundlanders will learn to acknowledge old-time talk for what it is – a legacy to be treasured but not something to nurture for modern every-day use.

5.4 Recent phonological and grammatical change

The Newfoundlanders are singularly sensitive about their speech. To record it, the observer has to work rapidly and refrain from questions. Ask the people to repeat a word or phrase, and they will usually try to recast it into their idea of conventional English. They seem to feel that the inquirer is 'tryin' to haul de cod off o' ("trick") we simple folk'. Some of them confided in me that 'us Newf'un'landers talks broken English'. (England 1925: 323)

In light of the generally held attitudes towards local varieties, along with extensive socioeconomic change in recent years, it should not be surprising that considerable language change has occurred over the past several decades. This section presents an overview of change in the areas of pronunciation and grammar; lexical and discourse-related change is discussed in section 5.5.

5.4.1 Phonetic change and its social patterning

Over the past quarter-century, a number of sociolinguistic studies have been conducted on the island of Newfoundland. Several (Clarke 1986, 1991; D'Arcy 2000, 2005; Hollett 2006) have focused on the province's capital and largest city, St. John's, while others have looked at the speech of small, outport fishing communities. Reid (1981) examined the patterning of several consonant and vowel features in Bay de Verde, a north shore Conception Bay community with fewer than 800 residents. Colbourne (1982a, 1982b) analysed socially conditioned language use on Long Island in Notre Dame Bay, on the northeast coast, with a total population of under 500. Newhook (2002) investigated the speech of Burnt Islands, a southwest coast community of just over 800. In 1994, Lanari examined the speech of the south coast town of Burin and neighbouring communities, with a total population of approximately 4000. An ongoing study under the direction of Gerard Van Herk (e.g. Van Herk et al. 2009) is investigating intergenerational language change in Petty Harbour/Maddox Cove, a former fishing community only 15 fifteen km from St. John's, whose residents increasingly find work in the capital city, if not outside the province. On a smaller scale, Richards (2002) examined the use of two traditional vowel features within a single family from a rural community on the Irish Avalon Southern Shore, by contrasting the speech of family members who remained in the community with those who had moved to suburban St. John's.

All of these studies have focused on phonological features, though several have also included local grammatical forms. All have investigated the effects of speaker age and gender on use of local features, along with the effects of socioeconomic status in larger communities (Clarke 1986, 1991; Lanari 1994). In two communities with mixed Irish–English settler origins, the effects of ethnicity have also been examined (Reid 1981; Clarke 1986, 1991). Despite early settlement on the island, ethnic divisions – which correlated to a large degree with religion, since most early Irish settlers were Roman Catholic, unlike most of the southwest English (cf. Wagner 2006–7) – continued to be fostered even in mixed communities by the existence of a religious-based denominational school system, which was finally abandoned only in 1998.

One notable finding highlighted by these studies – in particular those involving rural communities – is the high usage rates that continue to be displayed by many local features. In Colbourne (1982a), for example, TH-stopping – or the use of *t* and *d* rather than standard interdental fricatives in words like *thin* and *then* – was the overwhelming norm in casual speech, not only for voiced *then*-type words (where it occurred at an overall rate of 96 per cent), but also for voiceless *thin*-type words. In Burnt Islands, Newhook (2002) discovered initial *h*-deletion (e.g. *hair* pronounced *air*) to be the usual casual style pronunciation, occurring in 85 per cent of all *h*-initial lexical items. Even in St. John's, in a large corpus collected in the 1980s (cf. Clarke 1991), TH-stopping occurred in one-quarter to one-third of casual style tokens, depending on speaker group. In addition, many of the local vowel features discussed in Chapter 2 – fronted articulations of vowels in the lexical sets TRAP/BATH, LOT/CLOTH/THOUGHT and START, raising of the pre-*r* vowel in the SQUARE set (as in *bear*), and lowering in the POOR/CURE set (as in *tourist*) – were regularly used by a majority of St. John's speakers.

Yet whether urban or rural, all of these studies also point to the existence of relatively rapid phonological change across generations. The typical finding is a decline in the use of traditional local features on the part of younger and more upwardly mobile speakers in favour of increased adoption of more standard community external (supralocal) features. In St. John's, for example, a number of traditional Irish-origin features – among them 'clear' or palatal pronunciations of post-vocalic /l/ in words like *fill* and *pail*, and monophthongal variants of the tense vowels in words like *go* and *made* (see Chapter 2) – show dramatic decreases among younger speakers (Clarke 1991). Rather, younger generations favour pronunciations that are the norm in standard varieties elsewhere in North America: velar or 'dark' /l/, and upglided rather than 'steady' monophthongal pronunciations of the mid tense vowels. In addition, some younger St. John's speakers have been advancing features of pronunciation associated with 'trendy' mainland Canadian speech, in particular a more retracted version of the /æ/ vowel in words like *path* or *rack* (Clarke 1991; D'Arcy 2005). Similar overall results emerge from small outport communities. Most have noted a significant generational decline for the vast majority of traditional vowel and consonant features investigated.

Such age-related phonological change is not surprising, given the negative attitudes to local language varieties we have noted, and the realisation for many that traditional local economies are no longer viable; rather, the future lies in out-migration. Surveys (Ommer and Sinclair 1999; Palmer and Sinclair 2000) indicate that a very high percentage of high school students in rural areas of the province intend to leave their local areas, whether in search of economic advantages or higher education. The linguistic ramifications are obvious; as Newhook (2002: 95) puts it:

> Today, with the growing necessity to out-migrate, [the] self-conscious, negative evaluation of the Burnt Islands dialect may be growing with each generation. I spoke to one woman who said that she tried not to raise her children with a strong Newfoundland accent. It appears that there is little pride with respect to the local variety among those who plan to leave the community, and little concern about dialect preservation. There is more of a focus on the avoidance of local features, especially among teenagers.

However, linguistic change in rural communities is not simply a case of across-the-board intergenerational decline in local feature use. In all communities investigated, gender plays a major role; in small outport communities, it has proved more important than speaker age (Reid 1981; Colbourne 1982a; Newhook 2002). In general, though not exclusively, the Newfoundland studies show that females are approximately one generation ahead of males in the adoption of non-local features. In Colbourne's study, women in the over-fifty age group used supralocal pronunciations to about the same degree as younger (under-thirty) adults, whether male or female. For a number of pronunciation features in Burnt Islands, Newhook (2002) found a large gender gap not among the adults in her study, but rather among her adolescent group, aged thirteen to fifteen. While in their casual styles the teenage boys used such local features as vocalised post-vocalic /l/ (e.g. *milk* sounding like 'meok') and deletion of initial /h/ (e.g. *hear* pronounced 'ear') with a frequency approaching that of adults of both genders, teenage girls exhibited dramatically reduced rates, as Figure 5.1 illustrates. While this may reflect age-graded behaviour, it confirms the importance of gender roles among these adolescent speakers.

Despite the usual finding that Newfoundland females are spearheading the adoption of non-local features, this pattern does have exceptions. In Burnt Islands, Newhook (2002) observed that teenage females used two local vowel features significantly more frequently than teenage males. The first is the centralisation of the high tense vowel /u:/ (as in *do* or *loose*) to [ʉ:](i.e. 'GOOSE-centralisation', discussed in section 2.2.2.3). The second is the fronting of the nucleus of the /aʊ/ diphthong, as in *house* and *down*, to [æ] or [ɛ]. Both of these features figure prominently in

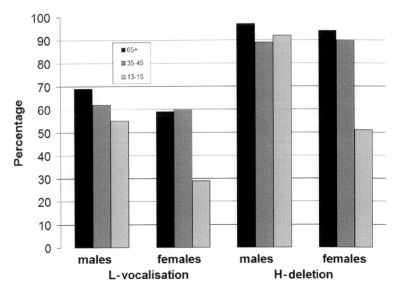

Figure 5.1 Casual style rates of L-vocalisation and H-deletion in the western south coast community of Burnt Islands (based on Newhook 2002)

the speech of Speaker 9, a young woman who comes from the western south coast portion of the island (see 7.5.2). What is striking about both features, however, is that not only are they are associated with females rather than males in adult generations, but they also coincide with innovative pronunciations in mainland Canadian English (e.g. Chambers and Hardwick 1986; cf. D'Arcy's 2005 study of pre-adolescent and adolescent girls in St. John's). Here, then, females appear to be advancing a feature that may carry with it connotations of non-localness and trendiness.

Yet not all rural Newfoundlanders appear to embrace such symbols. Consider a recent blog entry from a young rural resident who was outraged by the idea (posted in an earlier blog) that speech like hers might not be considered 'normal' by urban residents of the province:

What do you mean no one from Newfoundland talks like this? I'm from Newfoundland and I know thousands of people who talk with one of the many Newfoundland dialects, including myself. We're just talking the way we did for centuries, and I think it's a shame when you hear a Newfoundlander without their colourful accent. Why would someone who comes from such a deep rooted culture want to become so 'Americanized'? As Newfoundlanders we're so lucky to have such a distinct culture ... Anyone who don't embrace their Newfoundland culture is throwing away something that the majority of North Americans have already lost. (http://medium-info.livejournal. com/3461.html, posted by Anonymous, 26 March 2008; spelling and punctuation slightly revised)

This blogger goes on to claim that she is a Newfoundlander (definitely not a 'Newfie', which she considers a racial slur), and states, 'I'll hold my head high no matter where I go in this world.'

For such speakers, local identity is paramount; unlike the cases just outlined, such speakers appear to have little desire to assimilate to non-local norms. This loyalty to regional language and culture may clarify a gender-related finding that turns up in a minority of Newfoundland sociolinguistic studies: the greater attachment of rural women than rural men to several salient linguistic features that clearly signal local identity (Reid 1981; Lanari 1994). In the greater Burin area investigated by Lanari, one such feature is the pronunciation of tense /uː/ as a centralised diphthong, particularly before /l/, so that a word like *school* may be pronounced something like 'skew-wel' (see section 2.2.2.3). This pronunciation characterises Irish-settled communities in the area, and is locally well known and subject to parody. Lanari discovered that this feature, along with several others, was most associated not with working-class men, but with working-class women, especially in her younger (25–35) age group. Lanari attributes the unexpected adherence to such a marked local feature on the part of this younger female group to the strength of their local network ties. Unlike their middle-class counterparts, younger working-class women – most of whom were employed in the local fish plant – had dense and multiplex links within their community in terms of kinship, friendship and participatory networks (e.g. regular attendance at bingo games). In addition, unlike working-class males, whose jobs as dragger fishermen removed them from the community for weeks at a time, these women rarely travelled outside the region. Their orientation, loyalties and identity were clearly local, and their intent was to remain in the community – an option which, when Lanari's study was conducted in the early 1990s, still remained viable.

Lanari's findings represent one of the few NLE cases of intensification or 'concentration' of local features that has occasionally been noted in communities whose dialect varieties are undergoing rapid change and loss (Schilling-Estes and Wolfram 1999). A similar pattern has been observed in several Newfoundland studies for the feature of TH-stopping. Despite its overall decline in most communities where it has been investigated, in both St. John's (Clarke 1991) and Burin (Lanari 1994) it is associated to a higher than expected degree with younger working-class males, and in the community of Bay de Verde, with one group of younger women (Reid 1981). Nonetheless, the picture most frequently revealed by Newfoundland sociolinguistic studies is one of traditional feature decline across generations – or, in the terminology of Shilling-Estes and Wolfram, a pattern of 'dissipation'.

5.4.2 Variation across speech styles

Most of the local phonological features mentioned above do not enjoy overt prestige in that they are not the pronunciations sanctioned by standard English. They occur more frequently in vernacular and casual speech styles than they do in formal settings – that is, they are stylistically stratified. As the Newfoundland studies show, such features as TH-stopping, initial *h*-deletion and the pronunciation of words like *bed* as *bid* (on this last, see section 2.2.1.1) are subject to style shifting. A very small number of local features, nonetheless, are used at roughly the same rates across styles. This is the case, for example, for the vocalised articulation of post-vocalic /l/ (as in *milk* pronounced *meok*) in the northeast coast area investigated by Colbourne (1982a). Here, a vowel-like pronunciation is used at rates of over 90 per cent in all speech styles and thus constitutes the community norm. Yet in the south coast community of Burnt Islands (Newhook 2002), where the use of vocoid /l/ is much less frequent, this feature displays the expected stylistic stratification, occurring less often in careful than in everyday speech.

For a very small number of local features, usage increases from casual to formal styles. To date, all examples of this pattern involve features associated with women rather than men. In Burnt Islands, this is the case for the fronted [ɛʊ]-like realisation of the /aʊ/ diphthong, noted in the previous section. In St. John's, this pattern is found for the Irish-like slit fricative pronunciation of post-vocalic /t/, in words like *bit* or *better* (as described in Section 2.3.5.2). Though associated more with older than younger city residents, all groups tend to increase their usage in formal styles (Clarke 1986). However, unlike such features as TH-stopping or *h*-deletion, slit fricative /t/ is not stigmatised – in fact, it is viewed by some as representing 'clear' or 'proper' articulation.

One style-related observation that has emerged from several studies suggests that, despite fairly rapid intergenerational change, many local pronunciation features are in no danger of imminent disappearance. As Clarke (1991) points out for St. John's, a number of local features that are stratified by age display considerably greater generational differences in formal than in casual styles. Thus while in their careful speech

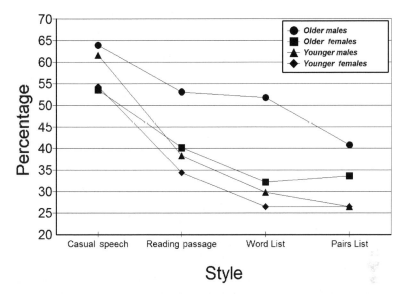

Style

Figure 5.2 Use of local phonetic features across styles, Long Island, Notre Dame Bay (based on Colbourne 1982a)

teenage and young adult speakers largely avoid TH-stopping in words like *thin*, *other* and *these* (using it in less than 5 per cent of *th* occurrences), they employ the stop pronunciation anywhere from four to ten times as frequently in casual style – in fact, at rates that are virtually as high as those found among older St. John's residents. Similarly, apparently innovative vowel pronunciations – such as the fronting of /aʊ/ in words like *now* and *mouth* – are making their way into the speech of younger generations initially via their formal styles (D'Arcy 2005).

The same top-down pattern, whereby supralocal features are diffusing into careful speech to a much greater extent than into everyday speech, has also been noted in rural contexts. Figure 5.2 summarises style shifting on the part of the four age and gender groups investigated by Colbourne (1982a) in rural Notre Dame Bay, across all the local phonological features he examined. In this figure, styles are arranged from left to right in terms of increasing formality. Figure 5.2 shows that younger speakers and older women use significantly fewer local features in their formal styles (elicited via three different reading tasks) than do the least standard speakers in the community, the older males. In casual style, however, these differences are much less apparent; in fact, casual style usage rates for younger males are remarkably similar to those of the older male group. In other words, younger speakers are not so much losing local pronunciations as they are becoming more adept at style shifting. Rather than abandoning their linguistic roots, these speakers have become more bidialectal, or more proficient at manipulating standard supralocal pronunciations alongside traditional community norms.

5.4.3 Grammatical change

As mentioned earlier, the social patterning associated with the use of local morphological and syntactic features has not been extensively investigated. However, studies generally confirm that local grammatical features are declining at an even more rapid rate than features of pronunciation. This is perhaps not surprising, since non-standard grammatical features are more subject to overt correction by the school system, and hence are often more salient than all but highly stigmatised phonological features. Thus on Long Island in Notre Dame Bay, Colbourne (1982a) investigated non-standard past tense/past participle usage (as in *I seen that, He done it already*), along with the application of grammatical gender to inanimates (e.g. the use of *'en* when unstressed or *he* when stressed in *Pick 'en /he up*, with reference to a book). Not only were these features used less frequently than all but the most stigmatised local features of pronunciation, they also displayed some of the greatest degree of usage difference (that is, sharper stratification) between the least standard and most standard speaker groups. As Figure 5.3 demonstrates, relative to these grammatical features the most standard users proved to be the women of the area, whatever their age group.

Likewise, in her investigation of the grammatical variable of pronoun exchange – the use of subject pronouns in stressed object position, as in *Do it for we* (see section 3.3.2.1) – Newhook (2002) found that this feature remained part of the casual style repertoire of Burnt Islanders, though not used as frequently as local pronunciation features. However, pronoun exchange was totally absent from the speech of teenage females. Yet for local phonological features (with a single exception, the highly stigmatised unrounded pronunciation of *-or-*, as in *born* pronounced *barn*) teenage females reduced their use of local variants rather than completely eliminating them, as they do in this instance (cf. Figure 5.1).

Yet despite the obvious decline in the use of local grammatical features, some remain very vigorous in rural contexts as well as in urban vernacular speech. One such feature is verbal *-s*, or the use of an *-s* suffix to mark any simple present-tense lexical verb, no matter what its subject

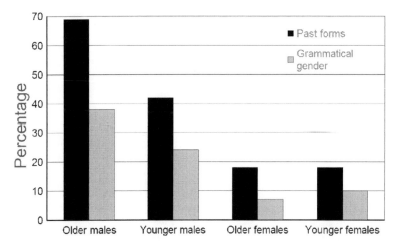

Figure 5.3 Use of non-standard past forms and grammatical gender by age/gender group on Long Island (based on Colbourne 1982a)

(e.g. *I goes there all the time; they loves it*, see section 3.2.2). Lanari's (1994) Burin corpus (analysed for this feature by Clarke 1997a) shows that the non-third-person-singular verbal -*s* form is the casual speech norm, occurring at an overall rate of 55 per cent. Given the salience of this feature, however, it is encountered much more rarely in careful speech styles, whatever the community. Apart from *is* and *was* forms of the verb *be*, the almost total absence of verbal -*s* with non-third-person singular subjects among the speech samples of Chapter 7 – which derive from radio interviews, along with relatively informal one-on-one interviews – stands in marked contrast to its high frequency in the Lanari corpus, which involves family and friendship group interactions in home settings. The iconic nature of verbal -*s* in the local context, however, makes it an eminently 'performable' feature, even on the part of speakers who otherwise would use it minimally, if at all, in their vernacular styles. Thus verbal -*s* may be regularly invoked to perform a range of discourse functions, from marking social identity (Van Herk et al. 2008) to parody.

One local syntactic feature is unusual in that it has actually increased its geographic range within the province over the past century. This is the *after*-perfect form, discussed in section 3.2.5. As noted, the *after*-perfect was not typically part of the grammars of traditional speakers in southwest English-settled parts of the province. Today, however, it is known and, to a degree used in all regions, though still most frequently in Irish-settled ones. Unlike a feature such as verbal -*s*, the *after*-perfect form is not stigmatised in NLE, and occurs commonly in the speech of middle-class urban residents. For at least some users, however, the form is largely restricted to negative or otherwise noteworthy events, among them changes in health and appearance (as in example 22 in Chapter 3).

5.5 Change at the levels of lexicon and discourse

Though many local features of pronunciation and grammar are undergoing considerable decline among younger generations, this tendency is even more noticeable in the areas of lexicon and discourse. As Chapter 4 shows, much traditional vocabulary is no longer known by younger speakers, particularly in urban contexts. Yet the waves of 'trendy' or 'slang' vocabulary that are spread via the media, internet chatrooms and face-to-face contact are highly evident in the speech of teenagers and young adults. Two decades ago, evaluative phrases like *totally awesome* and *way harsh* were the norm not only in California 'Valley Girl' talk, but also among many young Newfoundland females. These days, *awesome* and *cool* have been joined by the more recent imports *wicked* and *sweet*, frequently used as interjections (*I've got a ticket to the big game. Wicked!*). Just as in mainland Canada, among the current evaluators of choice is *brutal*, which may be used both negatively and positively; however, in Newfoundland it competes with *deadly*, which despite being known in Ireland is not well-known elsewhere in North America. Among younger females, the adjective *rotted* is a new import to express displeasure or disgust (as in *I'm rotted*, which competes with the more traditional Irish-inherited *I'm poisoned*). As to adverbial intensifiers, though *totally* and *way* have by no means disappeared from the speech of young Newfoundlanders, they are also in competition with newer arrivals. Thus *wicked* may now be employed as an adverbial intensifier (a use which appears to have originated in New England), as examples 80(a) and (b) indicate:

80.
(a)   Ever since the wet weather turned **wicked cold** . . . (young male CBC NL TV 'Here and Now' reporter, St. John's, 27 January 2009).
(b)   . . . and man, is it ever **wicked funny** ('Dav Net' column, *The Telegram*, 28 January 2009, B3).

Some younger Newfoundlanders even report use of the adverbial intensifer *hella* (as in *hella funny*), a form that is largely restricted to northern California, though it enjoyed some fleeting fame within North America through its associations with popular culture (see Bucholtz et al. 2007).

The path of diffusion of some lexical items into the vernacular speech of younger Newfoundlanders and Labradorians is less clear. Consider, for example, the word *razz*, used by younger speakers with the meaning 'riding around with friends in a car (or snowmobile), with no particular goal'. This meaning is not generally familiar to older residents of the province, and is largely unknown in North America. A very similar meaning does, however, occur in Britain and Australia, as in the following British online posting:

81. We find out about an exciting new craze that is seeing kids clad in leathers from Leamington **razzing around** on motorbikes. (http://www.bbc.co.uk/coventry/features/motor/mini-moto-crazy.shtml).

A small part at least of the vocabulary associated with younger speakers originates in local words that appear to have undergone recent meaning change. A good example is the word *skeet*. This term may be related to *skite*, which in neighbouring Prince Edward Island can mean 'a young scoundrel' (Pratt 1988), or to the American terms *skeester/skeeter*, defined by the *Dictionary of American Regional English* (Cassidy and Hall 1985) as 'rascal, rogue'. If older NLE speakers know this word at all, they would probably use it in this sense. Among younger speakers, however, it has much the same meaning as such British slang terms as *chav, charver* or *scally*, or even the North American *white trash*. The following online definition of *scally* (Bromley 2002) quite accurately describes the contemporary Newfoundland *skeet*:

[a person, usually male, who] wears sportswear (tracksuits, trainers, baseball caps) ... is in their teens or early twenties ... is usually working class or lower middle class ... loiters around in groups in town centres, not actually doing much ... is perhaps involved in petty crime (e.g. shop lifting, vandalism).

Other terms currently used by at least some Newfoundland youth appear to have taken on new meanings in the local context. The word *skully*, for example, refers to a person who is 'into' the heavy metal scene, and possibly also a lifestyle involving violence and drugs. Its origin is unclear. Could it be related to *scally*? Or might it derive from *skull*, given the skull-shaped tattoos favoured by some members of such non-mainstream groups? The positive evaluator *skint*, with a meaning of 'cool' or 'awesome', is used by younger generations in the area of Twillingate on the northeast coast of the island, yet appears to be unknown outside that region. In St. John's, the same meaning may be conveyed by the word *skunk*, though this usage is by no means wide-spread among St. John's adolescents.

Rapid change in NLE is also very much in evidence at the level of discourse. New quotative forms (roughly, forms which are the equivalent of *say* and which introduce directly quoted speech) are in evidence throughout the English-speaking world. The most usual of these, in North America at least, is *be like* (see e.g. Tagliamonte and D'Arcy 2004 for Toronto English). As D'Arcy (2004) indicates, *be like* has also found its way into St. John's youth speech and displays much the same distributional patterns as it does in Toronto; D'Arcy suggests that it may actually be further advanced in St. John's than in Toronto in its developmental path towards a full-function quotative. Henley et al. (2008) – analysing a data-set collected from Newfoundland university students, the majority from the greater St. John's area – found that these students used *be like* in three-quarters of their quotative contexts, and *say*, in only 8 per cent of occurrences; *be like* was particularly associated with females.

Quotative *be like* is by no means confined to urban residents. Examples 82(a) and (b) are drawn from interviews recorded in 2006 with students in their early twenties who grew up in rural Newfoundland and who were attending university in St. John's. Both were produced by female speakers – the first, from an isolated community on the island's westerly south coast (Speaker 9; see 7.5.2) and the second, from a northeast coast community.

82.
(a) So ah- everyone **was all like** 'Oh we're gonna be th[e] youngest people'.
(b) And **I'm like**, 'Oh my I don't have it ("frozen Christmas turkey") took out!' So I calls her father and **he's like** 'Well just put it in some water'.

The second example is of particular interest in light of its juxtaposition of local grammatical features (*took* rather than *taken; calls* rather than *call*, and a medial-object perfect, as outlined in Section 3.2.5) with 'trendy' innovative *be like*.

Another discourse feature that at first glance would appear to be a recent supralocal acquisition on the part of younger Newfoundlanders is the use of the conjunctions *and, but* and *so* as utterance finals. Final *so*, at least, has been noted to be increasing among younger speakers in Toronto (Tagliamonte 2006). These discourse tags are used to signal that the speaker has finished what she or he has to say, and typically invite a response from other conversational participants. The following

LANGUAGE ATTITUDES AND LANGUAGE CHANGE

examples were recorded in 2006 from students, both male and female, from various parts of the island who were attending university in St. John's:

83.

(a) That was our sort of place, we liked computer and technology sort of stuff **but** ... So we'd sort of hang out in there **and** ... (male, central Newfoundland).

(b) So these, you know, funny little stories coming up, I'm not really sure where they come from, **but** ... (female, south coast).

(c) ... I'm going to try and do four or five courses through the summer, it's just to hopefully get ahead if I can, **so** ... (female, northeast coast).

Yet as a glance at Chapter 7 indicates, utterance-final *and (ah)* ... and *but (ah)* ... are by no means restricted to younger speakers; they are also used by many traditional speakers in the province. Sentence-final *but* has been linked to British (particularly northern), Scottish, Irish and Australian English; in NL, it occurs readily among conservative speakers of English as well as Irish extraction. And while the greatest user of utterance-final *so* proves to be Speaker 8, a younger male, this feature also characterises two traditional speakers of NBE (see 7.1). What in fact the speakers featured in Chapter 7 illustrate is that a variety of turn-final discourse strategies are in play, and are favoured to different degrees by different speakers; in addition to the three listed above, these include the sentence-final tags *eh*, *right* and *you know*, and even, on the part of Speaker 6 from Labrador, ingressively articulated *yeah*. Clearly, the investigation of sentence-final tags in NLE provides a rich area for future research.

As the examples in 83 demonstrate, the particle *so* is also used with a turn-initial function as well as turn-finally. Further, as in innovative speech in many other parts of the English-speaking world (see e.g. Tagliamonte 2006; Bulgin et al. 2009), it is regularly used as an adverbial intensifier, particularly by younger females. The following utterance, on the topic of high schools in her city, comes from a university student from the west coast community of Corner Brook, and is typical of the discourse style of younger Newfoundlanders:

84. **So**, but they totally redid it, it's beautiful and so everybody's getting really mad that [*creaky voice*] Herdman is **so** old and they're going to take the time and renovate it and everything like that, and, Regina is [a] beautiful brand new school relatively now **and** ...

As the descriptor 'creaky voice' might suggest, the speech of younger Newfoundlanders is also characterised by the adoption of suprasegmental or prosodic features (see section 2.5) which characterise youth speech in mainland North America. Creaky voice involves a raspy quality of voice produced by reducing the amount of air passing through the vocal cords, which results in a non-pure or non-clear tone. It too carries a pragmatic meaning, often signalling the end of a turn, and is associated with younger female speech, as in examples 85(a) and (b) from the 2006 set of student recordings:

85.
(a) So, it was kind of petrifying and I will never drive around Burin without thinking of [*creaky voice*] these stories now (south coast).
(b) Yeah, but that's a little tiny [*creaky voice*] spot, yeh (northeast coast).

Examples of creaky voice can be heard in the online audio file for Speaker 9 (7.5.2).

Creaky voice phonation is a very recent import to the province; speech recorded prior to a decade or so ago gives no indication of it. The same, however, is not true of a second prosodic feature, the frequency of which has nonetheless dramatically risen locally in recent years: high rising tone, also known as 'uptalk'. This is the use of a rising, question-like intonation in what is actually a statement; it has been noted as a feature of innovative speech not only in the US and Canada, but also in Britain, Australia and New Zealand. Generally, in the English-speaking world, high rising tone is associated more with female than with male speech. This also appears to be the case in NLE, though it is by no means avoided by males, as its ready use by Speaker 3, a traditional NIE speaker from St. John's, attests (7.2.1). Examples 86(a)–(c), again drawn from the 2006 student recordings, illustrate this phenomenon:

86.
(a) ... because we were regulars in the computer lab so, there was this horrible bias to a certain extent? (male, central Newfoundland).
(b) Well there's one, there's a stretch of road there between Black Duck Cove and Long Cove, where the pharmacy used to be? (female, south coast).
(c) ... everyone goes there but, it's ('there's') only probably twenty people can get into the water [*laughs*] at one time because it's so small? (female, northeast coast).

As these examples show, the discourse or pragmatic function of high rising tone is to ensure listener comprehension and attention, and to create a positive interactive environment.

5.6 Concluding remarks

This chapter has shown that contemporary NLE is undergoing considerable change. Much of this change – involving the loss of community-related norms in favour of adoption of more widespread, supralocal forms – follows from the province's socioeconomic and demographic situation relative to the Canadian mainland. Yet at the same time, more salient traditional linguistic features may take on new social roles as markers of local identity on the part of younger speaker groups. Local words may undergo meaning change and be recycled among younger generations. Many of the province's younger rural residents have become adept style-shifters, moving with relative ease from local community norms to more standard regional and supralocal forms, as circumstances require. Thus despite much ongoing change, NLE retains a distinct identity within the North American context, as it will undoubtedly continue to do.

Web resources

Considerably more information on illustrative cases mentioned in this chapter may be found online:

Section 5.1

http://www.fairdealfornewfoundland.com/williamsresponse/
  A response to Margaret Wente's *Globe and Mail* column from the premier of the province, Danny Williams
http://www.kevinmccann.net/blog/index.php?p=16
  A response to Wente's column by national CBC commentator and native Newfoundlander Rex Murphy
http://www.youtube.com/watch?v=Mnf0VKMw6Vg
  Local reaction to the province's rise to economic 'have' status in November 2008, as encapsulated in Jody Richardson's video performance of 'Yes we have!', which was composed around the words of Premier Williams, hailed as a local hero for having stood up to 'big oil', thereby reaping substantial financial benefits for the province

Section 5.2

http://www.myspace.com/gazeebowunit
  Examples of the rap of Gazeebow Unit, grounded in traditional NL dialect
www.youtube.com/watch?v=3m-y-qAbpL0
  The Nissan 'Bonavista' SUV advertisement (see King and Wicks 2009)

http://www.youtube.com/watch?v=7c6_CBK4ufg
A parody of the Nissan Bonavista ad, made by a St. John's car dealership, featuring Newfoundland actor Pete Soucy in his locally well-known performance guise of 'Snook', a St. John's 'corner-boy'

Section 5.3

http://www.cbc.ca/nl/media/audio.html or http://johngushue.typepad.com/blog/2008/02/my-fair-bayman.html
The CBC NL 2007 radio documentary 'My Fair Bayman', containing commentary on, as well as performance of, a number of highly salient local features, notably, TH-stopping, initial *h*-deletion, and verbal -*s*

6 Survey of previous work

An English-language literature relating to Newfoundland has existed for well over 400 years. Richard Hakluyt the younger (1589) provides an account of sixteenth-century English explorations to the New World, including Newfoundland. The region figures in the documents of sixteenth-century explorers, notably those associated with the 1583 expedition of Sir Humphrey Gilbert, who claimed the island in the name of Queen Elizabeth I (see e.g. Quinn and Cheshire 1972). Early seventeenth-century Newfoundland is represented by the writings of its first English colonisers, among them John Guy of Bristol, who founded the first official colony in 1610, and Sir George Calvert, later Lord Baltimore (see Cell 1982). Mason (1620), in a tract written to promote investment in Newfoundland, contains a favourable description of the land and climate, as well as listings of local flora and fauna. Perhaps the most notable document of this period is the extensive 1620 treatise *A Discourse and Discovery of New-found-land* by Sir Richard Whitbourne, a Devonshire seaman and fishing merchant. The 1628 *Quodlibets* of Robert Hayman, former governor of the colony at Bristol's Hope/Harbour Grace, represents the first work of poetry to be written in the New World.

The eighteenth and nineteenth centuries saw the publication of various accounts by visitors to the area (Moyles 1975 represents a highly readable survey of some of the nineteenth-century descriptive literature). These ranged from members of the British Royal Navy (e.g. Chappell 1818; Thomas 1968 [1794]) to naturalists (among them Joseph Banks who, in 1766, documented local flora and fauna; see Lysaght 1971). Some early nineteenth-century works focused on the exploration of the then largely unknown interior of the island of Newfoundland; among these are Lieutenant David Buchan's account of attempts at contact with the local Beothuk Indians (Barrow 1818) and William Epps Cormack's narrative of the first expedition to successfully cross the island (Cormack 1928 [1822]). Later nineteenth-century literature included important publications on the island's geology, notably Jukes

(1842), as well as Murray and Howley (1881). While none of this literature had language and dialect as its prime focus, it provides extremely
valuable insights into local lexicon in particular; the manuscript notebook of the Newfoundland geologist J. P. Howley, written around
1900, for example (see Kirwin 1978; Kirwin et al. 1997; Kirwin and
O'Flaherty 2009), lists some eighty regional lexical items.

Even in the early twentieth century, the Newfoundland interior,
along with Labrador, remained sufficiently remote and unknown as to
attract explorers and scholars, whose published accounts provide information on local culture and, to a small degree, language. Millais (1907)
recounted an expedition to Newfoundland's interior and west coast,
while in 1908 Mina Hubbard, the widow of an American adventurer,
documented her exploratory voyage to previously uncharted regions of
Labrador. In the 1940s, the Finnish geographer Väinö Tanner published
an exhaustive geographic and cultural survey of Labrador, based on two
expeditions conducted in the 1930s.

The 1960s witnessed a dramatic increase in academic work relating
to the province's folklore, language, geography, history, anthropology
and sociology. The local focus continues to flourish in all of these disci-
plines. Links to some of this work can be found in the 'Web Resources'
section at the end of the chapter.

6.1 Observations on NLE prior to 1950

Despite the absence of early works focusing on local speech varieties, the unique character of NLE has been noted for over 400 years.
As McConnell (1979: 148) points out, an account of Sir Humphrey
Gilbert's 1583 expedition, written by one of his captains, Robert Hay,
includes new terminology which had arisen in conjunction with the
Newfoundland fishery, such as *green fish*, *corre* ('undried salted cod'), *skull*
('shoal or school of fish') and *gaunts* ('gannets').

Up to the 1950s, documentation of features of Newfoundland English
was largely confined to linguistically untrained observers, many of
them visitors to the region. Much of this related to local lexicon, though
there are a few brief descriptions of local pronunciation and grammar.
In addition, literary representations of NL vernacular speech are to be
found from the mid nineteenth-century.

6.1.1 Vocabulary

The journals of a number of seventeenth- and eighteenth-century
visitors attest to the existence of a unique NLE vocabulary, much of

it relating to the fishery, flora and fauna. The Newfoundland segments of the journal of the Plymouth surgeon James Yonge (written in 1663, 1669–70; see Poynter 1963) include such fishery terms as *flakes* and *stages*, names of local fish and birds (among the latter, *murr*, *noddy* and *ice bird*); and the word *rinds*, which Yonge glosses (Poynter 1963: 56) as 'bark stripped from trees'. All of these terms remain in use to this day. Thomas (1968 [1794]) describes local oddities such as the pitcher plant (now the province's floral emblem), for which he has no name, and the squid, along with a host of berries and 'water and land fowl', including *hegdowns*, *muirs* and *tuirs* [sic] (143ff.). The most extensive eighteenth-century documentation of local lexicon, however, is to be found in the 1792 journal of the Englishman George Cartwright, who resided in coastal Labrador from 1770 to 1786 (see Chapter 4). The three volumes of his journal are each prefaced by a glossary – the first glossaries of a regional language to be published north of the American colonies (Kirwin 1991).

The nineteenth century saw the publication of a number of works by visitors to the region which include a handful of local terms (e.g. Wix 1836; Tucker 1839; Wilson 1866). Two works by visiting clergy-men are however particularly worthy of note. The earlier of these was produced by the Rev. Julian Moreton, who spent almost thirteen years (1849–60) in the northern Bonavista Bay community of Greenspond. His *Reminiscences* (1863) contains a chapter listing some seventy words, plus a number of phrases, which he describes as either obsolete in his homeland (England), or of Newfoundland origin. In addition to terms designating the natural environment, these include items representing human qualities and activities, among them (pp. 30–3) *clever*, which he glosses as 'large, stout'; *stunned* ('dull of apprehension, stupid'); *turn* ('a burden, as much as a man will carry at one time'); and *ructions* ('an insurrection, any popular disturbance'). More than thirty years later, a visiting clergyman from Nova Scotia, the Rev. George Patterson, was also struck by the number of local words and phrases with which he was unfamiliar. Patterson produced three articles for the *Journal of American Folklore* (1895–97), which documented some 270 items, and attempted to link these to British and American regional lexicon.

Early twentieth-century glossarists include the American George Allan England, who appended a considerable list of local words and expressions to his 1924 novel *Vikings of the Ice*, based on the Newfoundland seal hunt. A consolidated glossary containing approxi-mately 1,000 items appears in England (1925). A prominent place is also occupied by the Newfoundlander P. K. Devine, whose 1937 volume on the folklore and word lore of Newfoundland contains entries for almost

1,000 local words and phrases, along with a list of proverbs, sayings and folk beliefs.

6.1.2 Pronunciation and grammar

In the early nineteenth century, Edward Chappell, a visiting lieutenant in the British Royal Navy, wrote of St. John's (1818: 52): 'Literature and polished manners are here unknown; and a stranger must not be surprised to observe a constant violation of the most ordinary rules of speech.' This constitutes one of the few early non-lexical comments on the English language in Newfoundland – perhaps not surprisingly, since much of the local population in the eighteenth and early nineteenth centuries would have been born in England and Ireland, and hence would not be expected to differ substantially in speech from their peers in the homeland. In 1838, for example, the New Englander Ephraim Tucker noted that 'all residents speak equally discordant in either an Irish or Devonshire accent' (Kirwin 1991: 232). However, one late eighteenth-century English visitor made perhaps the first mention of a local phonological feature: Thomas (1968 [1794]: 137) observes that the 'natives' (that is, people whose 'grandfathers were born in Newfoundland') 'speak English but they have a manner perculiar [sic] to themselves – the common people Lisp'. He goes on to state: 'for every Out-harbour I viseted [sic] on conversing with the people, they would on answering my enquirys [sic] say – "Yes, *dat* is the way" or "O no, we tant do it so; but *den* we do it the other way" . . .' He also notes the tendency of some residents of the island to use such (apparent hypercorrect) pronunciations as 'O *Th*ear, pay do not *thrubble* yourself' which he had previously observed in women 'of rank'. What Thomas seems to be referring to here, at least in part, is the long-standing NLE tendency towards TH-stopping (see Section 2.3.1).

Thomas's observations are based on his visits to communities on the southern (and, as he remarks, largely Irish-settled) Avalon Peninsula. Eighteenth- and early nineteenth-century commentary on the speech of areas settled by the southwest English is sparse. As reported in Story (1975, 1982), however, TH-stopping was also noted by the naturalist Philip Gosse, who during his stay in Newfoundland in the 1820s observed the 'inability' of English-origin (rather than Irish) settlers in Conception Bay North to pronounce *th*. A somewhat later observer (Moreton 1863) provides considerably more information relative to the speech of northern Bonavista Bay, an area largely settled by migrants from Wessex. Among the features noted by Moreton – in addition to TH-stopping – are the voicing of initial /f/ to [v]; final consonant cluster reduction (as in *topmasts* pronounced 'topmases'); insertion of an epenthetic vowel in syllable-final *-sts* and *-sks* clusters, as in *askes* and *ghostes*, along with the aforementioned *topmases*, and metathesis of *-sp* in words like *clasp* (yielding the pronunciation 'claps').

Early descriptions of local grammatical features are fewer in number. Patterson (1895) notes the use of *he* and *she* to designate inanimate objects, along with second-person singular forms *thee/thou*, non-standard past tense verb forms (*runned, goed, doned*, etc.), and *a*-prefixing on present participles (as in *a-walking, a-hunting*). That such features must have existed in abundance, however, is evident from nineteenth-century literary representations of local dialect (see below); verbal *-s* outside the third-person singular, for example, occurs in the speech of an 'old hand' on the Labrador coast, as portrayed by de Boilieu (1969 [1861]: 50).

6.1.3 Literary representations (to 1950 and beyond)

For well over a century and a half, Newfoundland-based literature has included representations of local people speaking in their own words, via 'semi-phonetic' spellings – that is, the use of non-standard spellings to represent words as they would actually be pronounced (such as 'da' for *the*). The first well-known attempt is Robert Traill Spence Lowell's 1858 novel *The New Priest in Conception Bay*. Lowell, an American, served as a Church of England minister in Bay Roberts, Conception Bay, and the many local phonological and grammatical features that he exploits (see Hiscock 1982; Kirwin 1991) are characteristic of the area. However, he fails to represent the local feature of post-vocalic /r/-deletion, possibly because, as he came from Boston, this feature would have characterised his own (standard) speech variety.

Several early twentieth-century writers from outside NL also made extensive use of local dialect features to represent vernacular NLE speech. The Canadian author Norman Duncan set several of his works of fiction in the region, among them his 1904 volume *Dr. Luke of the Labrador*. In his 1924 novel, the American George Allan England created a detailed and reasonably accurate portrayal of the speech of northeast coast Newfoundland fishermen. England represented a number of phonological and grammatical features that are now highly recessive, among them an initial *y* glide in words like *hear* and *here*, and the use of *am* with the grammatical subjects *you* and *s/he* (i.e. *you'm, he'm*, etc.). This tradition, incidentally, continues to the present, as in the case of the American writer Robert Finch; Finch's misplacement of verbal *-s* in *I don't wants to play patience* (Finch 2007: 206), however, serves as a reminder of the limitations of literary representations from writers without insider knowledge of local forms.

It should be added that the tradition of dialect representation has also continued to this day among NL writers. The collections of tales from the fictitious Newfoundland outport of Pigeon Inlet (Russell 1975, 1977) provide an excellent example, as do the novels of the writers Helen Porter (e.g. *Below the Bridge*) and Bernice Morgan (*Random Passage, Waiting for Time*). The poetry of Mary Dalton (notably her 2003 volume *Merrybegot*) makes extensive use of traditional Newfoundland lexicon. Kirwin (1991) provides a good overview of the history of literary representation of NLE dialect forms, while Shorrocks (1996) documents the use of local dialect by the novelist Percy Janes.

6.2 Post-1950: linguistic approaches to NLE

The first systematic and linguistically-grounded studies of NLE date back to the late 1950s and emerged out of the department of English Language and Literature of Memorial University in St. John's. Three faculty members in particular – together with their colleagues in Folklore, Herbert M. Halpert and John Widdowson – were instrumental in establishing collections of NL materials: these were Edgar Ronald Seary (family and place names), along with George M. Story and William J. Kirwin (lexicography and dialectology). Much of the material collected was deposited in Memorial University's Folklore and Language Archive (MUNFLA) and its affiliate, the English Language Research Centre (ELRC), where it remains available for consultation. The founding of a separate department of Linguistics at Memorial in 1967 led to a broadening of the scope of research into NLE, particularly in the form of sociolinguistic and variation studies, along with an increased emphasis on regional dialectology. Though the majority of post-1950 research on NLE has been carried out by those affiliated with Memorial University, the area has also been a focus for a number of scholars from outside the province, and from Europe in particular. The outcome is that NLE is the best documented of any variety of Canadian English.

Despite this, much basic work on NLE has appeared locally – including a number of unpublished Master's level theses – and has not up to now been readily accessible outside the local region. However, more and more is appearing online, as the 'Web resources' section at the end of this chapter indicates. An online bibliography, the link for which also appears in that section, lists more than 250 publications that deal with NLE.

6.2.1 *Lexical research, including place and family names*

Without doubt, the best-known volume on NLE is the *Dictionary of Newfoundland English* (*DNE*; Story et al. 1999 [1982]), also available online. The result of painstaking years of labour, during which its compilers collected and edited many thousands of potential entries from both print and oral sources, this publication represents the first scholarly collection of regional lexicography in Canada and stands as a model for future work.

The rich legacy of toponyms in NL had attracted interested laypersons well prior to the mid twentieth-century, as attested, for example, in the series of articles by Archbishop M. F. Howley, which appeared in a local periodical, the *Newfoundland Quarterly*, from 1901 to 1914. A detailed scholarly treatment of the place names of the Avalon Peninsula is to be found in Seary (1971), while Seary (2000) documents the toponyms of the Northern peninsula of the island. Hamilton (1996) briefly traces the historical origins of many of the place names of Atlantic Canada, with a chapter devoted to the province. Family names of the island of Newfoundland have been thoroughly documented in Seary (1998), a posthumous edition of a volume that originally appeared in 1977, corrected and expanded by W. J. Kirwin.

The popular literature on NLE also includes items of lexicographical interest. Young's (2006) *Dictionary of Newfoundland and Labrador* contains a glossary of local words and phrases, along with information on such topics as folklore and weather lore. Strowbridge (2008) constitutes a similar compendium. McConnell (1979), intended as a textbook on Canadian English for high school and university students, devotes a section to NLE, with a primary focus on lexicon.

6.2.2 *General descriptions of NLE, plus regional and community dialect studies*

Brief introductions to NLE and its features appear in a number of publications. Both Kirwin (2001) and Clarke (forthcoming) constitute general overviews of the history and structural features of NLE; the former also deals with lexicon. Shorrocks (1997) includes a survey of some of the previous research into the Irish roots of NLE. An overview of the phonology of present-day NLE may be found in Clarke (2004b, 2008); Clarke (2004c) outlines the principal morphological and syntactic features of vernacular varieties. Several of the chapters in Paddock (1982b) provide general, reasonably non-technical introductions to NLE and its regional varieties, in particular those by Story and by

Paddock (see also Story 1975). Halpert and Widdowson (1996) – a collection of folktales narrated by rural Newfoundlanders, many of whom were born in the late nineteenth century – also document a host of local phonological and morphological features, a number of which are now approaching obsolescence. The earliest descriptions of the phonology and morphosyntax of particular regional varieties of NLE date from the late 1950s. Drysdale (1959) discusses dialect areas within the province and outlines the phonology of a Conception Bay dialect, while Widdowson (1964) presents the major features of an NBE variety spoken in central Newfoundland. Seary et al. (1968) delineate four distinct dialect types on the Avalon Peninsula, and list their chief phonological and morphological correlates. One of these varieties, the NIE spoken in the Avalon's Southern Shore region, is further documented by Dillon (1968), particularly with respect to vocabulary. Widdowson (1968) reports on aspects of the phonology of an Irish enclave community on the island's northeast coast.

A handful of linguistic studies conducted largely within the framework of traditional regional dialectology describe community/regional varieties spoken in several areas of the island. As we have seen, Noseworthy (1971) deals with Grand Bank, an English-settled town near the tip of the Burin Peninsula on the island's south coast; his 1972 paper, based on his 1971 thesis, represents an overview of Grand Bank verb forms. Harris (2006) documents the NBE speech of now resettled islands within Bonavista Bay. Both of these studies contain glossaries of regional lexical items, along with descriptions of the principal phonological and morphosyntactic features of conservative vernacular speakers. Paddock (1981) (based on a 1966 thesis) analyses the speech of Carbonear, a Conception Bay town of mixed English-Irish settlement origin. Though essentially a community dialect survey, Paddock's description is based on adult speakers who differ as to socioeconomic status and education, as well as age.

Few studies of regional NLE present in-depth treatments of individual linguistic features. One exception is Whalen (1978), which examines both *h*-deletion and intrusive *h* among school students in an NBE community in northeastern Newfoundland, in terms of the linguistic factors which favour *h* presence and absence (see Section 2.3.2).

6.2.3 Sociolinguistic and applied studies

As we saw in Chapter 5, since the early 1980s a number of studies have analysed community-internal variation in NLE from a sociolinguistic or variationist perspective. Their overall aim has been to examine the effects of non-linguistic factors (speaker age, gender, social class and, occasionally, ethnicity; see section 5.4) on the use and maintenance of selected local phonological and grammatical features. Via an 'apparent time' methodology (that is, one which contrasts the usage of older and younger speakers at one and the same point in time), these studies draw inferences with respect to ongoing linguistic change within communities. Although quantitative sociolinguistic studies elsewhere have for the most part focused on urban speech, a number of NLE sociolinguistic studies have examined the patterning of local and supralocal features in rural communities with very small populations. As pointed out in Chapter 5, areas investigated include the English-settled northeast coast (Colbourne 1982a, 1982b) and south coast (Newhook 2002), as well as areas of mixed English–Irish settlement in northern Conception Bay (Reid 1981) and on the Burin Peninsula (Lanari 1994). Urban sociolinguistic studies of NLE have focused on the speech of St. John's (Clarke 1986, 1991; D'Arcy 2000, 2005; Hollett 2006) and environs (Lawlor 1986; Richards 2002). Currently, two community-wide studies are underway in the greater St. John's area; both involve former fishing settlements which today are serving more and more as dormitory communities for the capital city. These are Pouch Cove, to the north of St. John's, which is being investigated by Susanne Wagner, and Petty Harbour/Maddox Cove, to the south, under study by Gerard Van Herk (see e.g. Van Herk et al. 2009).

Many of the above-mentioned sociolinguistic studies have examined a range of local linguistic features, particularly phonological (Chapter 5 provides more details). Some, however, have concentrated on smaller feature sets. Wagner's ongoing study has examined the use of the *after*-perfect, non-standard verbal *-s*, and null or deleted subjects (as in *Went there yesterday* rather than *I went there yesterday*). Van Herk et al. have focused on TH-stopping, along with verbal *-s*. In St. John's, D'Arcy (2005) investigated the retraction and lowering of the TRAP vowel, along with the fronting of the MOUTH/LOUD diphthong, while Hollett (2006) investigated the spread of the set of lax vowel changes known as the Canadian Shift, which includes TRAP retraction/lowering. As we saw earlier, both Reid (1981) and Lawlor (1986) deal with post-vocalic /r/-deletion within communities in Conception Bay. The sociolinguistics of glide retention and deletion in words like *new* and *tune* are discussed by Clarke (1993a, 2006a).

As also indicated in Chapter 5, a number of studies (among them Clarke 1981, 1982; Hampson 1982a, 1982b; O'Dwyer 1982, 1985) have documented the language attitudes of Newfoundlanders to local speech varieties – varieties that, as we have seen, are negatively evaluated by mainland Canadians (cf. McKinnie and Dailey-O'Cain 2002). King and Clarke (2002) deal with the range of attitudes of Newfoundlanders towards the 'familiar' epithet *Newfie*, regarded by many residents of the province as an ethnic slur.

Several studies have focused on the social ramifications of the considerable phonological and morphosyntactic gulf between many rural NLE varieties and standard English. As we saw in Chapter 5, the difficulties faced by NL students in learning to read and write using only standard English models generated several (unsuccessful) calls in the 1970s for the school curriculum to incorporate local dialect systems into the teaching of reading and spelling (Walker 1975; Walker et al. 1975). Potential difficulties in doctor–patient interaction resulting from the misunderstanding of traditional and vernacular speakers on the part of doctors who come from outside the province – and, indeed, the country – have been taken up by O'Dwyer (1991).

6.2.4 Situating NLE within a (socio-)historical framework

In light of the generally conservative nature of NLE, the focus of a number of researchers has been the relationship of local features to those of their source varieties. The Irish underpinnings of NLE are investigated in Kirwin (1993), Shorrocks (1997), Clarke (1997c) and Hickey (2002). Kirwin and Hollett (1986) deal with aspects of the linguistic relationship between southwest England and Newfoundland, particularly with respect to the feature of initial /h/, while Clarke (2004a) examines linguistic links between Newfoundland/Labrador and its two principal source dialect areas, southwest England and southeast Ireland.

The parallels between NLE and African American English have likewise been noted by a number of scholars (among them Clarke 2006b and elsewhere). Perhaps the earliest statement of feature similarities between the two varieties is to be found in an unpublished paper by McDavid and Paddock (1971; see Paddock 1971).

A number of studies of individual NLE morphosyntactic features, or feature complexes, combine synchronic and diachronic approaches. Clarke (1997a) examines non-third-person singular verbal -*s*, and Clarke (1999), verbal representation of habitual aspect more generally. The latter topic is also investigated by Wagner (2007). Paddock (1991) examines change in pronominal grammatical gender assignment between southwest England and Newfoundland; Wagner (2004, 2005) provides a comprehensive treatment of gender in both varieties. The feature of pronoun exchange is the topic of Paddock (1994). Bismark (2008) examines the *after*-perfect in a southern Irish Avalon corpus and its relationship to *after*-perfect use in Irish English.

As to phonetic features, two recent studies of the pulmonic ingressive discourse particles *yeah, no, mmm* (Shorrocks 2003; Clarke and Melchers 2005) examine, among other things, the origins of such particles in NLE.

6.3 Ongoing and future research

As noted earlier, NLE is the best described of any variety of Canadian English. Nonetheless, its extensive regional and social diversity means that much important research remains to be done. Two major projects currently in progress (see Van Herk et al., along with Wagner, outlined above) focus on quantitative and social approaches to language change. Since the province's current period of socioeconomic change and restructuring may well be accompanied by rapid language change, particularly in rural communities, more of this type of work is highly desirable. Also very much needed are apparent time studies in the major towns of the island; to date, the sociolinguistic investigation of urbanised NLE has centred on the greater St. John's area. For example, are new regional standards developing outside the Avalon Peninsula, where the Irish input that has characterised St. John's speech is notably absent? Do such communities look more to St. John's or to the Canadian mainland for their linguistic models? And what of urban Labrador?

Other ongoing projects (see the 'Web resources' section at the end of the chapter) have as their primary aim the provision of linguistic links to the past and lay further groundwork for future studies of language change. These include the production of an online dialect atlas (DANL) of traditional NLE, plus the 'Voices of Newfoundland and Labrador' project, which will make available both sound-files and transcriptions for traditional and contemporary speakers in more than sixty (chiefly rural) communities. Efforts are also well underway to digitise the entire lexical file-card collection of Memorial University's English Language Research Centre (ELRC), less than one-third of which was directly utilised in the production of the *DNE*.

In several important areas, virtually no research has been conducted. As noted in Chapter 5, there have been very few discourse-oriented studies of NLE to date. This situation is changing, however, with the work of Gerard Van Herk and his students into such discourse features as intensifiers and quotatives (see the MUN Sociolinguistics

Laboratory (MUSL) website, along with Bulgin et al. 2009). Likewise, there are few sociophonetic studies of NLE and no in-depth studies of its prosodic features. Though, for example, intonational patterns differ between traditional speakers of Irish descent and those whose ancestors came from southwest England, there has been no systematic investigation of these differences. There has also been no systematic study of the segmental and suprasegmental features of contact varieties in the province, most notably the English spoken by descendants of the original aboriginal populations of Labrador (an example of which is provided by Speaker 7, in 7.4.2). Similarly, while in southwestern Newfoundland the English spoken by residents whose ancestors were speakers of French or Scots Gaelic is assumed to be much the same as that of speakers of English ancestry, this assumption remains to be investigated.

On a final note, it is unfortunate that despite their many decidedly non-standard structural properties, NLE varieties have not tended to inform current theoretical approaches or models in syntax or phonology. One exception may be found in Siemund and Haselow (2008), who examine several morphosyntactic features of NLE in terms of their status relative to linguistic typology and cross-linguistic language contact; see also Wagner (2004).

Web resources

NL language-related materials

http://collections.mun.ca/index.php
   The Digital Archives Initiative (DAI) of Memorial University, which is making available online an increasing number of the local linguistic materials referred to in this chapter, among them *Regional Language Studies ... Newfoundland* (*RLS*), plus all Memorial University theses
http://www.heritage.nf.ca/dictionary
   Dictionary of Newfoundland English (*DNE*) Online
www.mun.ca/linguistics/research/language
   Provides links to the author's bibliography of Newfoundland and Labrador English (with a focus on the post-1900 period), as well as a number of ongoing research projects on NLE
www.mun.ca/elrc
   Memorial University's English Language Research Centre (ELRC)
http://www.mun.ca/folklore/munfla
   Memorial University Folklore and Language Archive (MUNFLA)
http://musl.ling.mun.ca
   Memorial University Sociolinguistics Laboratory (MUSL)

NLE speech samples

http://www.cbc.ca/nl/programs
   Provides links to various radio and television programmes produced by the
   CBC in Newfoundland and Labrador, including 'The Morning Show',
   'Radio Noon' and 'The Fisheries Broadcast', along with programme sound
   archives
http://www.cbc.ca/nl/media/audio.html
   CBC NL's 'Media Archive', containing audio for a number of media stories
   and interviews from various parts of the province, from Sheshatshiu in
   Labrador to the southern Avalon Peninsula community of Branch
http://www.cbc.ca/nl/features/unclemose/index_mose.html (See the 'Stories'
   link)
   A site featuring twelve of the 'Chronicles of Uncle Mose' monologues, narrated by their author Ted Russell (as originally broadcast on local CBC
   radio, 1953–61). These monologues provide a fairly good – if somewhat
   formal – representation of the vernacular speech of Conception Bay North,
   where the author was born and raised
http://profile.myspace.com/index.cfm?fuseaction=user.
   viewProfile&friendID=203591912
   Excerpts from *Letters from Uncle Val* (a fictional outport resident now residing
   in St. John's), created and performed by St. John's actor Andy Jones

Other NL sites of linguistic and historical interest

Early texts
http://www.mun.ca/rels/hrollmann/relsoc/16th.html
   Includes such early tracts as Mason (1620) and Whitbourne (1620)
http://www.mun.ca/rels/native/index.html
   Links to J. P. Howley's *The Beothucks or Red Indians: the Aboriginal Inhabitants of
   Newfoundland*, containing excerpts from many early European explorers and
   colonisers, relative to the region's aboriginal inhabitants
http://books.google.com
   Digitised versions of several nineteenth-century volumes mentioned in this
   chapter (Chappell 1818; Wix 1836; Tucker 1839; Moreton 1863)

General
http://www.heritage.nf.ca
   The Newfoundland and Labrador Heritage website
http://www.library.mun.ca/qeii/cns/index.php
   The Centre for Newfoundland Studies (CNS), Memorial University
http://www.library.mun.ca/qeii/cns/pab.php
   A searchable bibliography of all Newfoundland/Labrador-related periodical
   articles, maintained by the CNS

7 Sample texts

The nine texts presented in this chapter constitute a representative sample of speakers of NLE. Since many examples of contemporary NLE are accessible online (see e.g. the CBC NL sites listed in the 'Web resources' section at the end of Chapter 6), this chapter's primary focus is the more traditional speech of the province. Section 7.1 contains transcriptions of two conservative rural NBE speakers, while two speakers of conservative NIE from the Irish-settled Avalon Peninsula appear in section 7.2. Section 7.3 presents a traditional NBE speaker from the post-vocalic /r/-deleting area of Conception Bay North. Section 7.4 has two examples of fairly traditional speech from coastal Labrador, the second representing an ethnically mixed community in which English came into contact with Inuktitut, as spoken by the region's earlier inhabitants. Speech samples from two young contemporary Newfoundlanders are provided in section 7.5.

Accompanying audio files for all nine speech samples can be accessed online at http://www.lel.ed.ac.uk/dialects.

In the texts that follow, the following transcription conventions have been adopted:

Bold font indicates words and phrases drawn from these samples to illustrate linguistic features presented earlier in the volume, particularly in Chapters 2 and 3. Bold may also indicate illustrative words noted for any particular speaker in the comments immediately preceding each text below. Bold is generally restricted to the first occurrence of a word or phrase.

Pauses A **hyphen** represents a false start or a hesitation, as well as an interrupted sequence. A **question mark** indicates a pause accompanied by rising intonation. A **comma** indicates a short pause, while a longer pause (particularly when sentence-internal) is represented by a **dash**. Given the many pauses in these samples, **periods** are also used, in the normal fashion, for ease of reading. **Three dots** . . . indicate an incomplete clause, in particular one involving a turn-final conjunction (notably *and* . . . or *but* . . .).

Parentheses ( ) represent a sound deleted by the speaker, though normally pronounced in standard North American English. Parentheses are largely restricted to the initial *h* of a word like *(h)eld*, the post-vocalic *r* of *fa(r)*, and the vowel of the definite article *th(e)*, and thus highlight several salient regional features occurring in these texts.

Square brackets [ ] indicate a fairly inaudible syllable or syllables; [?] marks a best-guess transcription.

Angle brackets < > enclose the words of an interviewer, including small interjections (<Mmm>, <Yeah>, etc.). Italics within angle brackets represent: (i) non-verbal or suprasegmental features (<*laughter*>, <*ingressive*> speech, <*creaky voice*>); (ii) simultaneous speech, noted <*sim.*>; (iii) glosses of local words (as in <*'thing'*>, for the word *machine*), along with local pronunciations, particularly those involving *h*-insertion (as in *hamber* glossed as <*'amber'*>); and (iv) proper names, noted <*name*>.

No attempt has been made below to represent the many phonetic reductions that are also commonplace in the casual styles of 'standard' speakers. These include final *t/d* deletion (as in *and, friends, next-door*), along with consonant deletion in such words as *that's, it('s), of* and *probably*. Also not generally represented is the reduction or schwa-like pronunciation of vowels in unstressed syllables (as in *ya* for *you, ta* for *to*, or *ther* for *there*). However, the following well-known **reduced forms** are regularly utilised: *in'* (as in *walkin'*); *'em* ('them'); the forms *gonna, wanna, dunno*, and, of course, such usual contractions as *'ll* ('will') and *'d* ('would'). Reduced traditional forms are also represented as such, notably *'tis* ('it is'), *'twas* ('it was'), and *'en* ('him, it').

7.1 Conservative NBE

The two speakers in this section exhibit many of the chief phonetic features of traditional NBE. These include TH-stopping (2.3.1); deletion of historical /h/ and, in the case of Speaker 2, non-historical [h]-insertion (2.3.2); dark or velar realisations of post-vocalic /l/ (2.3.3); DRESS raising and KIT lowering (2.2.1.1); TRAP/BATH raising (2.2.1.2); LOT/CLOTH/THOUGHT fronting (2.2.1.3); and GOOSE centralisation (2.2.2.3).

7.1.1 Speaker 1: northwest coast

Sex	Year of birth	Occupation	Recording information
Male	1930s	Fisherman	Interview segment, 'Fishermen's (now Fisheries) Broadcast' (CBC NL radio, May 1978)

Along with a fairly rapid speech tempo, this speaker also displays occasional post-vocalic /r/-deletion in unstressed lexical items (*far*), as well as function words (*their, there's*) (2.3.4). Syntactically, in addition to the complementiser *for to* (3.5.4), he makes use of a conditional clause without overt use of the conjunction *if*, in *There's no problem t(o) gettin' the fishermen to take be(tt)er care of thei(r)lobsters [if] they're gonna get the price.*

<<*name* > you've been part of the organisation[al?] of a lot of the
meetings that went into ah- tryin' to determine what kind of a price
you were gonna get for lobsters this year, it's all done now, the price
is a dollar eighty. Do you think people are pretty happy with
that?>
Yes – the people (h)ere you know is – is really (h)appy with it, it's that
you know they got- they got the- the (h)ardest [about?] the fishermen
(h)ere you know is they- they can't believe it really (h)appened you
know, they've been talkin' about ['im?] for years and years you know
gettin' a – a dollar eighty or a dollar ninety or two dollars a pound and
ah … It (h)appened this year you know and ah – and they can't
(h)ardly believe it (h)appened and they're really (h)appy with the
price and ah … As fa(r) as payin' a dollar eighty I'm sure that he's
gonna get ah – ninety per cent of all the lobsters caught on th(e)
north-west coast this year.
<<*name*>, I was talkin' to a couple of people who were ah – they were
leery, they said, 'We don't know this man, we never heard of (h)im
before'. Do y- is there any of that kind of feeling around your area?>
Ah, no … I- I- I don't think you know that we've got that feeling around
our area, uh … We (h)eld meetings and explained to 'en and ah – the
buyer (h)imself came in and ah – met with the fishermen and ah … I
think the fellow that's gettin' this goin', I- I'd say if it's <*name*> you
know s- that (h)ave been (h)ere all the time you know they're tryin'
to make the fishermen ah – you know tryin' to get the fishermen [at
this?] – go against this fellow and [there's?] tellin'- tellin' 'em you
know that he got no money and ah … I been told that myself, you

know ah – they got no money uh, [**they're a-?**] **watchin'**, you know,
bees all this kind of stuff. If (h)e comes payin' cash you know (h)e-
he- (h)is **cash** got to be good.

<<*name*>, what was your impression, you were – involved in setting the
    meetings up you-you know a fair bit what was going on, what was
    your impression do you think he can follow through?>
Oh yeah I b(e)lieve[s?]- I really believe (h)e could follow through you
    know or (h)e- (h)e wouldn't (h)ave come up with the price, payin' a
    dollar eighty you know that's uh . . . Uh – no man in (h)is right mind
    as far as **I'm concerned** would come in and pay a dollar eighty for –
    (h)alf the season you know and then uh – not be able to follow
    through with it you know ah . . . And ah the [?] (h)ave ah – checked
    'en out good and ah – ah, (h)e could – there's no [odds?]- there's no
    two ways about it, (h)e could.

<<*name*>, I guess this means too that ah people are gonna have to
    take better care of their lobsters if they're gonna get that kind of
    price.>
Uh yeah, I believe (h)e's gonna want the lobsters **ban(de)d** now the-
    there's no problem years ago (h)ere they- they **ban(de)d** 'em (h)ere.
    About this last – six or **seven** year I guess the bands w- (h)ave been
    gone out but ah . . . All the time before that people ban[d]ed 'em and
    ah . . . There's no problem t(o) gettin' the fishermen to take be(tt)er
    care of **thei(r)** lobsters they're gonna get the price that's no problem
    the fisherman you know (h)e's willin' to go through – extra [?] for to
    get the extra money there's no two ways about that.

<<*name*>, what about the collection along the shore it's ah been a
    problem in the past do you think you'll be able to cope with
    that?>
Oh – yeah, I- I think so because ah- you know if we- even ah- I've been
    talkin' to (h)im myself and ah – I b(e)lieve he's comin' back next week
    and ah . . . Well I don't know that much about it we've collected lob-
    sters for buyers for a few years and ah . . . ah – Some fellows (h)ere
    we're gonna (h)elp (h)im set up you know uh, we've told (h)im **what**
    (h)e's gonna need and ah – (h)e's comin' in and ah . . . We're gonna
    (h)elp (h)im set it up, you know and (h)elp (h)im – set up (h)is **col-**
    lectin', say agencies (h)e's gonna (h)ave for different- various places
    same as th(e) other fellas, so ah . . . I don't see no problem there. (H)e
    should (h)ave a good set-up.

<<*name*> generally you'd say up and down the coast they're pretty
    happy with it.>
Oh yeah, they're- you know they're more than (h)appy you know the
    fishermen is mo(re) than happy **the(r)e's** – you know the(r)e's no two

ways about [i]t they're just – more than (h)appy that's all you can say.

7.1.2 Speaker 2: northeast coast

Sex	Year of birth	Occupation	Recording information
Male	1930s	Fisherman	Recorded in 1978 in the speaker's home community in Notre Dame Bay, by a community member

Despite a one-on-one recording session, this speaker of NBE displays a slow and careful style, given his awareness that his speech would be used for a university research project, and given the unusual nature of the speech task (the description of a range of common household objects). Yet although his grammatical features are reasonably standard (apart from the form *haves*, the past tense *come*, the frequent use of stative *into* and *onto* rather than *in* and *on*, and the use of *a one* rather than simply *one*), he produces many traditional NBE pronunciation features. In addition to those listed at the beginning of section 7.1, these include NORTH unrounding, as in 'cark' for *cork* and 'shart' for *short* (see 2.2.4.1). This speaker is particularly noteworthy for his degree of backing (and rounding) of the PRICE/PRIZE diphthong, in words like *high* and *wine*. He also uses a number of regional lexical items: *stopper* 'bottle cap, bottle top'; *slice* 'wooden cooking utensil'; *crispy* (stripes) 'crinkly'; and *tumbler* with the generalised meaning of 'any drinking glass'.

I (h)ave a **stopper** in my (h)and horange – orange stopper – two inches in diameter – three **quarters** inch (**h)igh**. I (h)ave a stopper – very **small** – three quarters inch in diameter. I (h)ave another stopper, in my (h)and – that **come** off – of some kind of a **bottle**. You don't see many bottles today with ah – **cork** stoppers **into** 'em, 'tis mostly screw sto- screw stopper. And also there's a- a can opener **onto** it – for opening **cans** – [h]and a bottle opener as well. Hand <'*and*'> ah – I (h)ave a bottle opener (h)ere – much smaller only about ah two and a (h)alf inches **long** – for opening bottles, pop bottles or- anything that (**h)aves** – that kind of a stopper onto it.
And I ho- also (h)ave (h)ere a big ah large – **spoon**. Now I wouldn't know **exactly** the name of it but ah – for taking **potatoes** – out of- out of a pot [and] – such things as that like **vege(ta)bles**. And I have a – a

dessert spoon – **large** dessert spoon, probably height inches – eight inches long. And ah, hi <*T*> (h)ave a – a **slice** – or probably you might call (i)t some kind of a **pie** knife – for taking pie – off of the **plate** and – you (h)ave it cut up.

I (h)ave a, milk jug in my (h)and, **clear** glass – with **crispy** stripes, into it. **Three** inches (**h)igh**, three and a (h)alf inches in diameter. I (h)ave a teacup, with beautiful **roses** – pink in colour – (a)bout three inches high. That's **a one** for drinking tea. I (h)ave a tumbler – **wine, wine** in colour. I **presume** it's a – a wine- wine **tumbler**, for drinking your wine.

I (h)ave, a screwdriver – flat **head**, screwdriver, with a rubber handle, light **red, trimmed** with black. I (h)ave another, screwdriver, very small, very slender – (a)bout six inches long with a – a **hamber** <*'amber'*> – (**h)andle**. I (h)ave another screwdriver, very **short**, inch and a (h)alf – with a – **amber** – (**h)andle**.

I (h)ave a file – three-corner file – a one for using – filing **saws**: (h)and saws, rip saws, lock saws etcetera. Eight-inch file.

7.2 Conservative NIE

Speaker 3 below represents traditional working-class St. John's speech, while Speaker 4 represents a small rural Avalon Peninsula community some fifteen km to the south of the city. Both samples contain many of the pronunciation features associated with traditional NIE. These include TH-stopping (2.3.1); use of 'clear' rather than 'dark' post-vocalic /l/ (2.3.3); non-upglided realisations of the tense FACE and GOAT vowels (2.2.2.1); KIT tensing and DRESS raising (2.2.1.1); TRAP/BATH raising (2.2.1.2); and fronting of LOT/CLOTH/THOUGHT vowels (2.2.1.3).

7.2.1 Speaker 3: St. John's

Sex	Year of birth	Occupation	Recording information
Male	1914	Carpenter, barber, shopkeeper, etc.	Recorded in St. John's in December 1980, by a student interviewer

In the following passage, which involves relatively formal style and slow delivery, the speaker recounts his memories of former businesses on New Gower Street in downtown St. John's, a street which had undergone extensive urban renewal. His many local Irish-inherited features of pronunciation also include NORTH and CHOICE unrounding, as in, respectively, *corner* pronounced 'carner' and *Voisey's* pronounced 'Vizey's'. Grammatical features include the use of existential *they* as well as *it* (3.3.2.3), the definite article in such instances as *they used to sell the candy* (cf. 3.3.3), and verbal *-s* (*I forgets*). In addition, this speaker makes extensive use of high rising intonation in statements (see 5.5), as signalled in the text below by the use of clause-final question marks.

Now I'm gonna tell you about all [of] **New** Gower Street. Now all New Gower Street all the **houses** were **tore** down – all the shops and – barber shops, and everything. And then I'll – tell a- tell you- all the names now the most [at?] all the stores were there – from ah – West End, New Gower Street? There was th(e) old fire hall West End Fire Hall they tore that down? There on the **corner** of Horwood's **Lane**? Eh? And then there was Malone's grocery store? And ah **White's** hot **beer** shop – was there? And then there was Noah's – a dry goods store they had there and then on the corner of Springdale Street **they were** – Goobie's grocery store? And **Casey's** butcher shop? And there was Malone's grocery store? And then there was, **George's** Street church was there, that's th(e) only one that's standin' there now. And then you keep on further on down – there was another White's bar, ah – hot beer shop – and ah – Leo Woods's barber shop down [on] the corner of Buchanan <*pronounced 'Buckaddan'*> Street. And they were ah – Smith's – '**Dead**-eye Smith' they used to call (h)im. He (h)ad a butcher shop and a grocery store. And then we had Chaytor's the butcher – Blackler's the butcher – and Dooley's the butcher. And ah – Browman's the grocery store. We (h)ad Anthony's the grocery store. All them were tore down on the, south side of New Gower Street.

Now I'll come down the, **north** side – west. We had ah-ah – the laundry, th(e) Chinaman's – the laundryman. And then we had ah – Andrews' the grocery store. And then we had Power's the candy store, they used to sell **the candy**, the homemade candy **and that**. And then we had Wadden's. They used to sell all the cigarettes and – tobacco – and – **and stuff like that**. And then we had on the corner of Springdale Street – we (h)ad another hot beer shop, **Voisey's** owned it, there. People used to go in and get their – **pint** of beer for five cents. All hands 'd sit around, talkin' and **jokin'**. But I never used to go in there.

But then we go round the other corner of Springdale Street was

a **confectionery** store there. Then we fu- go further on and Smiths'
– they (h)ad a- a good[s] <*'dry goods store?'*>. And then we had Burfitt's
drugstore. And we (h)ad **Michael's** – another Michael's with their
store- small store. And then we (h)ad Parson's the grocery store.
Then on the other corner of Brazil Street – Brazil Street yeah we had
ah, Bristol **(H)otel**. Then on the other corner – of Brazil Street we
had ah – Michael O'Brien, he had the fruit store – there, and that's
gone out. Then was- next to that – there was Moore's, Ralph Moore's
– he (h)ad another confectionery store. And next to that then was the
old Belmont <*pronounced 'Belmount'*> – whe[re] used to be a little star
one time. Joey Judge had it – the fella used to have all the racin'
horses – goin' on the **go**.

Now we go over – [to] the foot of Casey Street. We had another confec-
tionary store there on the bottom of Casey Street. And then next to
that – **I forgets** their names, but next to that **it was** another big dry
goods store.

7.2.2 *Speaker 4: Irish Avalon*

Sex	Year of birth	Occupation	Recording information
Male	1930s	Fisherman	Interview segment, 'Fishermen's (now Fisheries) Broadcast' (CBC NL radio, June 1980)

In addition to the features noted at the beginning of 7.2, this speaker
exhibits the well-known local Irish-inherited features of post-vocalic
/t/ frication, as in some of his pronunciations of *water* (see 2.3.5.2);
the *after*-perfect and 'extended present' perfect forms (3.2.5); and the
unusual stress pattern found in experiMENTin' (2.5). Though he displays
considerable /r/-colouring in a word like *works* (see 2.3.4), he also –
unlike Speaker 3 – occasionally deletes post-vocalic /r/ in unstressed
syllables (*cheaper, after, we're, there*). His pronunciation of the sequence *at
all* as [ətʰ ɐ:l] is typical of NLE.

<How long does it take now, to clean out a salmon net like that?>
Overnight – overnight, you can ah-ah – **untangle** 'em the next day and
– put 'em out in the water – again, for- for fish you know? For
salmon. But now ah- ah – I'd sooner spend two or three hours –
down there untanglin' 'em eh? – than- than over in the river beatin'
'em. <Mmm> Now that's a- that's an **awful job** over in the river.

<chuckles> No [hundred?] fishermen in the harbour don't like that at all.

<Well now that's what you used to do before you used to let 'em soak in- in the river, eh?>

Yeah, let 'em soak for three or four days. And then go over and beat it out of 'em on the water, you know? Squish 'em back and forth in the **water** and – beat the slub out of 'em that way.

<But this system you got now of tying them on down in the landwash <*'area of shore between high and low tide marks'*>, you don't have to beat 'em at all.>

No, you don't have to beat 'em **at all.** Just untangle 'em and – they're ready for – salmon fishin' again.

<It ah- cleans 'em right- clean as a whistle, eh?>

Clean- **clean as the whistle.** Now there might be a bit of sand left in 'em but the sand'll come out when it goes in the water, anyway – you know.

<<*name*> how did you come up with that system? Who thought that up?>

Well now we – we, I tell you now ah me and <*name*> have been – and another fisherman here, <*name*> – we've been doin' some **experi-MENTin'** with th(e) high pressure **hoses** and – one thing and another you know? And ah – we came up with the idea that, when a net is [cable-laid?] on the water you know? After a breeze of **wind?** Th(e) nets roll up. <Yeah> And when we take 'em **in** then, after (th)ey're rolled up – we un- heave the rolls out of 'em – and put them back in the water again they're as clean as the whistle. <Mmm> So that squishing – that's done out on the water – **works** the same way in the landwash. And it gives it a – **sandpaper** effect you know? And all this slub is washed out.

<Now – could you do it on a- another kind of beach? You say you've got sand among the rocks down there that seems to be the answer.>

Yeah, (th)at's- that's- that's what it looks like to us you know?

<So would i- would it be effective on a beach with just ah – heavy rocks?>

It may- it may you know if the rocks are, you know if the net **don't** tangle too much in the **rocks** you know? But after – the sea goes out here after the, water falls you know? The net is left and it's, half buried with sand. And dig it out of the sand and untangle it – wash the sand off of it and untangle it and – th(e) net is as good as **new.**

<<*name*> after all that, trying over the last two or three years to come up with a good system it's as simple as that eh?>

Well I s(up)pose most ah- answers – you know – for them problems are

– lies in nature anyway you know? Because ah- ah – you know – nature takes care of **itself** anyway uh? I guess that's another way of tellin' us that – it can be done that way.

<Use your head. <*chuckles*>>

Yeah <*laughs*>, it's as simple [as that is?] you know. And this is not – an expensive method either you know. [It] **don't** cost the fishermen no money and – you know... [They're in?] systems that – you know high pressure hoses. [Them?] are – three or four thousand dollars and a fisherman can't be involved in that you know. Uh, you know if the salmon are scarce it wouldn't be worth his **while** you know.

<Could you use that same system with a cod trap?>

Not for the cod trap because – cod traps are – a lot **larger** you know? But you could use it on herring nets or – [some?] fish nets or something like that you know. I think it'd work on them, just as **well**.

<Are there fishermen in your area doin' the same now with their salmon nets?>

Fishermen here on the beach **today** uh now and all- this past two or three days here. And there's a fine lot of salmon here and ... They're cleanin' their nets as fast as they can and puttin' 'em out again – changin' 'em again – for <'*because of*'> the slub you know?

<Hmm. <*name*> you say you've had a good spring with the salmon.>

We have, yes we had an excellent spring here in Petty Harbour at th(e) salmon. And ah – this morning now we have – a trap out this – **we (h)ave it out since Monday now**. And we'(r)e afte(r) **haulin'** it three or four times **the(re)** but we had a fine sign of fish this morning. We (h)ad five or six hundred **pound** and uh ... **Boats** out hand-linin' after jiggin' – you know three and four hundred **pound** that way you know? <Mmm> That's the first sign of fish we had now this- this week you know?

<Well <*name*> that's great to hear that you've come up with that sort of an answer. Now there you go, it's hard to beat you.>

<*laughs*> Oh yeah, well you got to be always – thinkin' at this racket. <Mm-hmm> You know tryin' to come up with a new system or [a] **cheape(r)** system anyway – you know.

7.3 Conservative NBE r-deleting: Speaker 5

Sex	Year of birth	Occupation	Recording information
Male	1930s	Fisherman	Recorded in 1980 in the Conception Bay community of Port-de-Grave

This speaker is an excellent example of the NBE post-vocalic /r/-deleting variety spoken in Conception Bay North. Though the recording task was designed to elicit fairly 'emotionally neutral' speech via the description of household objects (cf. Speaker 2 above), this speaker provides a narrative by contextualising the items in question in terms of earlier times and traditional lifestyles. In addition to /r/-deletion (2.3.4) after a full range of vowels, his notable linguistic features include many of those documented for Speakers 1 and 2, along with not infrequent glottalisation of /t/ (see 2.3.5.3).

Now I notice you got a- a reel of **cotton** (h)e(re) – but I don't see **th**(e) **needle**. <*laughs*> Well ah – well I tell you [when?] ah what I just – mentioned (h)e(re) about **th**(e) **apple** and **th**(e) **orange**. Now when we were growin' up most of our ah – clothes we'd **wea**(r) then'd be made, eh? Handmade. I tell you it was no trouble to see a – a woman – sat down sewin' then – old sewin' machine out – with the, no electric then – with the (h)andle on it, the cranker I **call** it – crankin' it around, sewin' away. Makin' **our ah** – coats, **and that** and –'d make **ou**(r) winte(r) clothes and ou(r) **summe**(r) clothes and... And that was it then in **them times** you (h)ad to do it, eh? You (h)ad to do it. [It] wasn't uh – it wasn't **so prosperous** then as it is today. You know, you know [it's a?]- it's a great age we're livin' in now, I know that. And it wasn't too bad them times. We were (h)appy and – everybody was friends and – next-doo(r) neighbou(r)s they were hin <*in*> and out hin and out all th(e) time and – you know, **quite a** difference from what it is today, I don't know, probably . . . You know we were more uh contented, I don't know what it is but ah . . . Like I say we ah – we was **small** I can remembe(r), you'd go in any (h)ouse at all. And ah, you'd see different women makin' – different things for thei(r) – children, winte(r) clothes and then when the **winte**(r) goes th[ey'd] be makin' summe(r) clothes and . . . Even make ou(r) pa(r)kas then. Make the hood and all, to go up over our (h)ead. Put the string into 'em, the reevin' string, I call it. Pull it in tight, till it gets out – yeah.

And then ah – I notice you got some **ya**(r)**n** the(r)e. And that's anothe(r) thing. Yea(r)s ago we'd (h)ave our own knitted cuffs. Them times we wouldn't e- wouldn't – see a **nylon** glove then even ah to go fishin' eh and – we used to be at the traps then- cod traps and ah . . . Mom she'd always knit the- the cuffs **for us** – to go pull the traps with, no gloves then all cuffs. Single cuffs we call 'em. And then ah – when fishin' was ove(r) then in the winte(r) then we'd go **up** in the woods. And she'd knit the **wa**(r)**me**(r) cuffs for us goin' back and fo(r)th on the (h)o(r)se. 'Twas no – pick-ups then no trucks. [Wa]s all out in th(e) open – in the cold. She used to − knit the − the double cuffs then with the diamond backs we used to call 'em. You know, **patte(r)n** on the back − diamond. That's the ones she (w)ould knit for jou(r)neys goin' back and fo(r)th we used t(o) keep our (h)ands **warm** on the- on th(e) **(h)o(r)se stretchin'** out to the [ho(r)ns?] of the sleigh. So ah − they used to be [at?] ah − well now the- the double cuffs we used to call them the good cuffs eh the real good ones ah − ou(r) dress cuffs I s(up) pose you'd call 'em. Used to be different colou(r)s 'd be white − and − red − and blue and all different colou(r)s into 'em you know. [They] used to look good, too. [Sh(e)] used to **knit** 'em just to − keep our (h) ands warm goin' to chu(r)ch. We walked to chu(r)ch then eh? No such things as gettin' in your ca(r) then, goin' to chu(r)ch, always . . . Go through the **snow**, no plows nothin' to open the roads then. Everybody'd be dressed up wa(r)m, cuffs on and . . . We- but we used to **enjoy** it everyone seemed like used to be (h)appy them times. You know n-, not sayin' now we're not, (h)appy today but [it] seem[ed] like ah − **I don't know like**, them times we used to appreciate every- thing. [We] used to ce(r)tainly appreciate it.

7.4 Conservative NBE Labrador speakers

While Speaker 6 comes from a more southerly and less ethnically mixed Labrador coastal community than does Speaker 7, the speech of both is clearly representative of NBE. This is evident from their *h*-deletion and (non-historical) *h*-insertion patterns (2.3.2), their various vowel pronunciations, and, in the case of Speaker 6, such grammatical features as the use of *he* to designate an inanimate object, a bailing tool for boats (3.3.2.2). Both speakers also display occasional post-vocalic /r/-deletion (2.3.4) in unstressed syllables.

7.4.1 Speaker 6: southern Labrador

Sex	Year of birth	Occupation	Recording information
Female	c. 1920	Housewife	Segment from fieldwork interview for Harold Paddock's NLE dialect atlas research project (lexical component; see 4.4). Recorded in 1982 in Cartwright by Paddock's research assistant, a young female from Gander

Though Cartwright, in the southern portion of coastal Labrador, has a somewhat mixed ethnic heritage, this traditional speaker displays NBE phonetic features typical of those on the island of Newfoundland, as exemplified by the speakers in section 7.1. Among her other noteworthy features are use of the ingressively articulated discourse particles *yeah* and *no* (2.5), her negative habitual form (3.2.4) *don't be (much flowers to it)*, and her use of third-person singular *haven't* (3.2.3) in *she haven't got her coat back.*

<Well how far away from here would you have to go to, find any difference in words and that, that people use?>

My you wouldn't (h)ave to go **very** far, just south as far as – uh- uh **Batteau** and- <That close> **Yes,** that close..

<A lot of people> Yeah <from Batteau moved up here, didn't they?>

Oh yes, a lot of [us (h)ere?] go back in the summertime.

<Did their speech change or are they still . . .>

Yeah I think they did some. <Now *<interviewer in background>>* Since they come (h)ere in Cartwright guess they've been **(h)e(re)** **fo(r)** some time – **yeah** *<ingressive>*.

<And people – I s(up)pose a lot of Cartwright people went to, Goose Bay didn't they?>

Yes, some of us, when Goose Bay **started-** *<interviewer in background>* just about everybody went to the Base. <And everyone [?]> Mostly still down **the(re)**, the ones that went down – when the Base started – yeah *<ingressive>*.

<Segment of interview skipped>

<What do you call a wooden hammer?

A mallet.

<And that's the little one for in the boat. Uh what about the bigger one for say, drivin' fence stakes?>

Oh ah – this is a maul. <Maul for- > Yeah, for drivin' – ah **postes** down – yeah *<ingressive>*, yeah.

<Segment of interview skipped>

<How about- what do you call th(e) two types of weeds that sting your skin? Like one type only grows low but the other type – is->

Sting **nettle**? One was called a sting *<interviewer in background>* – that's a high one. And ah-ah, those are not here very much anyway. <Yeah?> No not in Labrador, are they? *<male voice.* No> Gracious you never see those, those sting nettles (h)ere – no *<ingressive>*. Not the small ones or the- <or the big ones> big ones no.

<What about ah- did you used to grow or do you still grow your own vegetables, or . . . ?>

I- we never, no.

<Wh- the ones who do grow 'em what do they use for fertiliser like what local things do they use?>

Oh well they use **kelp** and fish (h)eads and – fish insides and ... <Whatever they can-> Whatever they can get.

<D(o) they ever use caplin?>

Well caplin is not that plenty around here. Like here in Cartwright now you **gotta** go **outside** to get them and mostly people just go out and get a few for their own, like for food.

<D(o) you salt and dry them?>

Oh yes, salt and dry them.

<What about ah – d(o) you ever grow any- d(o) people grow flowers around here or do they bother with flowers or ...?>

Oh yes, (h)ere a few people (h)ave just a few flowers?

<Do they get- tulips or the ones with the – bu-[bulbs?]>

No, **don't be much flowers to it** no. [It']s only something that uh stays in the ground all the **winter** and comes up every year with a little yellow flower-er onto [it?]. <Whatever you ...> Oh yeah yes 'tis ah- <Not- not too much botherin' with it.> No that's true – and the season's not long enough to grow anything. I mean it's the last of June b(e)fore the frost and the – and the snow is gone, off the ground mostly. <Yeah [and?]> And then **during** the summer we get a little frost every once in a while of course that kills everything.

<What about- did – people ever used to keep animals?>

Oh long time ago, people used to- like over (h)ere **to** the Grenfell Mission they used to (h)ave pigs and they (h)ad a **cow** and ... Right there now there's a **horse** and- *<laughs; interviewer in background>* ah-h <She's a coloured horse?> She lost (h)er coat and then she's ah- **she (h)aven't** got her coat back. She's black.

<People who used to keep animals, did they grow their own hay for them or ...?>

No, they would have their hay come in.

<Come in in boat.> Uh-huh. <That's hardly worth [it?]>

Not it's not *<interviewer in background>* worth the expense. That's more or less just a **pet**. <Not a [workhorse?]> And s- and they order all their grass they claim this is no good for them. When 'tis dried. It's the wrong kind and ...

<[She] seems to like it *<laughs>*>. Yes.

<Segment of interview skipped>

<And what about if they wanna protect their boat against ice, what'd they do?>

Well there's no boats left out here in the hice <*'ice'*>. <They haul 'em

all up.> They (h)aul 'em all up. <*interviewer's words unintelligible*> No
– no <*ingressive*>. No, they just (h)ave 'em more or less on a cradle
launch, as they call a cradle – or on sticks – now and roll them – they
roll as you (h)aul the boat in.
<What about ah- when the boat's all ready to go in the water you say
that she's ready to what?>
Lanch (*'Launch'*).
<And what about after she's in the water you gotta check (h)er t[o] see
if she's got any what?>
Leaks, uh?
<What about what names <*interviewee clears throat*> [do you have for?]
containers used by hand to get th(e) water out of the bottom of the
boat?>
Oh, just a bailer. <*addressing male listener*> But what was this wooden
machine <*'thing'*> they used to have special for bailin' out boats what
was (**h**)**e** called? [A] spudgel.

7.4.2 Speaker 7: Labrador Métis

Sex	Year of birth	Occupation	Recording information
Male	c. 1930	Trapper, photographer, etc.	Interview segment, 'Radio Noon' (CBC NL radio, March 2006)

The interviewee, a community elder, describes the traditional use of
sealskin and seal parts in Makkovik, a small Labrador coastal community of mixed Inuit–European heritage where Inuktitut has become a
second language, though taught in the local school. He exemplifies the
conservative contact variety of NBE as spoken by older residents of the
community, and uses at least one feature that is highly recessive on the
island: the past form *floatied*, which ends in [iːd] rather than standard [əd]
(see 3.2.1). Also unusual is his disyllabic pronunciation of *June* and, variably, *our*, along with his vowel in the word *south*. His apparent use of *will*
rather than *would* (as in *you'll go right to the top of your boots*) merits further
investigation, as do several rather unusual syntactic features which may
result from language contact (e.g. *tight enough for that man to get on (h)im,
helpin' (h)im*).

Of course, the uh women ['ll?]make **boots**. They'd make ah – sew the
s- – sew them up. And they'd never leak. **You'll** go right to the top of

your boots, your boots 'd never leak – you know. I- I['ll?] tell you one t- just a short story about ah – what- what – what can be done **with-with** sealskin. <Yes please.> When I was goin' to school I heard, Dad talkin' about a- a family now **the(re)** used to be – always two o(r) three families up to the **south** of us – what they called ah – Lance [Ground?] – and they was from Nain. And they was- there was a family comin' down after it got hopen <*'open'*, i.e.,*'after the winter ice broke up*>, comin' down to Makkovik here   and they **land[ed]** on **the island** – **land[ed]** on the- to boil up I guess o(r) something. Anyway – their boat drove away their- their small boat their, big boat [where?] – all their belongin's – were- were [tight?] moored off. And the small boat drove away. Now how in the world was they gonna get- get aboard there? There was no radios or anything like that you know to let them kn- no ah satellite ra- <*chuckles*>
<So what did they do?>
Well what did they do for sure? This man, he took a thought – and of course (h)is- **(h)is** woman was a expert ah **makin'**- boot-maker and ah clo(th)in'. And they could – sew – so neat stitches you could (h)ardly see it. Sure he- (h)e was still wearin' – ah sealskin **trouse(r)s**. Because they'd wear that right up to **June** you know <Mmm> sealskin trouse(r)s with the – fur on outside. Sh- she softened it – and sewed it up – and they blowed up them trouse(r)s. (And) she and- and (h)er daughters – I s(up)pose between 'em all – they blowed up them trouse(r)s and she sewed it up – tight enough for that man to **get on (h)im,** helpin' (h)im. He couldn't **swim.**
<He could float then out to the boat.>
That's it **floatied** out to the boat like that.
<That's a great story.>
That's one thing that's a true story, just not- not made up at all just – one true story.
<Uncle <*name*>, it was a pleasure to talk to you, about using the seal.>
Yes ma'am uh, it was a very important thing the seal fishery – and- and I think it still is but ah – they don't make boots any more and things [for?] that- that **sort** of thing uh s- uh seems to be gone which is – losin' part of **our** culture our tradition.

7.5 Contemporary younger speakers

The following two extracts represent a more urban (7.5.1) and a more rural (7.5.2) variety of contemporary NLE, as spoken by younger

Newfoundlanders who come from communities outside the Avalon Peninsula. Though their phonetic features are considerably more standardised than those of the traditional speakers presented above, the speech of both these younger samples remains unmistakably NLE – not least in terms of their more raised and/or fronted vowel pronunciations in the TRAP/BATH and LOT/CLOTH/THOUGHT sets, relative to their mainland Canadian peers. In addition, both speakers occasionally use the local feature of TH-stopping (2.3.1) in unstressed function words. Nonetheless, their discourse features – including clause-final *so* (Speaker 8) and quotative *be like*, along with discourse *like* and creaky voice (Speaker 9) – indicate obvious participation in youth-led tendencies within global English.

7.5.1 Speaker 8: urban

Sex	Year of birth	Occupation	Recording information
Male	1977	University student	Interviewed in St. John's in March 2006 by Philip Hiscock, a member of Memorial University's Folklore department, and a St. John's native

This younger speaker, from the central Newfoundland town of Grand Falls, moved to St. John's in 2002 to attend university. Like many traditional speakers in English-settled areas of the province, he displays an obvious Canadian Raising pattern for the MOUTH/LOUD diphthong (see 2.2.3.1). His use of a disyllabic pronunciation in the verb *tends* (approaching 'tend-ez') may either be idiosyncratic, or an indication of a generalisation of the [əz] verbal suffix which in standard varieties of English is restricted to verbs ending in a sibilant , as in *pushes, freezes* and *touches*.

<Actually – I mean we were just talkin' about your cam- your new camera, so> Yeah <ah – the ah- how come you bought that, is that-?>
Uh – Well I- it's sort of a pseudo birthday gift – and uh-
<Just a second your birthday is this [week?]>
Yeah, it's today actually. Yeah <*laughs*> <*sim.* Happy birthday!> Thank you.

<How old are you?>
Ah, twenty-nine. And- and it's twenty-nine on the twenty-ninth so it's
   – <*sim*. twenty-nine on the twenty-ninth> one of those mysterious
   champagne birthdays – that no one knows anything **about** – but
   everyone knows **about** <*laughs*>.
<[So?] let's see you were born then in nineteen eighty – no, nineteen
   seventy seven >
Yeah, yeah. **So- ah** …
<*sim*. So you thought you'd buy yourself a birthday gift.>
Yeah I bought myself an early birthday gift because I **knew** I was gonna
   <*slightly creaky voice*> get a digital camera anyway so … So I ah –
   went **out** and – had a look **around** and I was lookin' for something
   with – video and – and still because, I have a – still film camera, but
   – it's such a pain for getting – personal photographs off of that? It- it's
   great for – you know doin' things like – actual formal – type of pictures for archival work **and things like that** but- but not – so effi-
   cient if you just want pictures of parties <*laughs*> or- or anything
   that – is more personal so I figured well I'll get a digital one uh …
   Tha- tha- that's the **ultimate** in convenience as far as being able
   <*laughs*> to send people pictures of those – you know? **So** …
<Did that one come with a-uh pod or did- > Ah <you have to plug it
   into your computer to-> It- <have it backed up [or?]>
It does have a- it does include a – a little charging stand, basically, it
   doesn't come with anything- any way of charging it aside from
   hooking it up to the computer which is … Although – actually the
   base of it does plug into a wall, so – I would assume even if it wasn't
   plugged in to a USB it would probably charge? <Mmm> I would
   hope anyway <*laughs*>. <Right> Uh – not that I usually **unplug** the
   USB thing because it's all built into the base so – why ah- why bother?
   <*laughs*> You know? The thing is it's gonna be there and – play AC
   it's gonna reach – plugged in on the USB s[o] it's just as well for it to
   sit there with- ah <*laughs*>- with the-
<Is the- is the pod carriable, can you put that in your pocket?>
<*sim., interviewer in background* > Not really, naw. No, it's not – it's sort
   of – oddly-shaped it's got a L sort of shape to it, and there's, quite a
   protrudance on the bott(om). I guess it's because the **camera's** sort
   of top-heavy? It- it slides in there sort of at a – maybe a thirty-
   degree angle or so and … And it **tends** to be <*laughs*> a little
   wobbly?
<So it's got a [?] for the university for the fieldwork and stuff> Yeah.
   <how- how long you could use it, you know.>
Uh – I've **found** it lasts a pretty good time but I'm not **sure**. <What's

that?> Uh – I'd say it probably – it depends on if you're shootin' video, or – or ah – full-on photography? Or ah – rather – still photography rather? Um. But – I think for the stills it- it maybe lasts seven or eight hours? <Mmm> And for video, two or three, somethin' like that which is probably pretty standard as far as digital – video goes <*laughs*> you know? <Mmm> So. It- it's certainly not – it's certainly not bad time by any means, um . . . I've got a one-gig card with it so . . . That's – quite a bit of storage in the [end?] I think. Somewhere around – <*interviewer in background*> two **thousand** five point one megapixels. And up to I think it's about – close on to an hour of video I think about fifty minutes or somethin' like that so- <*interviewer in background*> it's-it's – good enough for my purposes. <Mm-hmm> It's not as if I'm gonna be going out shooting any documentaries with it <*laughs*>.

7.5.2 *Speaker 9: rural*

Sex	Year of birth	Occupation	Recording information
Female	1988	University student	Interviewed in St. John's in February 2008 by Philip Hiscock

This younger female, who came to St. John's in 2006 to attend university, is from the small and relatively isolated western south coast community of Burgeo, which had no road link with the rest of the island until 1979. As noted in Chapter 2, among her most striking linguistic features are a fronted nucleus in the LOUD diphthong (2.2.3.1), along with vowel centralisation in GOOSE words (2.2.2.3). Her occasional deletion of word-initial historical /h/ (*it (h)appened*), along with glottalisation of postvocalic /t/ (see 2.3.5.3), represent maintenance of traditional NBE features. She also appears to display (cf. 2.2.2.1) a vowel contrast within the FACE set, by distinguishing words spelled with *ay* and *ey* (*away*, *play(ground), Grey (River)* – that is, words which contained a diphthong in Middle English – from other items in this set (e.g., *grade, strange*). In the former, her vowel nucleus is considerably lower than the NLE norm, and approaches [æ]. This speaker thus appears to maintain a distinction within the FACE set that disappeared from standard varieties of English several centuries ago (cf. Wells 1982: 192ff., on the FACE merger).

<In your time, growin' up in, Burgeo, has there been a lot of change?> Ahmm – from when I was little – yeah, the **population**, <*creaky voice*> was a **lot** – bigger. <Yeah> But . . .

<What was the population?>

Ah, it was like **two thousand** and now it's gone **down** to like – thirteen hundred or ... But it's- it's bigger- In the winter like everyone goes away? <Oh is that right?> Oh a big- yeah, a big portion of people go away. <*creaky voice*> But ah...

<So – uh, what was it like growin' up there – as a child in Burgeo how did- what did you think of the place?>

Ahmm – <*coughs*> Well there's not really much to **do**. I know like for the young people now – really ... Like a lot of people – just walk **around**, just ah hang around like the local- <Mm-hmm> sit down and ... There is one spot where there's like a **pool** table or – **stuff like that**, but ... And there is a- a playground for like younger – with swings **and stuff** but ...

<*Segment of interview omitted*>

Well, when I was – in elementary **school** there was **a elementary** school and a high school. But see ah – like the population just gradually went down. Like my **class** – in kindergarten, there was twenty-two people. And I graduated with – fourteen. So ... So yeah they ah- I think, I was in grade **seven** – and – that's when they formed **the all-grade** school. So ah- **everyone was all like** 'Oh we're gonna be th(e) youngest people' but what **(h)appened** was, they just – formed a big school so we ended up <*interviewer in background*> not havin' to be – grade seven. <*laughs*> Yeah <still have younger ones.> Yeah.

<That was a big community, it- it> Yeah <drew in people from all across the southwest coast>.

It did.

<*Segment of interview omitted*>

Grey River – is like ah, two hours away from – Burgeo and- and Francois <*pronounced 'Fransway'*>, which is like, they're all in a row, **right?** <Mmm> And the Grey River **accent is** so **strange** like it's so different.

<Can you imitate it?>

Not really. <*laughs*> I don- one thing they do do is though, they'll say like, 'ships' and 'sheezies' and 'shicken'. <*laughs*>

<Oh is that right, so it's 'ships'.>

Yeah <*sim.* Yeah> <*laughs*> Yeah it kind of gets made fun of, a little bit.

<And that's just the people from Grey River. >

Yeah – strange.

<What about the people [from] Francois?>

Oh! One thing they do a lot is – they don't say – like 'I am', 'you are', 'we'- they say 'you'm' – like 'You'm goin' there' and 'We'm- we'm goin' over th(e) road'.

<*Segment of interview omitted*>

Grey River gets made fun of a lot. <Mm-hmm> Ahmm – for some reason – Ramea, right, with **the island** ... Ah – for some reason there's always been like a kind of war between **Ramea** and Burgeo like, the young people I found? **Like** 'Oh you're from Ramea'!

<How do they speak? How d- how do Burgeo people make fun of the Rameans?>

Ah I don't know if it's really **about** [the?] speaking. I don't know. **But I** can't really think of any like distinct – way of the speech but I know if, I hear a Ramea person talk like 'Oh – that's – th(e) <*interviewer in background*> same a[s] Ramea'. Mmm.

References

All websites noted below were accessible as of 10 February 2009

Amulree, William W. M. (1933), *Newfoundland Royal Commission Report*, London: His Majesty's Stationery Office. (Also at http://www.heritage.nf.ca/law/amulree/am_report.html).

Anderwald, Lieselotte (2001), '*Was*/*were* variation in non-standard British English today', *English World-Wide* 22.1: 1–21.

Barrow, John (1818), 'Mr. Buchan's expedition into the interior of Newfoundand', in *A Chronological History of Voyages into the Arctic Regions*, London: John Murray.

Barry, Michael V. (1982), 'The English language in Ireland', in Richard W. Bailey and Manfred Gorlach (eds), *English as a World Language*, Ann Arbor: The University of Michigan Press, pp. 84–133.

Bennett Knight, Margaret (1972), 'Scottish Gaelic, English and French: some aspects of the macaronic tradition of the Codroy Valley, Newfoundland', *Regional Language Studies . . . Newfoundland (RLS)* 4: 25–30.

Bismark, Christina (2008), '"There's after being changes": *Be after* V-*ing* in Placentia Bay, Newfoundland', *Arbeiten aus Anglistik und Amerikanistik (AAA)* 33.1: 95–118.

Boberg, Charles (2005), 'The North American Regional Vocabulary Survey: new variables and methods in the study of North American English', *American Speech* 80.1: 22–60.

Boberg, Charles (2008), 'Regional phonetic differentiation in Standard Canadian English', *Journal of English Linguistics* 36.2: 129–54.

Bromley, Sarah (2002), 'In the name of the charver: an investigation into the regional variation and etymology of the words used to refer to a "scally"', http://www.sarahbromley.co.uk/scally/academic.html

Bucholtz, Mary, Nancy Bermudez, Victor Fung, Lisa Edwards and Rosalva Vargas (2007), 'Hella Nor Cal or totally So Cal? The perceptual dialectology of California', *Journal of English Linguistics* 35.4: 325–52.

Bulgin, James, Nicole Elford, Lindsay Harding, Bridget Henley, Suzanne Power and Crystal Walters (2008), 'So really variable: social pattering of intensifier use by Newfoundlanders online', *Linguistica Atlantica* 29: 101–16.

Byrne, Pat (1997), 'Booze, ritual and the invention of tradition: the phenomenon of the screech-in', in Tad Tuleja (ed.), *Usable Pasts: Traditions and Group Expressions in North America*, Logan: Utah State University Press, pp. 232–48.

Cartwright, George (1792), *A Journal of Transactions and Events During a Residence of Nearly Sixteen Years on the Coast of Labrador*, 3 vols., Newark: Allin and Ridge.

Cartwright, George (1911) [1792], *Captain Cartwright and his Labrador Journal*, ed. Charles W. Townsend, Boston: Dana Estes.

Cassidy, Frederic G. and Joan Houston Hall (eds) (1985), *Dictionary of American Regional English*, vol. 1, Cambridge, MA: Belknap Press of Harvard University Press.

Cell, Gillian T. (ed.) (1982), *Newfoundland Discovered: English Attempts at Colonisation, 1610–1630*, London: The Hakluyt Society.

Chambers, J. K. (1975a), 'The Ottawa Valley "twang"', in Chambers (ed.), pp. 55–9.

Chambers, J. K. (ed.) (1975b), *Canadian English: Origins and Structures*, Toronto: Methuen.

Chambers, J. K. (1987), 'The complementizer "cep' fer"', *American Speech* 62.4: 378–9.

Chambers, J. K. (1998), 'Social embedding of changes in progress', *Journal of English Linguistics* 26: 5–36.

Chambers, J. K. and Margaret Hardwick (1986), 'Comparative sociolinguistics of a sound change in Canadian English', *English World-Wide* 7.1: 23–46.

Chappell, Edward (1818), *Voyage of His Majesty's Ship Rosamond to Newfoundland and the Southern Coast of Labrador*, London: J. Mawman.

Charbonneau, Paul M. and Louise Barrette (1994) (translated by Mike Luke), *Against the Odds: A History of the Francophones of Newfoundland and Labrador*, St. John's, NL: Harry Cuff.

Clarke, Sandra (1981), 'Dialect stereotyping in rural Newfoundland', in T. K. Pratt (ed.), *Papers from the Fifth Annual Meeting of the Atlantic Provinces Linguistic Association*, Charlottetown: University of Prince Edward Island, pp. 39–57.

Clarke, Sandra (1982), 'Sampling attitudes to dialect varieties in St. John's', in Paddock (ed.), pp. 90–105.

Clarke, Sandra (1986), 'Sociolinguistic patterning in a new-world dialect of Hiberno-English: the speech of St. John's, Newfoundland', in John Harris, David Little and David Singleton (eds), *Perspectives on the English Language in Ireland*, Dublin: Trinity College, pp. 67–81.

Clarke, Sandra (1991), 'Phonological variation and recent language change in St. John's English', in Jenny Cheshire (ed.), *English Around the World: Sociolinguistic Perspectives*, Cambridge: Cambridge University Press, pp. 108–22.

Clarke, Sandra (1993a), 'The Americanization of Canadian pronunciation: a survey of palatal glide usage', in Clarke (ed.), pp. 85–108.

Clarke, Sandra (ed.) (1993b), *Focus On … Canada*, Amsterdam/Philadelphia: John Benjamins.

Clarke, Sandra (1997a), 'English verbal -*s* revisited: the evidence from Newfoundland', *American Speech* 72.3: 227–59.

Clarke, Sandra (1997b), 'Language in Newfoundland and Labrador: past, present and future', *Journal of the Canadian Association of Applied Linguistics (CAAL)* 19.1–2: 11–34.

Clarke, Sandra (1997c), 'The role of Irish English in the formation of New World Englishes: the case from Newfoundland', in Jeffrey Kallen (ed.), *Focus on Ireland*, Amsterdam and Philadelphia: John Benjamins, pp. 207–25.

Clarke, Sandra (1999), 'The search for origins: habitual aspect and Newfoundland Vernacular English', *Journal of English Linguistics* 27.4: 328–40.

Clarke, Sandra (ed.) (2002), *Papers from the 26th Annual Meeting, Atlantic Provinces Linguistic Association*, St. John's: Memorial University of Newfoundland.

Clarke, Sandra (2004a), 'The legacy of British and Irish English in Newfoundland', in Hickey (ed.), pp. 242–61.

Clarke, Sandra (2004b), 'Newfoundland English: phonology', in Schneider et al. (eds), pp. 366–82.

Clarke, Sandra (2004c), 'Newfoundland English: morphology and syntax', in Kortmann et al. (eds), pp. 303–18.

Clarke, Sandra (2006a), 'Nooz or nyooz? The complex construction of Canadian identity', *Canadian Journal of Linguistics* 51.2/3: 225–46.

Clarke, Sandra (2006b), 'From cod to cool (Newfoundland, Canada)', in Walt Wolfram and Ben Ward (eds), *American Voices: How Dialects Differ from Coast to Coast*, Malden, MA: Blackwell, pp. 203–9.

Clarke, Sandra (2008), 'Newfoundland and Labrador English: phonology and phonetic variation', *Anglistik* 19.2: 93–106. Special issue, 'Focus on Canadian English', ed. Matthias L. G. Meyer.

Clarke, Sandra (forthcoming), 'Newfoundland English', in Edgar Schneider, Daniel Schreier, Peter Trudgill and Jeffrey P. Williams (eds), *The Lesser Known Varieties of English*, Cambridge: Cambridge University Press, pp. 72–91.

Clarke, Sandra, Ford Elms and Amani Youssef (1995), 'The third dialect of English: some Canadian evidence', *Language Variation and Change* 7.2: 209–28.

Clarke, Sandra and Philip Hiscock (2009), 'Hip-hop in a post-insular community: hybridity, local language and authenticity in an online Newfoundland rap group', *Journal of English Linguistics* 37.3: 241–61.

Clarke, Sandra and Ruth King (eds) (1982), *Papers from the Sixth Annual Meeting of the Atlantic Provinces Linguistic Association*, St. John's: Memorial University of Newfoundland.

Clarke, Sandra and Gunnel Melchers (2005), 'Ingressive particles across borders: gender and discourse particles across the North Atlantic', in Markku Filppula, Juhani Klemola, Marjatta Palander and Esa Penttilä (eds), *Dialects Across Borders: Selected Papers from the 11th International Conference on Methods in Dialectology (Methods XI), Joensuu, August 2002*, Amsterdam and Philadelphia: John Benjamins, pp. 51–72.

Colbourne, B. Wade (1982a), 'A sociolinguistic study of Long Island, Notre Dame Bay, Newfoundland', MA thesis, Memorial University of

Newfoundland. (Also at http://collections.mun.ca/cdm4/document.php? CISOROOT=/theses&CISOPTR=255768&REC=8).

Colbourne, B. Wade (1982b), 'A sociolinguistic study of Long Island, Notre Dame Bay, Newfoundland, in Clarke and King (eds), pp. 9–25.

Cormack, William Epps (1928) [1822], *Narrative of a Journey across the Island of Newfoundland in 1822*, ed. F. A. Bruton, London: Longmans Green & Co.

Dalton, Mary (2003), *Merrybegot*, Montreal: Véhicule Press.

D'Arcy, Alexandra (2000), 'Beyond mastery: a study of dialect acquisition', MA thesis, Memorial University of Newfoundland.

D'Arcy, Alexandra (2004), 'Contextualizing St. John's Youth English within the Canadian quotative system', *Journal of English Linguistics* 32.4: 323–45.

D'Arcy, Alexandra (2005), 'Situating the locus of change: phonological innovations in St. John's English', *Language Variation and Change* 17.3: 327–55.

Davey, William and Richard MacKinnon (2002), 'Atlantic lexicon', in Clarke (ed.), pp. 157–69.

de Boilieu, Lambert (1969) [1861], *Recollections of Labrador Life*, ed. Thomas F. Bredin, Toronto: The Ryerson Press.

Devine, P. K. (1937), *Devine's Folk Lore of Newfoundland in Old Words, Phrases and Expressions, Their Origin and Meaning*, St John's, NL: Robinson & Co. Facsimile edition, 1997, Memorial University of Newfoundland Folklore and Language Publications.

Dewling, Clarence Brown (comp.) and Graham Shorrocks (ed.) (1999), 'Words, phrases and pronunciations used in Trouty (Trinity Bight, Trinity Bay)', *Regional Language Studies . . . Newfoundland (RLS)* 16: 2–21.

Dillon, Virginia M. (1968), 'The Anglo-Irish element in the speech of the Southern Shore of Newfoundland', MA thesis, Memorial University of Newfoundland. (Also at http://collections.mun.ca/cdm4/document.php? CISOROOT=/theses&CISOPTR=239634&REC=1).

Drysdale, Patrick D. (1959), 'A first approach to Newfoundland phonemics', *Journal of the Canadian Linguistic Association* 5: 25–34.

Duncan, Norman (1904), *Dr. Luke of the Labrador*, New York: Revell.

Edwards, John and Maryanne Jacobsen (1987), 'Standard and regional standard speech: distinctions and similarities', *Language in Society* 16: 369–80.

England, George Allan (1924), *Vikings of the Ice*, New York: Doubleday.

England, George Allan (1925), 'Newfoundland dialect items', *Dialect Notes* 5.8: 322–46.

English, L. E. F. (1975) [1955], *Historic Newfoundland*, 8th edition, St. John's: The Newfoundland Department of Tourism.

Filppula, Markku (1999), *The Grammar of Irish English*, London and New York: Routledge.

Finch, Robert (2007), *The Iambics of Newfoundland: Notes from an Unknown Shore*, Berkeley, CA: Counterpoint.

Flowers, Joey (2007), 'The LabVocab project: a lexical survey of Labrador English', Linguistics 520 undergraduate student paper, McGill University, Montreal, December 2007.

Foster, F. Gilbert (1979), 'Irish in Avalon: an investigation of the Gaelic language in eastern Newfoundland', *Newfoundland Quarterly* 74: 17–22.

Foster, F. Gilbert (1982), 'Gaeldom and Tír (N)úr – "the New-found Land": sociological patterning of Scottish Gaelic in western Newfoundland', in Paddock (ed.), pp. 14–41.

Gold, Elaine (2008), 'Canadian *eh*? From *eh* to zed', *Anglistik* 19.2: 141–56.

Hakluyt, Richard (1589), *The Principall Navigations of the English Nation*, London: Imprinted by George Bishop, Ralfe Newberrie and Christopher Barker.

Halpert, Herbert and J. D. A. Widdowson (1996), *Folktales of Newfoundland* (2 vols.), St. John's: Breakwater (for the American Folklore Society).

Hamilton, William B. (1996), *Place Names of Atlantic Canada*, Toronto: University of Toronto Press.

Hampson, Eloise Lemire (1982a), 'The dialect stereotypes of schoolchildren and teachers in the Bay Roberts area of Newfoundland', MA thesis, Memorial University of Newfoundland.

Hampson, Eloise Lemire (1982b), 'Age as a factor in language attitude differences', in Clarke and King (eds), pp. 51–62.

Handcock, Gordon (1977), 'English migration to Newfoundland', in Mannion (ed.), pp. 14–48.

Handcock, Gordon (1989), *Soe Longe as There Comes No Women. Origins of English Setlement in Newfoundland*, St. John's: Breakwater.

Handcock, Gordon (1994), 'Settlement', in Cyril F. Poole and Robert H. Cuff (eds), *Encyclopedia of Newfoundland*, vol. 5, St. John's: Harry Cuff, pp.133–42.

Handcock, Gordon (2000a), 'Population', http://www.heritage.nf.ca/society/population.html

Handcock, Gordon (2000b), 'The West Country', http://www.heritage.nf.ca/society/west_country.html

Handcock, Gordon (2000c), 'Patterns of settlement', http://www.heritage.nf.ca/society/patterns_settlement.html

Harris, Linda (2006), 'Two island dialects of Bonavista Bay, Newfoundland', MA thesis, Memorial University of Newfoundland.

Harris, Martin B. (1967), 'The phonology and grammar of the dialect of South Zeal, Devonshire', PhD thesis, University of London.

Hay, Jennifer, Margaret Maclagan and Elizabeth Gordon (2008), *New Zealand English*, Edinburgh: Edinburgh University Press.

Hayman, Robert (1628), *Quodlibets, Lately Come Over from New Britaniola, Old Newfound-land*, London: Elizabeth Allde.

Henley, Bridget, Meghan Hollett, Elizabeth Ingram and Gerard Van Herk (2008), 'Grey's Anatomy viewers as a community of choice (seriously!)', Paper presented at NWAV-27, November 2008, Houston, TX.

Henry, P. L. (1957), *An Anglo-Irish Dialect of North Roscommon*, Dublin: University College, Department of English.

Henry, P. L. (1958), 'A linguistic survey of Ireland, preliminary report', *Lochlann* 1: 49–208.

Hewett, Sarah (1892), *The Peasant Speech of Devon*, 2nd edition, London: Elliot Stock.

Hewson, John (1978), 'Micmac place names in Newfoundland', *Regional Language Studies . . . Newfoundland (RLS)* 8: 1–21.

Hickey, Raymond (1986), 'Possible phonological parallels between Irish and Irish English', *English World-Wide* 7.1: 1–21.

Hickey, Raymond (2002), 'The Atlantic edge: the relationship between Irish English and Newfoundland English', *English World-Wide* 23: 283–316.

Hickey, Raymond (2004a), 'Development and diffusion of Irish English', in Hickey (ed.), pp. 82–117.

Hickey, Ramond (ed.) (2004b), *Legacies of Colonial English*, Cambridge: Cambridge University Press.

Hickey, Raymond (2007), *Irish English: History and Present-Day Forms*, Cambridge: Cambridge University Press.

Hiscock, Philip (1982), 'Dialect representation in R. T. S. Lowell's novel, *The New Priest in Conception Bay*', in Paddock (ed.), pp. 114–23.

Hollett, Pauline (2006), 'Investigating St. John's English: real- and apparent-time perspectives', *Canadian Journal of Linguistics* 51.2/3: 143–60.

Howley, M. F., Bishop (1901–14), 'Newfoundland name-lore', *Newfoundland Quarterly* 1–14. Reprinted in vols. 32–9, 48–51: and 64–5. (Also at http://collections.mun.ca).

Hubbard, Mina (1908), *A Woman's Way through Unknown Labrador*, Toronto: William Briggs.

Ito, Rika and Sali Tagliamonte (2003), '*Well* weird, *right* dodgy, *very* strange, *really* cool: layering and recycling in English intensifiers', *Language in Society* 32.2: 257–79.

Jones, Malcolm and Patrick Dillon (1987), *Dialect in Wiltshire*, Trowbridge: Wiltshire County Council, Library and Museum Service.

Jukes, Joseph Beete (1842), *Excursions in and about Newfoundland, during the Years 1839 and 1840* (2 vols.), London: John Murray. Reprinted 1969, Toronto: Canadiana House.

Kallen, Jeffrey L. (1995) 'English in Ireland', in Robert Burchfield (ed.), *The Cambridge History of the English Language*, vol. 5, Cambridge: Cambridge University Press, pp. 148–96.

Kennedy, W. R. (1885), *Sport, Travel and Adventure in Newfoundland and the West Indies*, Edinburgh and London: W. Blackwood.

King, Ruth and Gary R. Butler (2005), 'Les Franco-Terreneuviens et le franco-terreneuvien', in Julie Auger and Albert Valdman (eds), *Le français en Amérique du Nord*, Québec: Presses de l'Université Laval, pp. 169–87.

King, Ruth and Sandra Clarke (2002), 'Contesting meaning: *Newfie* and the politics of ethnic labelling', *Journal of Sociolinguistics* 6.4: 537–56.

King, Ruth and Jennifer Wicks (2009), '"Aren't we proud of our language?" Commodification and the Nissan Bonavista TV commercial', *Journal of English Linguistics*, 37.3: 262–83.

Kirwin, W. J. (1978), 'A glossary of c. 1900 by J. P. Howley (1847–1918)', *Regional Language Studies . . . Newfoundland (RLS)* 8: 22–7.

Kirwin, W. J. (1982), 'Folk etymology: remarks on linguistic problem-solving and who does it', in Paddock (ed), pp. 106–13.

Kirwin, W. J. (1991), 'The rise and fall of dialect representation in Newfoundland writings', in Thomas and Widdowson (eds), pp. 227–44.

Kirwin, W. J. (1993), 'The planting of Anglo-Irish in Newfoundland', in Clarke (ed.), pp. 65–84.

Kirwin, W. J. (2001), 'Newfoundland English', in John Algeo (ed.), *English in North America. The Cambridge History of the English Language*, vol. 6, Cambridge: Cambridge University Press, pp. 441–55.

Kirwin, W. J. and Robert Hollett (1986), 'The West Country and Newfoundland: some SED evidence', *Journal of English Linguistics* 19.2: 222–39.

Kirwin, William J. and Patrick A. O'Flaherty, with the assistance of Robert C. Hollett (eds.) (2009), *Reminiscences of Forty-two Years of Exploration in and about Newfoundland (1868–1911)* by James P. Howley. http://collections.mun.ca/cdm4/browse.php?CISOROOT=%2Fhowley

Kirwin, W. J. and G. M. Story (2008), Dictionary of Newfoundland English; lexical files: supplementary (computer file), English Language Research Centre (ELRC), Memorial University of Newfoundland.

Kirwin, W. J., G. M. Story and Patrick O'Flaherty (eds) (1997), *Reminiscences of J. P. Howley: Selected Years*, Toronto: The Champlain Society (Also available online, http://www.champlainsociety.ca/index.php/publications).

Kortmann, Bernd and Benedikt Szmrecsanyi (2004), 'Global synopsis: morphological and syntactic variation in English', in Kortmann et al. (eds), pp. 1142–1202.

Kortmann, Bernd, Edgar W. Schneider, Kate Burridge, Rajend Mesthrie and Clive Upton (eds) (2004), *A Handbook of Varieties of English*, vol. 2, Berlin and New York: Mouton de Gruyter.

Labov, William, Sharon Ash and Charles Boberg (2006), *The Atlas of North American English*, Berlin and New York: Mouton de Gruyter.

Lanari, Catherine E. Penney (1994), 'A sociolinguistic study of the Burin region of Newfoundland', MA thesis, Memorial University of Newfoundland.

Lawlor, Judy A. (1986), 'A sociolinguistic study of St. Thomas' and St. Philips', BA Honours thesis (Linguistics), Memorial University of Newfoundland.

Lowell, Robert Traill Spence (1858), *The New Priest in Conception Bay* (2 vols.), Boston: Phillips, Sampson & Co.

Lumsden, James A. (1906), *The Skipper Parson on the Bays and Barrens of Newfoundland*, London: Charles H. Kelly.

Lysaght, Averil M. (1971), *Joseph Banks in Newfoundland and Labrador, 1766: His Diary, Manuscripts and Collections*, London: Faber and Faber.

Macaulay, Ronald K. S. (2006), 'Pure grammaticalisation: the development of a teenage intensifier', *Language Variation and Change* 18: 267–83.

MacLeod, Malcolm (1990), *A Bridge Built Halfway: A History of Memorial University College, 1925–1950*. Montreal and Kingston: McGill-Queen's University Press.

Mannion, John J. (1977a), 'Introduction', and 'Settlers and traders in western Newfoundland', both in Mannion (ed.), pp. 1–13, 234–75.

Mannion John J. (ed.) (1977b), *The Peopling of Newfoundland*, St. John's: Institute of Social and Economic Research, Memorial University of Newfoundland.

Mannion, John J. (2000), 'The Irish in Newfoundland', http://www.heritage.nf.ca/society/irish_newfoundland.html

Mason, John (1620), *A Briefe Discovrse of the New-fovnd-land*, Edinburgh: Andro Hart.

Matthews, William (1939), 'Southwestern dialect in the Early Modern period', *Neophilologus* 24: 193–209.

McConnell, R. E. (1979), *Our Own Voice: Canadian English and How it is Studied*, Toronto: Gage Educational Publishing.

McDavid, Raven I., Jr. and Harold Paddock (1971), '"Black English" in Newfoundland?', Paper presented at the annual meeting of the Canadian Linguistic Association, St. John's, May 1971.

McKinnie, Meghan and Jennifer Dailey-O'Cain (2002), 'A perceptual dialectology of Anglophone Canada from the perspective of young Albertans and Ontarians', in Daniel Long and Dennis R. Preston (eds), *Handbook of Perceptual Dialectology*, vol. 2, Amsterdam and Philadelphia: John Benjamins, pp. 279–96.

Millais, J. G. (1907), *Newfoundland and its Untrodden Ways*, London: Longmans, Green & Co. Reprinted 2005 by Boulder Publications, St. John's, NL.

Montgomery, Michael (2006), 'Notes on the development of existential *they*', *American Speech* 81.2: 132–45.

Moreton, Rev. Julian (1863), *Life and Work in Newfoundland: Reminiscences of Thirteen Years Spent There*, London: Rivingtons (Available at http://ngb.chebucto.org/Articles/hist-007.shtml).

Morgan, Bernice (1992), *Random Passage*, St. John's: Breakwater.

Morgan, Bernice (1994), *Waiting for Time*, St. John's: Breakwater.

Moyles, R. G. (1975), *'Complaints is Many and Various, but the Odd Divil Likes it': Nineteenth Century Views of Newfoundland*, Toronto: Peter Martin Associates.

Murray, Alexander and James Patrick Howley (1881), *Geological Survey of Newfoundland*, London: Edward Stanford.

Murray, James A. H. (1873), *The Dialect of the Southern Counties of Scotland. Its Pronunciation, Grammar, and Historical Relations*, London: Philological Society.

Newhook, Amanda (2002), 'A sociolinguistic study of Burnt Islands, Newfoundland', MA thesis, Memorial University of Newfoundland.

Noseworthy, Ronald G. (1971), 'A dialect survey of Grand Bank, Newfoundland', MA thesis, Memorial University of Newfoundland. (Also at http://collections.mun.ca/cdm4/document.php?CISOROOT=/theses&CISOPTR=187353&REC=3).

Noseworthy, Ronald G. (1972), 'Verb usage in Grand Bank', *Regional Language Studies . . . Newfoundland (RLS)* 4: 19–24.

O'Dwyer, Bernard (1982), 'A perception of the speech of a Newfoundland speech community', in Clarke and King (eds), pp. 63–75.

O'Dwyer, Bernard T. (1985), 'A study of attitudes with specific reference to language attitudes among "three Newfoundland dialects"', PhD thesis, University of Edinburgh.

O'Dwyer, Bernard T. (1991), 'Medical language and dialect variation in Newfoundland English', *Canadian Family Physician* 37: 2088–9.

Ommer, Rosemary E. (1977), 'Highland Scots migration to southwestern Newfoundland: a study of kinship', in Mannion (ed), pp. 212–33.

Ommer, Rosemary and Peter Sinclair (1999), 'Outports under threat: systemic roots of social crisis', in Reginald Byron and John Hutson (eds), *Local Enterprise on the North Atlantic Margin*, Aldershot: Ashgate, pp. 253–76.

Paddock, Harold (1966), 'A dialect survey of Carbonear, Newfoundland', M.A. thesis, Memorial University of Newfoundland. (Also at http://collections. mun.ca/cdm4/document.php?CISOROOT=/theses&CISOPTR=159601& REC=19).

Paddock, Harold (1971), 'Black English in Newfoundland?' *Memorial University of Newfoundland Gazette* 4 (cf. also *Regional Language Studies...Newfoundland (RLS)* 4: 33, 1972).

Paddock, Harold (1981), *A Dialect Survey of Carbonear*, Alabama: University of Alabama Press for the American Dialect Society. Revised version of 1966 MA thesis, Memorial University of Newfoundland.

Paddock, Harold (1982a), 'Newfoundland dialects of English', in Paddock (ed.), pp. 71–89.

Paddock, Harold (ed.) (1982b), *Languages in Newfoundland and Labrador*, 2nd edition, St. John's, NL: Memorial University of Newfoundland.

Paddock, Harold (1984), 'Mapping lexical variants in Newfoundland English', in Helmut Zobl (ed.), *Papers from the Seventh Annual Meeting of the Atlantic Provinces Linguistic Association*, Moncton, New Brunswick: University of Moncton, pp. 84–103.

Paddock, Harold (1991), 'The actuation problem for gender change in Wessex versus Newfoundland', in Peter Trudgill and J. K. Chambers (eds), *Dialects of English*, London/New York: Longman, pp. 29–46.

Paddock, Harold (1994), 'From CASE to FOCUS in the pronouns of some Wessex-based dialects of English', in E. Engberg-Pedersen, L. F. Jakobsen and L. S. Rasmussen (eds), *Function and Expression in Formal Grammar*, Berlin and New York: Mouton de Gruyter, pp. 255–64.

Palmer, Craig T. and Peter R. Sinclair (2000), 'Expecting to leave: attitudes to migration among high school students on the Great Northern Peninsula of Newfoundland', *Newfoundland Studies* 16.1: 33–46.

Patterson, Rev. George (1895), 'Notes on the dialect of the people of Newfoundland', *Journal of American Folklore* 8: 27–40. Part II in *Journal of American Folklore* 9: 19–37 (1896); Part III in *Journal of American Folklore* 10: 203–13 (1897).

Pope, Peter (2004), *Fish into Wine: The Newfoundland Plantation in the Seventeenth Century*, Chapel Hill, NC: University of North Carolina Press.

Porter, Helen (1979), *Below the Bridge: Memories of the South Side of St. John's*, St. John's: Breakwater.

Poynter, F. N. L. (1963), *The Journal of James Yonge, Plymouth Surgeon* [1647–1721], London: Longmans.

Pratt, T. K. (1982), 'I dwell in possibility: variable (ay) in Prince Edward Island', *Journal of the Atlantic Provinces Linguistic Association* 4: 27–35.

Pratt, T. K. (ed.) (1988), *Dictionary of Prince Edward Island English*, Toronto: University of Toronto Press.

Pringle, Ian (1985), 'Attitudes to Canadian English', in Sidney Greenbaum (ed.), *The English Language Today*, Oxford: Pergamon Press, pp. 183–205.

Quinn, David B. and Neil M. Cheshire (eds) (1972), *The New Found Land of Stephen Parmenius*, Toronto: University of Toronto Press.

Reid, Gerald D. (1981), 'The sociolinguistic patterns of the Bay de Verde speech community', MPhil paper (Linguistics), Memorial University of Newfoundland.

Richards, Dawn (2002), 'Vowel variation in Cappahayden, an Irish Southern Shore Newfoundland community', in Clarke (ed.), pp. 171–85.

Rogers, Norman (1979), *Wessex Dialect*, Bradford-on-Avon, Wiltshire: Moonraker Press.

Russell, Ted (1975), *The Chronicles of Uncle Mose*, St. John's: Breakwater.

Russell, Ted (1977), *Tales from Pigeon Inlet*, St. John's: Breakwater.

Scargill, M. H. (1974), *Modern Canadian English Usage. Linguistic Change and Reconstruction*, Toronto: McClelland and Stewart.

Schilling-Estes, Natalie and Walt Wolfram (1999), 'Alternative models of dialect death: dissipation versus concentration', *Language* 75.3: 486–521.

Schneider, Edgar W. (2004), 'Synopsis: phonological variation in the Americas and the Caribbean', and 'Global synopsis: phonetic and phonological variation in English-world wide', both in Schneider et al. (eds), pp. 1075–88, 1111–37.

Schneider, Edgar W., Kate Burridge, Bernd Kortmann, Rajend Mesthrie and Clive Upton (eds) (2004), *A Handbook of Varieties of English*, vol. 1, Berlin and New York: Mouton de Gruyter.

Seary, E. R. (1971), *Place Names of the Avalon Peninsula of the Island of Newfoundland*, Toronto: University of Toronto Press for Memorial University of Newfoundland.

Seary, E. R. (1998), *Family Names of the Island of Newfoundland*, ed. William J. Kirwin, St. John's and Montreal: J. R. Smallwood Centre, Memorial University of Newfoundland/McGill-Queen's University Press.

Seary, E. R. (2000), *Place Names of the Northern Peninsula. A New Edition*, ed. Robert Hollett and William J. Kirwin, St. John's: Institute for Social and Economic Research (ISER), Memorial University of Newfoundland.

Seary, E. R., G. M. Story and W. J. Kirwin (1968), *The Avalon Peninsula of Newfoundland: An Ethno-linguistic Study*, Ottawa: Bulletin No. 219, National Museum of Canada.

Shorrocks, Graham (1996), 'Language in Percy Janes' novella, *The Picture on the Wall*', *Journal of English Linguistics* 24.3: 220–33.

Shorrocks, Graham (1997), 'Celtic influences on the English of Newfoundland and Labrador', in Hildegard L. C. Tristram (ed.), *The Celtic Englishes*, Heidelberg: Carl Winter, pp. 320–61.

Shorrocks, Graham (2003), 'Pulmonic ingressive speech in Newfoundland English: a case of Irish-English influence?', in Hildegard L. C. Tristram (ed.), *The Celtic Englishes III*, Heidelberg: Carl Winter, pp. 374–89.

Siemund, Peter and Alexander Haselow (2008), 'Newfoundland English morpho-syntax: universal aspects and trends', *Anglistik* 19.2: 201–14.

Statistics Canada (2007), 2006 Census of Canada, available at http://www12.statcan.ca/english/census06/data/profiles/community

Stenström, Anna-Brita, Gisle Andersen and Ingrid K. Hasund (2002), *Trends in Teenage Talk*, Amsterdam: John Benjamins.

Story, G. M. (1975), 'Newfoundland dialect: an historical view', in Chambers (ed.), pp. 19–24.

Story, G. M. (1982), 'The dialects of Newfoundland English', in Paddock (ed.), pp. 62–70.

Story, G. M., W. J. Kirwin and J. D. A. Widdowson (eds) (1990) [1982], *Dictionary of Newfoundland English*, 2nd edition, Toronto: University of Toronto Press.

Strowbridge, Nellie P. (2008), *The Newfoundland Tongue*, St. John's: Flanker Press.

Tagliamonte, Sali A. (2006), '"So cool, right?" Canadian English entering the 21st century', *Canadian Journal of Linguistics* 51.2/3: 309–31.

Tagliamonte, Sali A. and Alexandra D'Arcy (2004), '*He's like, she's like*: the quotative system in Canadian youth', *Journal of Sociolinguistics* 8.4: 493–514.

Tanner, Väinö (1947), *Outlines of the Geography, Life and Customs of Newfoundland-Labrador*, Cambridge: Cambridge University Press.

Thomas, Aaron (1968) [1794], *The Newfoundland Journal of Aaron Thomas, 1794*, ed. Jean M. Murray, Don Mills, Ontario: Longmans.

Thomas, Gerald and J. D. A. Widdowson (eds) (1991), *Studies in Newfoundland Folklore: Community and Process*, St. John's: Breakwater.

Thornton, Patricia (1977), 'The demographic and mercantile bases of initial permanent settlement in the Strait of Belle Isle', in Mannion (ed.), pp. 152–83.

Troike, Rudolph C. (1986), 'McDavid's law', *Journal of English Linguistics* 19.2: 177–205.

Tucker, Ephraim (1839), *Five Months in Labrador and Newfoundland*, Concord, NH: Israel S. Boyd and William White.

Upton, Clive and J. D. A. Widdowson (2006), *An Atlas of English Dialects*, 2nd edition, London/New York: Routledge.

Van Herk, Gerard, Becky Childs and Matthew Sheppard (2008), 'Work that -s! Drag queens, identity and traditional Newfoundland English', Paper presented at NWAV-37, November 2008, Houston, TX.

Van Herk, Gerard, Becky Childs and Jennifer Thorburn (2009), 'Identity marking and affiliation in an urbanizing Newfoundland community', in

Papers from the 31st Annual Meeting of the Atlantic Provinces Linguistic Association (PAMAPLA/ACAPLA 31), Fredericton, NB, pp. 85–94.

Waddell, Eric and Claire Doran (1993), 'The Newfoundland French: an endangered minority?', in Dean R. Louder and Eric Waddell (eds), *French America. Mobility, Identity, and Minority Experience across the Continent*, Baton Rouge and London: Louisiana State University Press, pp. 212–28.

Wagner, Susanne (2003), 'Gender in English pronouns: myth and reality', PhD thesis, University of Freiburg, Germany. (Available at http://www.freidok. uni-freiburg.de/ volltexte/1412/).

Wagner, Susanne (2004), '"Gendered" pronouns in English dialects: a typological perspective', in Bernd Kortmann (ed.), *Dialectology Meets Typology: Dialect Grammar from a Cross-Linguistic Perspective*, Berlin and New York: Mouton de Gruyter, pp. 479–96.

Wagner, Susanne (2005), 'Gender in English pronouns: southwest England', in Bernd Kortmann, Tanja Herrmann, Lukas Pietsch and Susanne Wagner (eds), *A Comparative Grammar of British English Dialects: Agreement, Gender, Relative Clauses*, Berlin and New York: Mouton de Gruyter, pp. 211–367.

Wagner, Susanne (2006–7), 'The Tocque formula and Newfoundland English', *Linguistica Atlantica* 27-28: 141–6.

Wagner, Susanne (2007), 'Unstressed periphrastic do – from Southwest England to Newfoundland?', *English World-Wide* 28.3: 249–78.

Wakelin, Martyn F. (1986), *The Southwest of England (Varieties of English around the World, T5)*, Amsterdam and Philadelphia: John Benjamins.

Wakelin, Martyn F. (1988), 'The phonology of South-Western English 1500–1700', in Jacek Fisiak (ed.), *Historical Dialectology*, Berlin, New York and Amsterdam: Mouton de Gruyter, pp. 609–44.

Walker, Laurence (1975), 'Newfoundland dialect interference in oral reading', *Journal of Reading Behaviour* 7.1: 61–78.

Walker, Laurence, Harold Paddock, Lloyd Brown and Ishmael Baksh (1975), 'Nonstandard dialect and literacy: an in-service project in Newfoundland', *Interchange* 6.3: 4–10.

Warkentyne, H. J. (1971), 'Contemporary Canadian English: a report of the Survey of Canadian English', *American Speech* 46.3/4: 193–9.

Wells, J. C. (1982), *Accents of English* (3 vols.), Cambridge: Cambridge University Press.

Whalen, John (1978), 'The effects of varying contexts on the adding and dropping of [h] by Grade IV and Grade IX students on New World Island, Newfoundland', MEd thesis, Memorial University of Newfoundland. (Also at http://collections.mun.ca/cdm4/document,ogo?CISOROOT=/theses& CISOPTR=238509&CISOSHOW=238401&REC=10).

Whitbourne, Richard (1620), *A Discourse and Discovery of New-found-land*, London: Felix Kyngston for William Barret. (Also at http://collections.mun. ca/cdm4/document.php?CISOROOT=/cns&CISOPTR-23942&REC=1).

Widdowson, J. D. A. (1964), 'Some items of a central Newfoundland dialect,' *Canadian Journal of Linguistics* 10: 37–46.

Widdowson, J. D. A. (1968), 'The dialect of Fortune Harbour, Newfoundland: a pronouncing glossary', *Folia Linguistica* 2: 316–26.

Widdowson, J. D. A. (1991), 'Lexical retention in Newfoundland dialect', in Thomas and Widdowson (eds), pp. 245–58.

Widén, Bertil (1949), *Studies on the Dorset Dialect*, Lund: C. W. R. Gleerup.

Wilson, H. Rex (1975), 'Lunenburg Dutch: fact and folklore', in Chambers (ed.), pp. 40–4.

Wilson, William (1866), *Newfoundland and its Missionaries*, Cambridge, MA: Dakin and Metcalf.

Wix, Edward (1836), *Six Months of a Newfoundland Missionary's Journal*, London: Smith, Elder & Co.

Wolfram, Walt, Kirk Hazen and Natalie Schilling-Estes (1999), *Dialect Change and Maintenance on the Outer Banks* (*PADS* 81), Tuscaloosa and London: University of Alabama Press for the American Dialect Society.

Wolfram, Walt and Natalie Schilling-Estes (1997), *Hoi Toide on the Outer Banks*, Chapel Hill, NC: University of North Carolina Press.

Young, Ron (2006), *Dictionary of Newfoundland and Labrador*, St. John's: Downhome Publishing.

Index